UNEMPLOYMENT IN IRELAND

AF738711

Unemployment in Ireland

Alternative perspectives

Edited by
CHARLES M.A. CLARK
CATHERINE KAVANAGH

Routledge
Taylor & Francis Group
LONDON AND NEW YORK

First published 1998 by Ashgate Publishing

Reissued 2018 by Routledge
2 Park Square, Milton Park, Abingdon, Oxon, OX14 4RN
52 Vanderbilt Avenue, New York, NY 10017

Routledge is an imprint of the Taylor & Francis Group, an informa business

Copyright © Charles M.A. Clark and Catherine Kavanagh 1998

All rights reserved. No part of this book may be reprinted or reproduced or utilised in any form or by any electronic, mechanical, or other means, now known or hereafter invented, including photocopying and recording, or in any information storage or retrieval system, without permission in writing from the publishers.

Notice:
Product or corporate names may be trademarks or registered trademarks, and are used only for identification and explanation without intent to infringe.

Publisher's Note
The publisher has gone to great lengths to ensure the quality of this reprint but points out that some imperfections in the original copies may be apparent.

Disclaimer
The publisher has made every effort to trace copyright holders and welcomes correspondence from those they have been unable to contact.

A Library of Congress record exists under LC control number:

ISBN 13: 978-1-138-36049-5 (hbk)
ISBN 13: 978-0-429-42926-2 (ebk)

Contents

List of tables and figures

List of contributors

Frank Barry is Senior Statutory Lecturer in the Economics Department at University College Dublin. He has held visiting appointments at the Universities of Stockholm, California and New South Wales and was Trade and Industry Advisor to the Indonesian Ministry of Finance with the Harvard Institute for International Development. He has published widely on macroeconomics and international trade issues.

Charles M.A. Clark is Professor of Economics at St. John's University, New York. His previous positions include Visiting Professor of Economics at University College Cork. He has published extensively in the fields of history of economics, inequality, basic income policies, unemployment and measures of economic progress.

Aoife Hannan is currently studying for a Ph.D at the University of British Columbia, Vancouver, Canada. Her former positions include Lecturer in Economics at University College Dublin and Quantitative Analyst with Allied Irish Bank Investment Managers. Her publications are in the areas of CGE modelling, foreign direct investment and the impact of the European Single Market on the economics of the European Union periphery.

Catherine Kavanagh is Lecturer in Economics at University College Cork. She is currently completing a Ph.D at the University of Aberdeen. She has published on such topics as the impact of public capital expenditures, unemployment, basic income policies, measures of economic progress and the political economy of European Monetary Union.

Ella Kavanagh is Lecturer in Economics at University College Cork. She has published in the areas of exchange rate arrangements, macroeconomics and the economic implications for Ireland of European Monetary Union.

Kieran A. Kennedy has recently retired as Director of the Economic and Social Research Institute, having served 25 years in the post. He previously worked in the Department of Finance and the Central Bank of Ireland. He has published extensively in areas such as economic development, productivity, industrial policy, employment and unemployment, European integration and fiscal policy.

Terrence McDonough is Lecturer in Economics at University College Galway. He has published extensively in the areas of American economic history, the Irish nineteenth century, the history of economic thought and the philosophy of economics.

Anthony Murphy is Lecturer in Economics at University College Dublin. He previously worked at the Northern Ireland Economic Research Centre, Belfast and Nuffield College, Oxford. He has published widely on topics such as labour market discrimination, the incidence and duration of unemployment, and the effects of the housing market on inter-regional mobility.

Francis O'Toole is Lecturer in Economics at University of Dublin (Trinity College). His current research interests include economic and legal aspects of competition policy and the economics of compulsory voting. He has published widely in the area of taxation.

Eric A. Strobl is Lecturer in Economics at University College Dublin. He previously worked as Lecturer in Economics at University of Dublin (Trinity College). His research interests include labour economics, law and economics and regional economics.

Brendan M. Walsh is Professor of National Economics of Ireland at University College Dublin. He previously worked at the Economic and Social Research Institute, Dublin, and with the Harvard Institute for Economic Research in Iran and The Gambia. He has published extensively on various aspects of the Irish economy, including migration, unemployment and the growth of women's employment.

Patrick P. Walsh is Lecturer in Economics at University of Dublin (Trinity College). He previously worked as Lecturer at University College Dublin and as Research Officer with the Economics of Industry Group at the London School of Economics. He has published widely on various aspects of the Irish labour market including unemployment, the real wage gap and labour market policies. His current research interests include environmental economics and accounting, trade policy, and the impact of legislation on female unemployment.

Acknowledgements

We would first like to thank Edward Shinnick for his invaluable help in organising the Second Cork Economic Policy Symposium, where these papers were first presented. His enormous effort and efficient diligence contributed immensely to the success of the event. We gratefully acknowledge the support, advise and assistance of Professor Connell Fanning of the Department of Economics at University College Cork. He was particularly instrumental in getting the Cork Economic Policy Symposium series off the ground. In addition, his guidance and encouragement with this book is much appreciated. We owe a particular debt of gratitude to Mary Maguire, John Considine, Dorothy Comer and Eoin O'Leary for their participation in the symposium and the members of the Department of Economics at University College Cork for their support and assistance. We are especially grateful to the administrative staff - Sheila O'Driscoll, Margaret Clayton and Bernadette Fitzgerald. We wish to thank Dr. Michael Mortell, President of University College Cork, for his gracious opening remarks at the symposium. The success of a symposium like this requires support from all levels of a University and we are very lucky that such support is willingly and generously provided at University College Cork, and in particular, at the Department of Economics.

A word of thanks to Noel Woods for his help in formatting the papers into chapters and to the editorial staff at Avebury, in particular Rachel Hedges and Anne Keirby, for their cheerful help and assistance. We also wish to thank Charles Kronke, former Dean, College of Business Administration, St. John's University, New York, for his support and encouragement which will be greatly missed at St. John's.

Finally, we wish to thank the contributors for their participation in the symposium and their efforts in turning the papers into a book.

Preface

The problem of unemployment is clearly Ireland's most serious economic and social issue. It is the major contributor to poverty, exclusion and social decay. Even with the recent successes of the "Celtic Tiger", and the surprising growth in employment that has accompanied it, the number of unemployed persons remains stubbornly high. This is particularly the case for the long term unemployed and those with low levels of skill attainment. The pressing need to better understand this issue was the motivation behind the Second Annual Cork Economic Policy Symposium, hosted by the Department of Economics, University College Cork on July 12, 1996 and entitled "Unemployment in Ireland: Diagnoses and Prescriptions". The papers from the symposium are the subject matter of this book and it is hoped that they will encourage discussion and research into the problem of unemployment.

The main contribution this book makes towards understanding the problem of unemployment in Ireland is in the bringing together of a diverse collection of economists representing different perspectives. This is especially significant for the problem of unemployment. The theoretical perspective determines how we think about issues such as: how to define labour market slack (unemployment and underemployment); how to conceptualise the labour market (market clearing model, segmented market model, macro or micro perspective, or non-equilibrium perspective); how to organise empirical observations (measure and collect data); and what policies should be pursued to address the problem. Unfortunately, economists with different perspectives rarely interact and exchange ideas. However, the range of different perspectives was a highlight of the symposium. We feel that an important issue such as unemployment, with its persistence and resistance to standard economic policy solutions, warrants discussion and debate from as many perspectives as possible.

The symposium began with a presentation on the historical perspective of the unemployment problem in Ireland by Professor Joe Lee of University College, Cork (not a chapter in the book). In his presentation, Professor Lee highlighted the duration of the problem of labour slack for Ireland,and the various policies which the government has suggested and implemented to address it.

The book begins with Chapter 1 by Professor Charles M.A. Clark who argues that the current level of unemployment in Ireland is both the result of the general levels of labour slack in the advanced Capitalist economies and the result of factors specific to the Irish economy. He examines both of these sets of factors from a post-Keynesian/institutionalist perspective. Clark claims that the assumptions of neoclassical theory which lead to the conclusion that the labour market clears are not valid and hence, cannot explain adequately the rise in Irish unemployment. According to Clark, the post-Keynesian perspective, which does not assume that the labour market has any natural mechanism to clear the market, but rather, emphasises demand deficiency as an explanation of unemployment, offers a superior framework for analysing the problem. Clark concludes that Irish unemployment can in part be explained by the fall in aggregate demand which was more pronounced in Ireland during the 1970s and 1980s than in most other OECD countries.

In Chapter 2, Anthony Murphy and Professor Brendan Walsh address the very important issue of measurement of labour market conditions. They suggest that although overt unemployment is the main measure of labour market slack in Ireland, non-participation may also reflect difficulty in obtaining employment, especially among prime age males. They document the decline of market unemployment among Irish males over the recent past and investigate the reasons for this decline. Using the 1993 Labour Force Survey (LFS), Murphy and Walsh then explore the individual characteristics associated with different labour market outcomes such as unemployment, non-participation and non-employment. The extent to which unemployment, retirement and permanent invalidity should be regarded as complementary measures of labour market slack is investigated and the importance of discouragement and hidden unemployment assessed.

Catherine Kavanagh, in Chapter 3, examines the role of active labour market policies (ALMPS) and the contribution they can make to alleviating unemployment. These policies are playing an increasingly important role in the move to fight unemployment in many OECD countries, including Ireland. ALMPS are aimed at improving labour market efficiency and equity by enhancing labour market mobility, strengthening the job search process, and combating social exclusion. Kavanagh reviews the international literature on possible macroeconomic and microeconomic effects of ALMPS and provides a summary of Irish studies which have attempted to evaluate the effectiveness of individual labour market programmes. She concludes that ALMPS have to be effective if increased expenditure on them is to be justified. However, there appears to be little evidence to suggest that ALMPS have been effective in reducing Irish unemployment. Kavanagh advocates the establishment of an independent government body to review and monitor individual labour market programmes and to coordinate the activities of the various different groups involved.

In Chapter 4, Dr. Francis O'Toole comments on the first four papers that were presented at the symposium. Fully in the spirit of the symposium, O'Toole attempts to show the parallels and the divergences of the four papers.

Dr. Frank Barry and Aoife Hannan begin Chapter 5 by noting that the demand for unskilled labour has fallen sharply right across the industrialised world in the last two decades, while the demand for skilled labour has risen. In the US, this shows up as a fall in the real wages of poorly educated workers, while in Europe, and in particular Ireland, it has led instead to an increase in their rates of long term unemployment. In both cases, the real wages of more highly educated workers have increased. Barry and Hannan document these changes for the Irish case, and show how they relate to the other explanations of Irish unemployment offered in the literature. The analysis leads to what the authors feel are two quite profound policy conclusions. First, individuals who are poorly qualified are likely to be poor and unemployed. Second, if individuals are poor and unemployed, then the likelihood is that their children will be poorly qualified. This means that deprivation and unemployment can cross the generational divide leading the authors to express concern for improvements in education and training.

In chapter 6, Eric Strobl and Patrick Walsh examine the magnitude and composition of the male unemployment flows and trace their contribution to the build up of long term unemployment in Ireland. They first document the underlying flows that have induced movements both in the overall level of male unemployment and that of the long term unemployment in Ireland. They then develop a methodology to construct male flows to and from the Live Register. Their innovative methodology allows a comparison of the characteristics of males in the stocks with those in the flows and also allows for the dynamics to be traced by these characteristics. Strobl and Walsh argue their results indicate that heterogeneity in the unemployment inflow was a major cause of the build-up and persistence of long term unemployment in the 1980s. Specifically, those that become long term unemployed are inherently different to those who are unemployed for short spells. They suggest that heterogeneity in the inflow, in the form of older males with redundant human capital, was due to the changing occupational structure of employment.

Chapter 7 by Professor Kieran Kennedy assesses Irish unemployment in a European context. He argues that relative to Europe, recent employment performance in Ireland has been remarkable. As a result, the Irish unemployment rate since 1993 has fallen by four percentage points and could, he argues, be down to the EU average by 1998. Further reduction requires sustained growth in employment. Convergence towards European levels of income per capita requires continued high growth in productivity. Both objectives, Kennedy suggests, can be achieved simultaneously only through strong growth in output in the face of moderate growth in the EU. He concludes that this outcome is attainable if a disciplined approach to economic management by the Irish government and social partners continues.

In Chapter 8, Dr. Ella Kavanagh focuses on how unemployment in a small country like Ireland is affected by the choice of exchange rate regimes, a topic of particular relevance in the lead up to European Monetary Union. In the first part of the chapter, Kavanagh reviews the theoretical literature. According to the "Optimum Currency Area" literature originating with Mundell (1961), negative asymmetric shocks will increase unemployment and/or increase emigration in the absence of wage/price or exchange rate flexibility. Drawing on open economy models in the literature, Kavanagh discusses the channels through which membership of particular exchange rate regimes affects unemployment and the structural features of the economy that make particular channels of transmission more or less important are examined. Given that the interest is in the policy implications for Ireland, the focus is mainly on three country models where one country is small and two countries are large. The channels of transmission discussed are (i) interest rates, (ii), exchange rates and (iii) wages and prices. The next part of the chapter provides empirical evidence for Ireland on the impact of membership of the exchange rate regime on unemployment. Using two econometric models, MULTIMOD (a world model) and HERMES-IRELAND, the impact on domestic and external unanticipated demand-side disturbances on Irish unemployment are examined, assuming (i) a flexible exchange rate regimes, (ii) a single currency peg to the DM, (iii) a single currency peg to sterling, and (iv) a composite peg arrangement. Kavanagh concludes that Ireland's exchange rate regime does matter for Irish unemployment as does the exchange rate regimes between the two larger countries, like the UK and Germany.

The final chapter by Dr. Terrence McDonough, both comments on the previous four papers and addresses the theoretical and political issues raised by the problem of unemployment in the developed capitalist economies. McDonough takes a very broad perspective and for this reason, this chapter is in many ways, a fitting conclusion to this volume. He argues that Irish unemployment is due to long term structural factors. Because of the depth of the problem, he suggests that marginal changes will only provide marginal improvement, and instead, calls for economic and cultural change. In particular, he challenges the neoclassical theory of the labour market and advocates change in the way we understand and evaluate labour market outcomes. However, McDonough concludes that solutions to the problem of unemployment and its associated problems of inequality and deprivation, require courage and audacity on the part of policymakers.

1 Unemployment in Ireland: a post-Keynesian/ institutionalist perspective

Charles M. A. Clark

Ireland's dual unemployment problem

The current level of unemployment in Ireland is both the result of the general level of labour slack in the advanced capitalist economies and of the specific historical and social context of the Irish economy. To understand the current labour slack and to design policies to fight high unemployment, it is necessary to address both sets of factors.

Unfortunately, the greatest barrier to reducing world unemployment is the very "science" which is charged with explaining and leading the fight against unemployment: economic theory. The current high levels of unemployment in the OECD countries, and the inability of the economics profession, or at least mainstream economists, are both the effects of the same cause: the economics profession's adherence to a pre-Keynesian view of the workings of capitalist economies.

Therefore, in order to get a clear idea of the economic, social and political forces behind the now decade long era of high unemployment we must, as Keynes suggested 50 years ago, again start the "long struggle of escape ... from habitual modes of thought and expression" (Keynes, 1936, p. viii). To aid in this endeavour, it will be helpful to briefly examine the neoclassical theory of unemployment, or more accurately the neoclassical theory of explaining away unemployment, and to contrast it with the post-Keynesian/institutionalist view.

Neoclassical and post-Keynesian/institutionalist views of unemployment

The two approaches to unemployment and the labour market to be considered here are the neoclassical market clearing model and the post-Keynesian/institutionalist (PKI) approach.[1] The neoclassical market clearing model is built upon pre-Keynesian economic theory, while the PKI approach builds on the insights of John Maynard Keynes, combined with the institutionalist's emphasis on historical and social context (institutions).[2]

Neoclassical perspective

Neoclassical economic theory treats the labour market in the same way that it analyses all markets, as the arena which co-ordinates the rational self-interest actions of individual economic actors. The buying and selling of labour is the same as the buying and selling of any other good or service, with its price (the real wage) being determined by the interaction of supply and demand. In the event that quantity supply and quantity demand are not equal, i.e. not in equilibrium, then the price of labour (the real wage) will adjust upward (to alleviate a shortage of labour) or downward (to alleviate a surplus) in order to re-establish the equilibrium market clearing price. The most important features of this theory are its market clearing assumption and its determination of factor prices. Market clearing is the process which leads to zero excess supply, which for the labour market means the existence of no involuntary unemployment.[3] This process is worked out through adjustments in relative prices (as described above), which, for the labour market to clear, entails the real wage, the return on capital (profit rate) and the rate of interest.

Both the supply and the demand for labour, according to this theory, are functions of the real wage. The supply of labour is based on the utility maximisation model. Individuals have preferences: they like income, they dislike work, and they like leisure. The decision to work (i.e. supply labour) is based on the labour/leisure trade-off, with the individual maximising her utility by choosing the level of labour supply which equates the marginal utility of income earned from an additional unit of work with the marginal disutility of an additional unit of labour (which is the same as saying giving up a unit of leisure). The real wage is the price signal, which the individual reacts to, i.e. it is the measure of the "utility" received from work.

The demand for labour is a similar utility maximising story, this time from the perspective of the firm (the employer). The firm wants to maximise revenue over costs. It will hire workers as long as the revenue generated by the worker (the marginal revenue product) is greater than the cost of hiring the worker (the real wage). Assuming diminishing returns to scale, at some point the additional revenue generated by additional employees falls, so that the firm will only hire additional employees if the real wage falls. The market demand for labour is the sum of all individual firms'demand for labour. Thus, there is an inverse relationship between the real wage and the demand for labour. The net result of this approach is that unemployment is either voluntary or due to barriers to flexible wages that would produce full employment. In effect, this theory has eliminated Keynesian involuntary unemployment.

Any deviation from full employment, if it persists beyond the short run, must be due to some market imperfection, with the most common being government intervention and the influence of trade unions. The obvious policy implication of this theory is to deregulate labour markets, that is, move them closer to the perfect competition model. Most neoclassical economists argue that making labour markets more flexible is the primary way for the government to promote employment.

The neoclassical theory of the labour market is supplemented by various versions of "Say's Law of Markets"(that is a natural level of output). Although the presentation of the new classical and new Keynesian macroeconomics is certainly more rigorous than Jean-Baptist Say's presentation of his theories, the fundamental proposition of a tendency of the economy to a "natural level of output" remains the same. The influence of the neoclassical pre-Keynesian perspective can be seen in the modelling of "wage equations" in an effort to discover what factors are preventing the real wage from reaching its full employment level. This whole approach is based on the assumption of a unique relationship between wage rates and levels of unemployment. From this proposition, it is only a short step to the theory that has dominated macroeconomic theory over the past three decades: that there is a unique relationship between the level of unemployment and inflation, an idea which started out as the "Phillips Curve,"evolved into the "natural rate" hypothesis and which is now called the "NAIRU" (Non-Accelerating Inflation Rate of Unemployment). The main purpose of this theory, along with the "rational expectations hypothesis" is to reassert the classical proposition of a vertical aggregate supply curve. The radical nature of Keynes'suggestion that the level of output adjusts to the level of aggregate demand, and has no level of central tendency, stems from its attack on the whole notion of equilibrium. It is an assertion that the economy does not possess dominant and persistent forces, which lead to a general equilibrium at a socially optimal level. That is, that the Invisible Hand doesn't work, and that social institutions must intervene to promote full employment and other socially desirable goals. We shall now turn to a post-Keynesian/institutionalist explanation of unemployment.

Post-Keynesian/institutionalist perspective

The post-Keynesian/institutionalist explanation of unemployment differs from neoclassical economics in two regards: (i) they have not forgotten the essential message of John Maynard Keynes, that the economy has no self-correcting mechanism to bring it to full employment; and (ii) they have a very different view of how labour markets behave. The basics of Keynes'macroeconomic theory should be widely known. Essentially it is the proposition that the level of output is determined by the level of aggregate demand, and that there is neither a "natural"or "long run equilibrium" level of output, nor a mechanism to adjust current levels to full employment. In Keynes'analysis, the problem of a tendency for unemployment (labour slack) stems from the institution of money. It is the essential properties of money, and the workings of the financial system, which keeps the money rate of interest too high to promote maximum employment.[4] We will see below that "money"and the workings of the financial system are still at the heart of the problem of mass unemployment.

The main difference between neoclassical economic theory and PKI theory is the treatment of historical and social factors, that is, the institutional structure of the society and economy. Neoclassical economic theory assumes a competitive market structure and assumes away the historical and social context in which economic activity takes place.[5] PKI theory is built upon the particular social and economic institutions which shape and direct economic activity. Thus, what neoclassical economics assumes away, PKI highlights. This is particularly important in the field of labour economics.

The difference between the PKI perspective and the neoclassical perspective can be quickly seen in the change in terminology. The PKI approach looks at labour *markets*, and *not* at a *single* homogenous or all-inclusive labour market. PKI analysis begins with the recognition that many sectors of the so-called "labour market" are in fact, to use John Stuart Mill's terminology, "non-competing groups." This fragmentation of the labour market into segments recognises the limited mobility and institutional barriers which separate different types of workers.[6] PKI theory also gives a very different analysis of the determinants of labour supply and labour demand: neither is a simple function of the real wage. In fact, the real wage does not play an important role in a PKI explanation of unemployment. The supply of labour is a cultural and social phenomenon and not merely a reaction to price signals. Working is an important aspect of social participation, and the value of a job goes beyond it being a mere pay-cheque. Self-esteem, status, social belonging, skills acquisition and many other factors influence job decisions and the desire to work.[7] Furthermore, the supply of workers cannot be separated from the demand for labour. Thus, the supply of labour, especially male workers and single female workers, will be relatively unresponsive to wage or income changes.

The PKI analysis of the demand for labour comes from post-Keynesian macroeconomic theory.[8] The demand for labour is a function of the aggregate demand for the goods and services in the economy. It is thus a *derived* demand. Contrary to the theories espoused by the neoclassical economists, there is no mechanism in the economy to ensure that the level of aggregate demand will be sufficient to employ all who desire employment. This means that there is no tendency towards full employment. Neither labour markets (through adjustments in the real wage), nor the investment market (through adjustments in the interest rate) has a mechanism in which the prices generated by each respective market (wages and interest rates respectively) will clear the market (labour or investment) at the full employment level.[9] Thus, involuntary unemployment is an expected outcome. Furthermore, neither theoretically nor empirically does PKI theory support the idea of an inverse relationship between the real wage and employment.

Eileen Appelbaum (1979, pp.115-6) has summarised the PKI approach.

> The labour market is not a "market", as that term is usually understood, for the labour market does not possess a market-clearing price mechanism. Variations in either money wages or in the real wage rate are unable to assure a zero surplus supply of labour, and thus eliminate unemployment. In the context of (i) an industrial structure that is largely oligopolistic, (ii) fixed technical coefficients in production and (iii) mark-up pricing, the demand for labour depends on the level of aggregate economic activity. It has little, if anything, to do with the marginal product of labour. The supply of labour, meanwhile, depends largely on demographic and other sociocultural factors, though it is somewhat responsive to changes in employment opportunities.

Furthermore, the distribution of income is largely determined by how market relations are instituted (relative power between workers and employers), and government policies, and not by impersonal market forces (Clark, 1996).

The existence and persistence of mass unemployment in the OECD countries is reason enough to reach the conclusion that labour markets do not spontaneously clear, nor do they show any tendency towards clearing in the long run. Yet such obvious evidence does not stop economists from applying the market-clearing model to the problem of mass unemployment, to which we return to soon. But before we examine the various explanations for the rise in unemployment, we must first examine the extent of the problem.

The problem of generalised labour slack

The statistics used to depict and explain the rise in unemployment certainly show the dramatic increase in mass unemployment. However, they do not fully show the extent to which there is slack in the labour market. To be unemployed typically means that one is without *any* job and one is actively looking for employment. This common definition of unemployment leaves out discouraged workers, part-time workers looking for full-time work and workers who are employed below their productive capabilities. In a recent publication, the OECD (1995) has given estimates of a more generalised labour market slack which includes traditional unemployment, discouraged workers and involuntary part-time workers, the results of which can be seen in Table 1.1.

John Eatwell (1995) has recently presented another measure of labour slack. Building on Joan Robinson's (1937) concept of disguised unemployment, Eatwell notes how labour slack manifests itself depends on the institutional context in which labour slack is presented.

Table 1.1
Unemployment and adjusted unemployment rates (%), 1983 & 1993

	Unemployment		Adjusted Unemployment	
Country	1983	1993	1983	1993
Australia	9.7	10.8	13.0	15.6
Belgium	11.4	8.1	12.8	11.4
Canada	12.0	11.3	15.3	14.8
Denmark	9.0	10.8	11.3	14.7
France	8.0	11.4	NA	14.0
Germany	6.9	7.7	7.4	8.5
Greece	8.1	9.6	10.0	11.4
Ireland	15.0	15.3	16.5	17.4
Japan	2.7	2.6	6.8	5.7
Netherlands	9.7	7.2	13.3	10.6
New Zealand	4.1	9.6	5.8	13.6
Norway	4.9	6.0	6.1	7.1
Portugal	8.8	5.5	10.5	6.5
Spain	20.8	22.4	22.4	23.1
Sweden	2.0	5.3	5.4	10.2
UK	11.2	10.3	13.3	12.5
USA	9.8	6.9	13.9	10.2
Average	9.1	9.5	11.5	12.2

Source: OECD *Employment Outlook* (1995, pp. 76-77).

Disguised unemployment is defined by Joan Robinson in the following manner.

> In a society in which there is no regular system of unemployment benefit, and in which poor relief is either non-existent or "less eligible" than almost any alternative short of suicide, a man who is thrown out of work must scratch up a living somehow or by means of his own effort. ...Thus, except under peculiar conditions, a decline in effective demand which reduces the amount of employment offered in the general run of industries will not lead to "unemployment" in the sense of complete idleness, but will rather drive workers into a number of occupations - selling match-boxes in the Strand, cutting brushwood in the jungles, digging potatoes on allotments - which are still open. ... Thus a decline in demand for the product of the general run of industries leads to a diversion of labour from occupations in which productivity is higher to others where it is lower. The cause of this diversion, a decline in effective demand, is exactly the same as the cause of unemployment in the ordinary sense, and it is natural to describe the adoption of inferior

occupations by dismissed workers as *disguised unemployment* (Robinson, 1937, pp. 83-84 quoted in Eatwell, 1995, p. 5).

Thus, if there is an extensive Welfare State in place, and with it adequate unemployment benefits and other types of social services, then we would expect a fall in aggregate demand to manifest itself fully, or mostly in the unemployment statistics, whereas in countries where the Welfare State is weak and where there are very limited and inadequate social protections against economic down-turns, then we would expect much of the displaced workers to go to low productivity employment instead of to the unemployment lines. This phenomenon partly accounts for much of the rise in low paying jobs in the United States.

If a country has a high average replacement ratio and high benefits coverage, then we would expect little disguised unemployment, whereas, if these are low, then we would expect a large amount of discouraged workers. John Eatwell has estimated the extent of discouraged workers for G7 countries and these results confirm the above proposition.[10] Furthermore, they show that the labour slack of the 1980-1990s is more generalised than is typically noted.

The experience of the United Kingdom is a good illustration of how important the institutional structure of the labour market is for how labour slack will be manifested. In 1979, the United Kingdom had a strong Welfare State with a high replacement ratio and wide benefit coverage. The Government instituted a policy to deregulate the labour market, thus causing disguised unemployment to rise from 0 per cent to 5.7 per cent of the labour force.

Table 1.2
Unemployment rates adjusted for disguised unemployment (%)

	1979		1990	
Country	Published	"True"	Published	"True"
Canada	7.4	24.0	7.5	29.0
France	6.0	9.5	8.9	11.9
Germany	2.9	5.1	4.9	5.5
Italy	7.8	14.5	11.1	16.5
Japan	2.1	18.3	2.1	18.7
United Kingdom	4.5	4.5	5.9	11.6
United States	5.2	7.1	6.2	11.1
G7 Average	5.2	11.9	6.7	14.9

Source: Eatwell (1995).

Eatwell's estimates (Table 1.2) raise important questions as to the supposed "successes" of the American model of job creation in the 1980s and 1990s, and the alleged benefits of "flexible" labour markets, a topic we will soon turn to.

Furthermore, they highlight another area where "official" economic statistics give a very misleading depiction of the actual state of the economy.[11]

Unemployment in the advanced capitalist economies: the usual suspects

Given that the neoclassical explanation of unemployment is based on a market-clearing model of the labour market, no one should be surprised that the most common "causes" of unemployment in neoclassical economics are various forms of market failures or government interventions in the labour market. Of the former category, labour market inflexibility is most frequently seen as the cause of high unemployment, with the solution being to increase labour market flexibility.[12] The latter set of diagnoses often add to the labour market inflexibility thesis, with the addition of government spending or programs creating the inflexibility in the labour market.

Simply put, according to the market-clearing model of the labour market, unemployment is caused by an imbalance in the supply and demand for labour. Such an imbalance can persist only if something (usually a government programme or labour union) is preventing real wages from performing their market clearing function. The more sophisticated of the neoclassicals, the self-styled "new Keynesians," are able to produce labour market rigidities without blaming government policy, via insider/outsider models. In such models, wages fail to fall either because of information co-ordination failures or because there is no way for those outside of the labour market (the unemployed) to express their willingness to employers to work for less, while those holding jobs have the incentive to keep wages high (they already have jobs and the benefits of a wage decease goes to the unemployed who would get the jobs created by a reduction in wages).[13]

The weakness of the inflexibility argument was first demonstrated by Keynes in the *General Theory* when he showed, via cumulative causation, how a reduction in wage rates increases, and not decreases, unemployment. Even if prices fell simultaneously with wages, and by the same amount, spending would not increase by enough to justify an increase in employment. For a reduction in wages not to lead to a fall in spending, employment would have to increase simultaneously. Yet employers will only hire more workers if their sales increase. Thus the unemployed workers will not be hired. Furthermore, they will be joined by more unemployed as employers lay workers off due to a build-up in inventories caused by the decline in spending (the result of a fall in wages). Moreover, a decline in prices would certainly lead to a decline in profits (since the goods being sold under the new price regime were produced under the old, higher costs, price regime). In either case, inventories would build up, causing employers to cut production and lay off more workers. Keynes could see the dynamic effects of a change in wages only by breaking free of the constraints of "equilibrium" theorising and its necessity of thinking in mechanical time. Keynes'theory is in historical time, where the sequence of events, and the historical and social structures are of primary importance (Clark, 1987-88). To this day, neoclassical economists still do not understand this essential point of *The General Theory*, the reason being their inability to "escape" the intellectual straightjacket of the concept of equilibrium.

The largest and most comprehensive empirical investigation into the recent rise in unemployment, the *OECD Jobs Study*, stated that "much unemployment is the unfortunate result of societies'failure to adapt to a world of rapid change and intensified global competition. Rules and regulations, practices and policies, and institutions designed for an earlier era have resulted in labour markets that are too inflexible for today's world" (OECD, 1994). These inflexibilities keep wage rates too high, which discourage employers from increasing employment, and which prevent the correct price signals from being sent to workers telling them to switch occupations. For all its insights and evidence (which are considerable), the OECD report could not produce any direct evidence to support the wage flexibility argument. The fact that they do not even look at inadequate aggregate demand as a possible cause of unemployment shows how constrained the authors are by the neoclassical theoretical perspective that pervades this study. Thus, they ignore the key factors in the recent rise of mass unemployment.

Related to the flexible labour market argument is the social protection argument. As stated above, social spending is often seen as interfering with the natural workings of the labour market as a market clearing mechanism. Various forms of social protection are seen as insulating workers from the discipline of the forces of supply and demand. While there is clear evidence (John Eatwell's earlier mentioned study) that the structure of the labour market will influence how labour slack will be manifested (standard unemployment or disguised unemployment), it is very hard to find any relationship between social spending and unemployment (especially when a broader measure of labour slack is used). Moreover, the levels of social spending and social protection have not changed all that much in the 1980s and 1990s, yet unemployment has increased significantly. Clearly, social spending cannot be the cause of mass unemployment. With both declining social spending throughout most of Europe, and labour markets becoming more flexible throughout the 1980s and 1990s, it hard to see how these could be the cause of the rise in unemployment.

Other common explanations of the rise of unemployment are: (i) the effects of the oil price shock; and (ii) foreign competition. The oil price shocks of the 1970s had a major effect on the advanced capitalist economies. According to the OECD, they reduced income in the developed countries by 20 per cent (Eatwell, 1994). While this is a significant reduction in aggregate demand, and is certainly part of the rise in unemployment, 80 per cent of this reduction must be found elsewhere. Furthermore, the oil price shock was not unprecedented. Other supply shocks have hit the OECD countries before, yet their effects were very limited. Why did the rise in oil prices have such a lasting effect? As we will see below, the answer to this question is not in economics, but in economic theory.

The rise in foreign competition, especially for third world countries, is frequently mentioned as one of the causes in the rise in unemployment. Yet international trade, which rose rapidly from the 1940s to 1975, has not increased all that much since the mid-1970s. Furthermore, most international trade is between rich countries, thus it could not be used as an explanation of the dramatic rise in OECD unemployment (Pressman et al, 1995).

PKI explanation of the rise in mass unemployment

Economies can be classified as either supply constrained or demand constrained. A supply constrained economy is one in which the central economic problems stem from the inability to produce enough goods and services. Pre-industrial revolution Europe was a supply constrained economy.[14] A demand constrained economy is one in which the central economic problems stem from the inability to absorb sufficient amounts of production to keep the economy fully employed and to keep profit rates and expectations high enough to prompt future levels of investment and economic activity. Modern capitalist economies are demand constrained economies. Under such an economic regime, the level of employment is a function of the demand for the goods and services which employed workers would produce. Since a modern capitalist economy can produce much more than what is sufficient for necessary consumption, the economy has a wide range of employment levels it can settle down to. Since labour markets do not possess market clearing attributes, there is no tendency for any one level of employment to be a long run equilibrium.

The level of employment will depend on the level of effective demand. The level of effective demand has no mechanism to bring it to full employment. The level of consumption can be kept artificially high through advertising and conspicuous consumption. The level of government spending could be keep artificially high through the military industrial complex, which can also stimulate the level of investment. Yet none of these are a built in mechanism for insuring that the level of consumption, investment or government spending will be at, or tend towards, the full employment level.

Following Keynes, the PKI perspective sees the problem of mass unemployment as an aggregate demand problem. Given this perspective, the question naturally becomes: Why has the level of aggregate demand been inadequate to sustain full employment?

A look at the decline in the rate of growth of real GDP in the G7 countries demonstrates this general fall in aggregate demand (see Table 1.3).

Table 1.3
Growth of real GDP - "the slowdown" (%)

	A. 1964-73	B. 1983-92	B/A
W.Germany	4.5	2.9	0.64
France	5.3	2.2	0.42
Italy	5.0	2.4	0.48
UK	3.3	2.3	0.69
USA	4.0	2.9	0.72
Canada	5.6	2.8	0.52
Japan	9.6	4.0	0.42

Source: Eatwell (1994, p. 9).

The decline in aggregate demand can be traced to many factors.

> Put simply, lower wages and greater wage inequality reduce consumption spending, fears of capital flight and trade deficits lead policy makers to employ restrictive domestic macroeconomic policy, inappropriate monetary policy stifles business investment, and fear of government budget deficits prevents fiscal policy from stimulating demand through tax cuts or greater government expenditures. With every component of aggregate spending being reduced, it is no wonder that unemployment has been rising throughout the world (Pressman et al, 1995, p. 127).

Four factors seem to underpin the inability of aggregate demand to keep up with potential production: (i) restrictive economic policies; (ii) the break-up of the Bretton Woods system; (iii) the dominance of speculation over productive investment in capital markets; and (iv) the rise in income inequality. All four of these factors have been legitimated by the dominant economic orthodoxy.

As stated before, the rise in oil prices had an effect on the rise in unemployment, but this effect was small, because of the 20 per cent reduction in OECD income. The primary effect that the oil shocks had was to make inflation the number one economic problem, with the restriction of aggregate demand (creating recessions) becoming the main anti-inflation instrument.

One should not ignore the "self-interest" involved in this type of policy. When Keynes suggested in chapter 24 of the *General Theory* that interest rates should be kept very low for a long time to keep investment high, an additional benefit he pointed out was that such a policy would have the effect of making capital less scarce, thus leading to the "euthanasia of the rentier class".Keynes discounted the importance of "vested interests" because such a low interest rate policy redistributes money downward.[15] The financial community has a "vested interest" in keeping capital scarce and favours high interest rates and recession over full employment and possible inflation.

The dominance of restrictive macroeconomic policies has been greatly aided by the two most important institutional changes to have taken place in the international economy in the past three decades: the break-up of the Bretton Woods system; and the increased mobility of capital. These two changes have greatly increased the amount of risk and uncertainty in the international economy, raising real interest rates and stifling investment. Furthermore, they have placed strict limits on the ability of governments to initiate stimulative economic policies, first because of the balance of payments constraint (Glyn and Rowthorn, 1994) which places pressure on the exchange rate when one economy grows faster than its trading partners, causing imports to rise and choking off the much of the multiplier effects, and second, because international investors and speculators can create a crisis for a nation's currency if they disagree with the country's policies. The world financial markets have become what Keynes warned us about: casino capitalism. As John Eatwell (1994, p. 10) recently noted:

> Financial markets are today dominated by short term flows that seek to profit from changes in asset prices, in other words, from speculation. The growth in the scale of speculation, relative to other transactions, has been particularly marked in the foreign exchange markets over the past twenty years. It is estimated that in 1971, just before the collapse of the Bretton Woods fixed-exchange-rate system, about 90 per cent of all foreign exchange transactions were for the finance of trade and long term investment, and only 10 per cent were speculative. Today, those percentages are reversed, with well over 90 per cent of all transactions being speculative. Daily speculative flows now regularly exceed the combined foreign exchange reserves of all the G7 governments.

Thus, the financial community's reaction to government policy is crucial for the success of any economic policy. If they feel that the policy will lead to inflation (that is lowering the real value of their assets) they can act in such a manner to counter the government policy. Specifically, a stimulative government policy will cause the financial community to expect higher inflation, or a change in currency values, thus causing a fall in the value of the currency. To prevent a capital flight, governments and central banks are forced to increase interest rates. Thus, adherence to pre-Keynesian economic theory is enough to prevent governments from attempting to increase aggregate demand. The buzzword dominating economic policy today is "credibility,"[16] with credibility meaning "market friendly," that is, "a policy that is in accordance with what the markets believe to be 'sound'" (Eatwell, 1994, p. 12). Thus, the need to have a credible policy forces governments to lower, or attempt to lower, government spending, deficits, and inflation, that is to pursue a restrictive macroeconomic policy. The extent of this restrictiveness for the G7 nations has been shown by Pressman (1995), who demonstrates how the fiscal impulse, a measure of whether a fiscal stance is expansionary or restrictive, has moved from mostly expansionary in the 1970s to largely restrictive in the 1980s.

Even without the credibility factor, the new international arrangements have a contradictory effect on macroeconomic performance. Under the Bretton Woods system, much of the risk in the international economy was transferred to the international agencies and governments. Pressures on currencies were mediated by central banks, thus eliminating the risk of a swing in values. This lowered real interest rates by reducing risk. Furthermore, since there was little economic incentive to speculate in currency values, there was much less uncertainty. Thus, interest rates were lowered further by a more certain future. The break-up of the Bretton Woods system thus caused a significant rise in real interest rates, which, along with the rise in monetarism and restrictive monetary policy, led to the high real interest rates of the 1980s and 1990s. Also, a rise in interest rates led to a reduction in investment activity, and with it a fall in aggregate demand.

The fourth factor which has lead to a rise in insufficient aggregate demand is the rise in the level of income inequality. In chapter 24 of the *General Theory,* Keynes argued that the "arbitrary and inequitable distribution of wealth and incomes" contributed to the problem of mass unemployment. Given that the marginal propensity to consume falls with increases in relative income, a shift in income towards the lower income classes leads necessarily to a rise in aggregate demand, while a shift upwards will have the opposite effect. Furthermore, the distribution of income can have an effect on the balance of trade if the propensity to import is higher among the more affluent than it is for those on lower incomes. Such differences seemed to exist for the United Kingdom (Arestis and Howells, 1994) and the United States.

Thus, we should not be surprised that the rise in mass unemployment coincided with a general rise in income inequality.[17] In fact, the rise in income inequality is partially the result of the same set of economic policies which have resulted in the rise in mass unemployment (Clark, 1996).

The case of Ireland

As stated at the outset of this chapter, Ireland's high unemployment rate, and its rise over the past two decades, must be seen as a dual problem. Much of Ireland's increase in unemployment is due to the general trends noted above, which have affected Ireland both as exogenous factors and as internal developments.

The rise in Irish unemployment can be explained by looking at changes in the level of aggregate demand. From 1973 to 1979, the average growth in real total domestic demand for Ireland was 5.4 per cent, whereas for 1980-1992 it rose at an average rate of 0.3 per cent (see Table 1.4). In these same time periods, Ireland's unemployment rate rose from an average of 7.34 per cent in the first period to 14.57 per cent in the latter. Investment was particularly weak. According to the OECD (1995), gross fixed capital formation had an average real increase of 0.0 per cent from 1984 to 1993, which is to say that during that period there was no capital accumulation in Ireland. The recent Forfás report *Shaping*

Our Future (1996), also notes this disturbing trend. In 1981, Irish non-residential fixed investment as a percentage of GDP was 24.1 per cent. This figure fell steadily during the 1980s to 12.5 per cent in 1992. The most dramatic aspect of this fall is the decline in business investment, which fell from 19.5 per cent in 1981 to 10.3 per cent in 1992. Some of this decrease can be accounted for, the report suggests, by the fall in profitability of Irish firms, a clear sign of inadequate aggregate demand, while much is accounted for by the increase in Irish firms acquiring financial assets and investing overseas. This, I would suggest, is a reflection of the new institutional arrangements of increased capital mobility and the dominance of speculation over productive investment. Capital formation has been shown to be a major determinant of employment (Rowthorn 1995), a point which is missed by those who view unemployment as solely a labour market problem.

Only Lee (1988), in the studies reviewed by Donal McGettigan (1994), mentions capital formation as an important factor in Ireland's increase in unemployment, suggesting that the fall in capital formation could be a cause of hysteresis in the Irish labour market. The dis-investing in Ireland, at a time when the EU average of non-residential fixed investment as a percentage of GDP increased marginally, should be seen as one of the primary factors explaining its differentially high unemployment rate.

Similarly, public consumption fell during the 1980s and 1990s, contributing to the rise in unemployment. From 1970 to 1979, real public consumption rose at an average annual rate of 6.2 per cent in Ireland, while from 1980 to 1992, its rate of increase was a mere 0.9 per cent. This is a much sharper drop than the average for the European Union, which fell from 3.7 per cent to 2.2 per cent. The contradictory effects of the government sector can also be seen by their fiscal stance, which was generally restrictive during the 1980s and 1990s.

The only aspect of aggregate demand which improved during the 1980s and early 1990s was the balance of trade, with the growth rate in exports rising, while the growth rate in imports fell to 50 per cent of the 1970s rate. This too can be attributed to weak domestic aggregate demand. If Ireland's aggregate demand shortage were not enough of a problem, the fact that a good portion of the social surplus (from which societies typically get the funds for capital accumulation) leaves Ireland for other countries, makes inadequate aggregate demand even more likely.

From 1988 to 1993, an average of 11.5 per cent of GDP leaked out of the Irish economy in the form of repatriated profits, dividends, royalties and net interest with profits, dividends and royalties accounting for 9.5 per cent and net interest for 1.9 per cent (OECD, 1995, p. 5). This far exceeds the amount of foreign investment and in many years is close to total domestic investment.

Although Ireland has one of the highest levels of income inequality in the OECD (Atkinson et al, 1995), and it witnessed an increased level of income inequality from 1987 to 1994 (Clark and Healy, 1997), it is difficult to say whether this has had a significant effect on aggregate demand. Certainly a more equal level of income distribution would change the composition of spending, leading to an increase in consumption spending. However, with Ireland's high degree of openness, it is hard to say how much of this would lead to the consumption of domestic production as opposed to the consumption of imports.

Table 1.4
Changes in Irish aggregate demand (%), 1970-1992

	A 1970-79	B 1980/92	B/A
Average annual growth in			
Real private consumption	4.5	1.7	0.37
Real public consumption	6.2	0.9	0.14
Total gross fixed investment	7.1	-0.4	-0.05
Total domestic demand	5.4	0.3	0.05
Real exports	7.5	8.3	1.10
Real imports	7.8	3.9	0.50
Unemployment rate	7.34*	14.57	1.99

* 1973-1979

Source: OECD *Economic Outlook*, 1996.

During the period when Ireland's unemployment rose dramatically, real unit labour costs fell, relatively and absolutely. This was caused by real wages not keeping pace with productivity gains. With real unit labour costs falling, it is difficult to argue that the rise in unemployment was due to wages being too high, or the inability of real wages to fall when unemployment was rising. Furthermore, Ireland's level of taxation and social spending are among the lowest in Europe, further questioning these commonly attributable causes of high unemployment.

The Celtic Tiger

The recent "success" of the Irish economy has, in the past two years, began to make significant reductions in the level of unemployment. In 1992, Ireland's unemployment rate was more than 50 per cent higher than the European Union average, while by late 1996, it was equal to this average. If the analysis of the effect of aggregate demand on rising unemployment is accurate, we should also expect aggregate demand to be able to explain the decline in unemployment. An examination of Table 1.5 illustrates that this is in fact the case. Thus, we see that Ireland's rate of unemployment fell by 3.6 percentage points, while the European Union's average rose slightly. While it is beyond the scope of this paper to examine Ireland's recent economic boom, we can see that the rise in investment, much of it spurred by the infusion of EU structural funds, has played an important role, as has Ireland's continued strong growth in exports.

Table 1.5
Per cent changes in Ireland's & EU's aggregate demand, 1993-96

	A Ireland	B Europe
Average annual growth in		
Real private consumption	4.43	1.30
Real public consumption	2.45	1.00
Total gross fixed investment	6.25	-0.30
Total domestic demand	4.60	1.10
Real exports	12.78	5.60
Real imports	10.95	3.58
Changes in the unemployment rate 1993 to 1996	-3.60	+0.30

Source: OECD *Economic Outlook* (1996).

Conclusion

A review of the developments in Ireland's aggregate demand suggest that one should have expected a dramatic rise in the rate of unemployment. An examination of how the other small European countries aggregate demand fared in the 1970s and through to the 1990s indicates that Ireland was not alone in facing falling aggregate demand. The growth in domestic demand for the small European countries fell from a rate of growth of 2.91 per cent in 1973-79 to 2.02 per cent in 1980-92, far less then what Ireland experienced (5.4 per cent to 0.3 per cent). The major difference between Ireland and the other small European countries was that Ireland's fall in private and public consumption was moderately larger than the other small European countries (with the drop in public consumption being much larger for Ireland), while the other small European countries increased investment by 85 per cent, with both exports and imports increasing marginally.

Can all of Ireland's unemployment problem be blamed on the fall in aggregate demand? Certainly not. Ireland's labour slack problem is centuries old. For hundreds of years, Ireland existed to provide England with cheap labour, and its social and cultural institutions reflect this long history. Furthermore, part of Ireland's labour force is particularly ill-suited to the employment needs of the 21st century, particularly those who are counted as the long term unemployed.

The overall labour slack in the world economy is not expected to improve in the near future, and most likely won't ever improve under existing institutional arrangements. The problem of mass unemployment is exasperated by the breakdown of the Bretton Woods system, the increase in capital mobility, the almost universal acceptance of restrictive macroeconomic policies and the neoclassical ideology which supports it. Yet the existence of a labour surplus is a common feature of all stages of capitalism, and is particularly the case in demand constrained, affluent economies. In the Golden Age of Capitalism (the end of World War II to 1971), a host of factors helped to artificially generate demand (the Cold War; the Marshall Plan; the rise of consumerism and conspicuous consumption and advertising; and the increased state spending from the full development of the Welfare State) so as to mask this fundamental problem. However, none of these individually or collectively can permanently mask the basic contradictions in modern capitalism: the ability of societies to produce more than they need to consume, and the assignment of incomes (social participation) based on ones contribution to this production process.

Such inherent problems will not be addressed by marginal analysis or marginal economic policies. Labour market reforms, i.e., increasing labour market flexibility, will not improve Ireland's glaringly inadequate aggregate demand. Furthermore, it will do little to help the long term unemployed, who need education and training and the hope of jobs if such activities are undertaken, and not more efficient "market signals", meaning lower wages for the already low paid and less government protection for those who already have little protection. What is needed is to escape from the old ideas and to rethink the nature of work, social participation and the purpose of economics.

References

Appelbaum, E. (1979), "The Labour Market", in Eichner, A. (ed.), *A Guide to Post Keynesian Economics*, M.E. Sharpe: Armonk, New York.

Arestis, P. and Howells, P. (1994), "Changes in Income Distribution and Aggregate Spending: Constraints on Full-Employment?" *Review of Political Economy*, Vol. 7, No. 2, April, pp. 150-163.

Atkinson, A., Rainwater, L. and Smeeding, T. (1995), *Income Distribution in the OECD*, OECD: Paris.

Clark, C.M.A. (1987-88), "Equilibrium, Market Process and Historical Time", *Journal of Post Keynesian Economics*, Vol. 10, Winter, pp. 260-71.

Clark, C.M.A. (1992), *Economic Theory and Natural Philosophy*, Edward Elgar: Aldershot.

Clark, C.M.A. (1996), "Inequality in the 1980s: An Institutionalist View", in Dugger, W. (ed.), *Inequality: Radical Institutionalist Perspectives on Race, Gender, Class, and Nation*, Greenwood Press, New York.

Clark, C.M.A. and Kavanagh, C. (1995), "Basic Income and the Irish Worker", in Reynolds, B. and Healy, S. (eds.), *An Adequate Income Guarantee for All: Desirability, Viability, Impact*, CORI: Dublin.
Clark, C.M.A. and Kavanagh, C. (1996), "Progress, Values and Economic Indicators", in Reynolds, B. and Healy, S. (eds.), *Progress, Values and Public Policy*, CORI: Dublin.
Clark, C.M.A. and Healy, J. (1997), *Pathways to a Basic Income*, CORI: Dublin.
Eatwell, J. (1995), "Disguised Unemployment: The G7 Experience", UNCTAD Discussion Paper.
Eatwell, J. (ed.) (1994), *Global Unemployment: Loss of Jobs in the 90's*. M.E. Sharpe: Armonk, New York.
Forfas (1996), *Shaping Our Future*, Forfas: Dublin.
Gly, A. and Rowthorn, B. (1994), "European Employment Policies", in Michie, J. and Grieve Smith, J. (eds.), *Unemployment in Europe*, Academic Press: London.
Heilbroner, R.L. (1985), *The Nature and Logic of Capitalism*, Norton: New York.
Keynes, J.M. (1973), *The General Theory of Employment, Interest and Money*, Cambridge University Press: Cambridge.
Lee, G. (1988), "Hysteresis and the Natural Rate of Unemployment", *Journal of the Statistical and Social Inquiry of Ireland*, Vol. 25, Part II.
Moore, B.J. (1989), "The Effects of Monetary Policy on Income Distribution", in Davidson, P. and Kregal, J.A. (eds.), *Macroeconomic Problems and Policies of Income Distribution: Functional, Personal, International*, Edward Elgar: London.
Niggle, C.J. (1989), "Monetary Policy and Changes in Income Distribution", *Journal of Economic Issues*, Vol. 23, No. 3, pp. 809-22.
OECD (1993), *Employment Outlook 1993*, OECD: Paris.
OECD (1994), *Employment Outlook 1994*, OECD: Paris.
OECD (1994), *Economic Outlook 1994*, OECD: Paris.
OECD (1994), *OECD Jobs Study, Evidence and Explanations, Part I*, OECD: Paris.
OECD (1994), *OECD Jobs Study, Evidence and Explanations, Part II*, OECD: Paris.
OECD (1995), *OECD Economic Surveys - Ireland*, OECD: Paris..
OECD (1996), *Economic Outlook 1996*, OECD: Paris.
Pressman, S. (1995), "Deficits, Full Employment and the Use of Fiscal Policy", *Review of Political Economy*, Vol. 7, No. 2, pp. 212-226.
Pressman, S., Seccareccia, M. and Lavoie, M. (1995), "High Unemployment in Developed Economies", *Review of Political Economy*, Vol. 7, No.2, April, pp. 125-32.
Ramstad, Y. (1993), "Institutional Economics and the Dual Labour Market Theory", in Tool, M. (ed.), *Institutional Economics: Theory, Method, Policy*, Kluwer: Boston.
Robinson, J. (1937), *Introduction to the Theory of Unemployment*, Macmillan: London.

Rowthorn, R. (1995), "Capital Formation and Unemployment", *Oxford Review of Economic Policy*, Vol. 11, No. 1, pp. 26-39.
Standing, G. and Tokman, V. (1992), *Towards Social Adjustment?* ILO: Geneva.
Weeks, J. (1992), "The Myth of Labour Market Clearing", in Standing, G. and Tokman, V. (eds.), *Towards Social Adjustment?*, ILO: Geneva.
Wilber, C. and Jameson, K. (1983), *Poverty of Economics*, University of Notre Dame Press: South Bend, Ind.
Woodbury, S. (1987), "Power in the Labour Market", *Journal of Economic Issues*, Vol. 21, No. 4, December, pp. 1781-1807.

Notes

1 We are combining aspects of post-Keynesian macroeconomics with institutionalist labour economics, following in the tradition of Wilber and Jameson (1983).

2 This section is largely taken from Clark and Kavanagh (1995).

3 This summary has benefited greatly from John Weeks (1992).

4 This is contrasted with the "rigid wages" interpretation of Keynes. Considering that Keynes explicitly assumes flexible wages, it is hard to see how this reading of Keynes has become so widely accepted.

5 For a history of how neoclassical economic theory became ahistorical and asocial, see Clark (1992).

6 For a history of this approach to labour, see Yngve Ramstads (1993).

7 See Appelbaum (1979) and Woodbury (1987) for introductions to post-Keynesian and institutionalist views, respectively, on labour markets.

8 Post-Keynesian economics is derived from Keynes, but differs from the neoclassical interpretations of Keynes in that post-Keynesians do not try to harmonise Keynes' insights with neoclassical microeconomic theory. Neoclassical macroeconomics is based on a rigid wage interpretation of Keynes, that is, that unemployment is due to a labour market imperfection (wages are not flexible). Keynes and post-Keynesians contend that unemployment would exist even if wages were flexible (which of course they are not).

9 This is also true of the money market which determines interest rates.

10 John Eatwell defined disguised unemployment as any increase in employment sectors of the economy which have a value of output per head of less than 80 per cent of the manufacturing sector.

11 The other area where this is the case is the use of GDP as a measure of economic and social well-being, a topic which is discussed in Clark and Kavanagh (1996).

12 Here, I am referring to wage flexibility only. There are many aspects of labour market flexibility, many of which are very important for the operation of the economy. It is unfortunate that neoclassical economists seem only to be interested in this one aspect of flexibility. See Clark and Kavanagh (1995, pp. 112-113) for a brief review of this issue.

13 The "neoclassicalness" of this variety of theorising is the necessity of having "individual maximising decision makers" as the final term of analysis.

14 An analysis of the differences between supply and demand constrained economies can be found in John Kenneth Galbraith's *The Affluent Society*, albeit with different terminology.

15 For an analysis of the effect of monetary policy on income distribution, see Moore (1989) and Niggle (1989). Their work is summarised in Clark (1996).

16 Credibility is essentially a blackmail relationship. The ability to withhold capital, an essential aspect of private property rights, has always been a fundamental component of the power relations in capitalism (Heilbroner, 1985). However, when capital mobility is limited to a nation, this ability to withhold capital is limited, for it cannot be in the interest of capitalists to let the means of production sit idle for too long. The increase in capital mobility largely removes this limit.

17 See Atkinson et al (1995) for an analysis of the changes in international income distribution levels.

2 Unemployment, non-participation and labour market slack among Irish males

Anthony Murphy

Brendan M. Walsh

Introduction

Despite the central place of the concept of unemployment in macroeconomics, economists devote relatively little attention to the problems attendant on its measurement. Most theoretical discussions assume that a well-defined measure of unemployment is available and econometric studies often use official published unemployment series without discussing their validity. However, specialists in labour economics are aware of the important complications that arise in the measurement of unemployment and of the fact that no single series provides an ideal measure of labour market slack. The issues that arise in this context have been reviewed in several specialised studies (Garvey, 1998; and Royal Statistical Society, 1995).

This chapter deals with the measurement of labour market conditions among Irish males over the period 1983-96. The central question addressed is how important is it to take account of other indicators of labour market slack to supplement the information conveyed by the conventional unemployment rate. As well as looking at the full range of time series evidence available from the published results of the Labour Force Survey (LFS), we use the detailed results of the 1993 Survey to explore the individual characteristics associated with different labour market outcomes. Attention is confined to male labour market outcomes because different, and more complex, issues arise in connection with women's labour force participation and employment. These have been studied separately (Murphy and Walsh, 1997).

Alternative measures of labour market slack

Labour force participation rates may be affected by the availability of employment opportunities. For this reason they should be used to supplement the evidence from unemployment rates when assessing the trend in labour market conditions. The non-employment rate captures the effects of both unemployment and non-participation.[1]

A rising rate of male non-employment has been widely observed in recent years. This reflects lower rates of labour force participation as well as higher rates of unemployment. In the United States, the fall in the employment rate of older males has been attributed to a combination of reduced labour supply and declining wages, with the former playing the main role in the 1960s, the latter in the 1980s (Juhn, 1992). In Ireland, a marked contrast between the labour market outcomes of men and women has been noted (Murphy and Walsh, 1997). Since the end of the recession of the early 1980s, the number of women at work has increased steadily. Between 1985 and 1996, female employment grew by 45 per cent. On the other hand, the number of men at work did not begin to grow until 1989 and by 1996 had increased by only 9 per cent. Over the same period there was a decline in the female unemployment rate relative to the male - in 1983 the female unemployment rate was 17 per cent higher than the male rate but since 1992, the male rate has been slightly higher than the female. Finally, there has been a sharp rise in labour force participation rates for women aged 20 and over while male participation rates have declined. These developments are part of a long run trend for the share of women in the labour force to grow, which has been attributed to factors such as declining family size, rising women's educational levels and shifts in the demand for labour in favour of traditionally female occupations (Walsh, 1993). A relative deterioration in male employment and earnings could also be due to increased exports of unskilled-labour-intensive products from low-wage countries, the empirical importance of which has been much debated recently (IMF, 1997).

International comparisons

The LFS and its US counterpart, the Current Population Survey, is the main source of modern labour market statistics.[2] It provides two measures of the population's labour force status - one based on the respondent's self-assessed principal economic status (PES), the other on his or her situation with respect to employment in a reference week prior to the survey. The latter forms the basis of the International Labour Office (ILO) definition of the labour force that is widely used in international comparisons and generally regarded as more meaningful, from an economic perspective, than the PES measure.[3] Table 2.1 presents data on an ILO basis on the unemployment rate, the labour force participation rate, and the non-employment rate among men aged 25-54 years in the 20 OECD countries in 1994. Ireland's unemployment and non-employment rates are surpassed only by Finland and Spain.

Table 2.1
Labour market indicators, males aged 25-44, OECD countries, 1994

Country	Labour force participation rate	Employment rate	Unemployment rate	Non-employment rate
Japan	97.5	95.5	2.0	4.5
Luxembourg	94.9	92.6	2.5	7.4
Greece	94.5	90.0	4.8	10.0
Portugal	93.6	89.1	4.8	10.9
Netherlands	92.6	87.4	5.6	12.6
US	91.7	87.2	4.9	12.8
Norway	90.6	86.3	4.7	13.7
Belgium	92.1	86.2	6.4	13.8
France	95.1	85.9	9.7	14.1
New Zealand	92.3	85.9	7.0	14.1
Denmark	91.9	85.7	6.7	14.3
Australia	91.4	84.5	7.5	15.5
UK	93.0	83.9	9.8	16.1
Germany	89.2	83.0	6.9	17.0
Sweden	89.8	82.8	7.9	17.2
Canada	91.4	82.7	9.5	17.3
Italy	87.0	81.8	6.0	18.2
Ireland	90.8	77.7	14.4	22.3
Spain	92.9	77.6	16.4	22.4
Finland	90.9	75.1	17.4	24.9

Source: OECD, *Employment Outlook* (1996), Tables 4.1, 4.2, and 4.3.
Note: The employment rate and the non-employment rate can be derived from the unemployment rate and the labour force participation rate. If E = employment, P = population, and U = unemployment, E/P = (1-U/(U+E))x(U+E)/P, that is, the employment rate equals 1 *minus* the unemployment rate *times* the participation rate.

It is evident from Figure 2.1 that high unemployment rates tend to be associated with low labour force participation rates. A regression of the log of the labour force participation rate, *y*, on the log of the unemployment rate, *x*, yielded the following result when all twenty OECD countries were included (absolute *t*-ratio in parentheses).

$$\hat{y} = 4.56 - \underset{(1.94)}{0.019x} \qquad R^2 = 0.19 \qquad (1)$$

The negative coefficient of the unemployment rate is expected, but it is not highly significant statistically. It is evident from the scatterplot in Figure 2.1 that Ireland, Spain and Finland are outliers, with relatively high labour force participation rates in view of their high unemployment rates.

Figure 2.1
Scatterplot of labour force participation and unemployment rates, males aged 25-54, OECD countries

When the regression is run excluding these three countries, the following result is obtained.

$$\hat{y} = 4.58 - \underset{(2.11)}{0.029\,x} \qquad R^2 = 0.23 \qquad (2)$$

There is an increase in the level of significance and the elasticity of the participation rate with respect to the unemployment rate is higher, although still very low. It may be concluded that there is some evidence from the international evidence that high unemployment rates depress male labour force participation rates, but that the effect is not large and the three countries with the highest unemployment rates, of which Ireland is one, are exceptions to this generalisation.

Trends in unemployment and non-employment in Ireland

Figure 2.2 presents the Irish male unemployment rate on the standard ILO basis and on the broader PES definition over the period 1983-1996. The two series convey the same information about the cyclical behaviour of the labour market since 1983. The unemployment rate reached a peak in 1987, fell sharply over the years 1987-1991, rose to a lower peak in 1993, and has fallen very rapidly since then. Although over the longer run an upward drift in the unemployment rate at comparable stages of the business cycle is apparent and has been taken as evidence of hysteresis (Leddin and Walsh, 1995), the series in Figure 2.2 show no evidence of an upward drift from peak to peak, or trough to trough, since 1983.

Figure 2.2
Unemployment rate, males

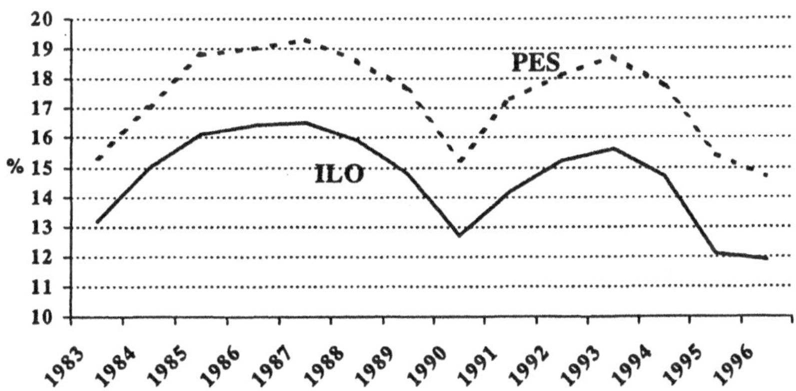

To establish the relationship between the two unemployment rates more precisely, we have regressed the log of the PES unemployment rate (y) on the log of the ILO unemployment rate (x) and a time trend, for the period 1983-96, with the following result (absolute t-ratios in parentheses).

$$\hat{y} = 0.36 + 0.92x + 0.0052Time \qquad (3)$$

$$(3.6) \qquad (25.6) \qquad (5.5)$$

D.W = 2.97
R^2 = 0.99

The elasticity of the PES rate with respect to the ILO rate is significantly less than unity (Wald test, Prob ^{2} < 0.05), indicating that the cyclical fluctuations in the PES rate are dampened slightly relative to those in the ILO rate. The positive trend is highly statistically significant, confirming that the PES rate has tended to rise relative to the ILO rate over time.

The reason why the PES unemployment rate exceeds the ILO rate is that many men who classify themselves as "usually unemployed" do not report any form of active job search and hence are classified as "inactive" rather than "unemployed" according to ILO conventions.[4] Our regression results indicate that, controlling for the level of unemployment as measured by ILO definitions, the proportion of the male population in the inactive categories has been increasing over time.

Figure 2.3
Non-employment rate, males aged 15-64

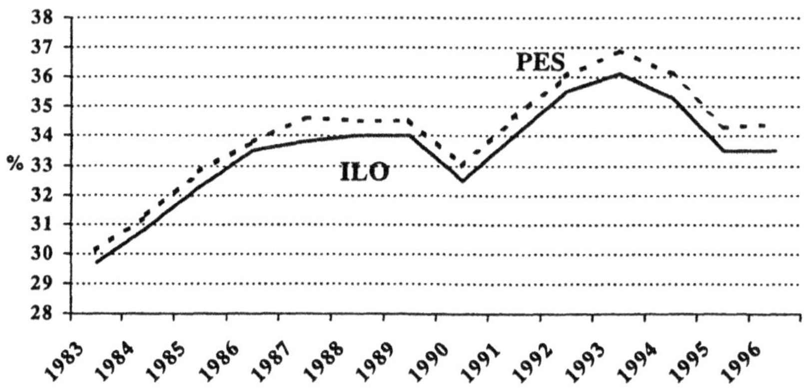

Figure 2.3 shows the male non-employment rate on a PES and ILO basis for the years 1983-96. The gap between the two measures of non-employment is much smaller than between the two unemployment rates, reflecting the fact that little of the discrepancy between the unemployment rates is due to the classification of employed males. The relationship between the two non-employment rates was explored by regressing the log of the PES rate (y) on the log of the ILO rate (x) and a time trend, for the period 1983-96, with the following result.

$$\hat{y} = -0.03 + 1.01x + 0.0004 Time \quad (4)$$
$$(0.3) \quad (33.0) \quad (1.2)$$

D.W. = 2.65
R^2 = 0.99

The elasticity of the PES unemployment rate with respect to the ILO rate is not significantly different from unity (Wald test, Prob $^2 > 0.05$), indicating that there is no significant difference between the cyclical behaviour of the two series. The trend variable is not significantly different from zero, which establishes that there has been no upward trend in non-employment that is not reflected in both series. While the cyclical pattern in the non-employment rates is similar to that in the unemployment rates, there is a marked upward trend in the former that is not evident in the latter. This reflects a falling trend in the rate of male labour force participation, which we discuss below. The closer concordance between the two non-employment rates bolsters the case for using this indicator, as well as the unemployment rate, in assessing the trend in labour market conditions.

Demographic factors are often believed to play an important role in labour market developments. The entry of the post-war baby-boom generation on the labour market in the 1970s tended to depress the opportunities for young workers, resulting in a downward movement in the age-earnings profile in the United States and a rise in the relative youth unemployment rate in many European countries.[5] Since 1980, these trends have been reversed in most OECD countries. In Ireland, however, the population aged 15-24 is still exceptionally high as a proportion of the population aged 25-54, at 44.9 per cent compared with an (unweighted) OECD average of 34.5 per cent (1994). Yet despite this, the youth unemployment rate as a percentage of the adult rate is relatively low in Ireland (see Figure 2.4). A factor that may help account for this is the relatively low labour force participation rate among Irish teenagers - only 26.4 per cent of the Irish male population aged 15-19 were in the labour force, compared with the OECD average of 36.4 per cent. Emigration has been very important in this age group. The openness of the labour market tends to stabilise the rate of unemployment.

Figure 2.4
Youth unemployment rates as a percentage of adult rates, OECD, 1994

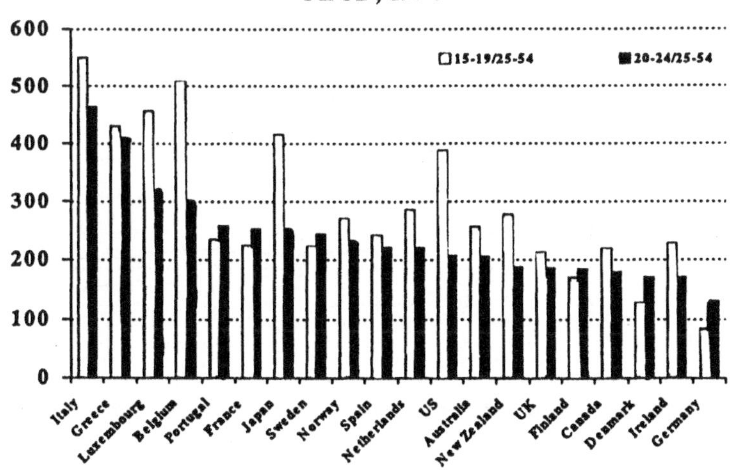

Conflicting views have been aired about the effect of Ireland's demographic structure on labour market outcomes. In the past, the high rate of growth of the labour force was often invoked as a factor contributing to the high unemployment rate, but in recent years it has been argued that the availability of an abundant supply of labour force entrants has contributed to the rapid growth of employment. The truth is difficult to establish due to the need to control for other influences. On the basis of a panel study of 20 countries over the period 1970-94 that took into account aggregate employment conditions, trend, and some country-specific influences, the OECD concluded that

> relative population [structure] has no statistically significant effect on teenage male employment and only a small effect on young adult men's employment rates (OECD, 1996, p. 141).

Other factors, such as the degree of labour market flexibility, are more important than purely demographic influences. Ireland has coped well up to now with the entry of the baby boom generation of the 1970s onto the labour market. In the mid-1980s, high emigration among school leavers eased the pressure on the labour market, but in recent years the growth of employment has been more than adequate to absorb the natural increase of the labour force.

Figure 2.5 displays the Irish PES and ILO unemployment rates by age in 1993. The PES unemployment rate is relatively flat over the interval 25-64, but the ILO rate continues to fall with advancing age. As a result, the discrepancy between the PES and ILO rates widens at the older age groups, reflecting the tendency for older men to continue to classify themselves as "usually unemployed" even when they have ceased any form of active job search.

Figure 2.5
Male unemployment rate by age group, 1993

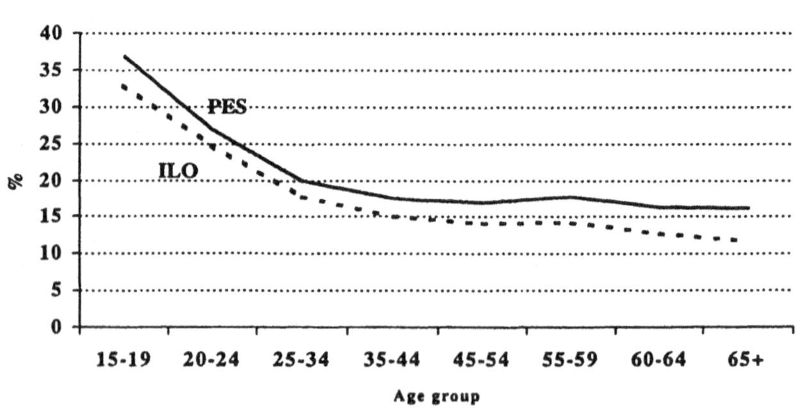

Figure 2.6 shows the pattern of the non-employment rate by age, which is very different from that of the unemployment rate.[6] Non-employment is high among those aged 15-24, reflecting the large proportion still in full-time education. The rate is flat over the range 25-54, and then rises sharply after age 55. (Only between ages 21 and 62 is half or more of the male population at work.)

Figure 2.6
Male non-employment rate by age group, 1993

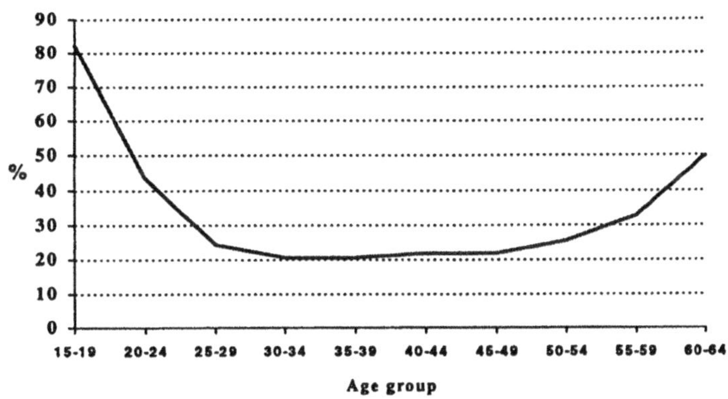

The rise in non-employment among older males provides the strongest evidence of the existence of hidden unemployment or labour market slack that is not reflected in the conventional unemployment figure. A perspective on the extent of this phenomenon is provided in Figure 2.7 which shows the proportions who classified themselves in the PES "usually unemployed", "retired", and "disabled, permanently ill, etc." categories in 1993. Over the interval from age 20 to 49, the total number of these three categories is roughly constant, with the numbers unemployed declining and those in the other two categories rising. After aged 50 the total rises sharply, as the decline in the numbers unemployed is more than offset by the rising numbers "retired" and "disabled". It is striking that in the age group 55-59, the numbers in each of these three categories are almost equal.

There is clearly an element of arbitrariness about the labour force status to which elderly men with poor employment prospects are assigned. Econometric analysis shows that the same factors are associated with non-participation and unemployment among males aged 20-59, namely being single, low educational attainment, living in local authority housing, and living in a household with other unemployed or inactive adults (Murphy and Walsh, 1996).

In Figures 2.8 (a, b, and c), we show the age-specific ILO unemployment and non-employment rates for the years 1983-96. The same cyclical pattern is common to all three age groups, but it is most pronounced among youths aged 15-24 and least pronounced among those aged 45-64. The age-specific non-employment rates display a similar but much less pronounced cyclical pattern to that revealed by the unemployment rates. Among younger and older males, a secular rise in non-employment has been the dominant feature.

Figure 2.7
Non-employed males by age group, 1993
(excluding students)

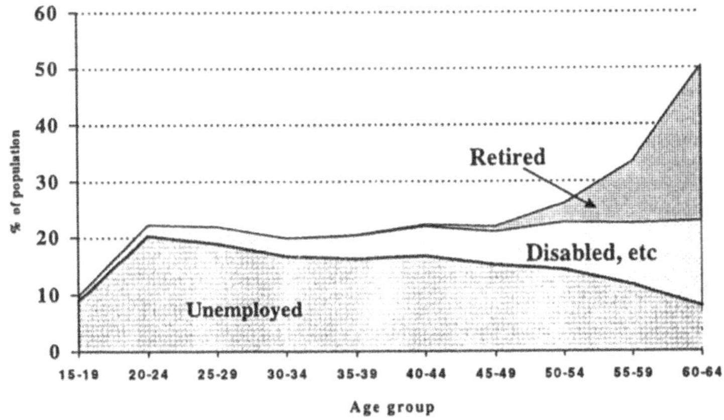

Figure 2.8a
Unemployment and non-employment rates,
males aged 15-24

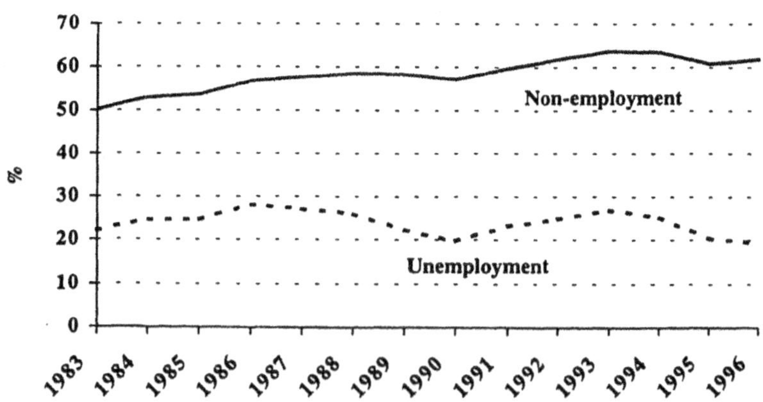

The recent fall in the youth unemployment rate should be interpreted in light of the continuing reduction in the labour force participation rate in this age group.

There was a sharp rise in the non-employment rate among males aged 45-64 in the first half of the 1980s and this has not been reversed during the recent boom. Since the late 1980s, about 30 per cent of the men in this age group are not employed and, as we noted above, a preponderance of them are either retired or permanently ill. Among the population of prime working age (25-44 years), unemployment is the dominant form of non-employment and the labour force participation rate has remained within a very narrow range (92.3 to 93.9 per cent). As a consequence, there is a very close correlation between the non-employment and unemployment rates in this age group. The recent pronounced fall in both the unemployment and non-employment rates in this age group is unambiguous evidence of an improvement in labour market conditions.

Figure 2.8b
Unemployment and non-employment rates,
males aged 25-44

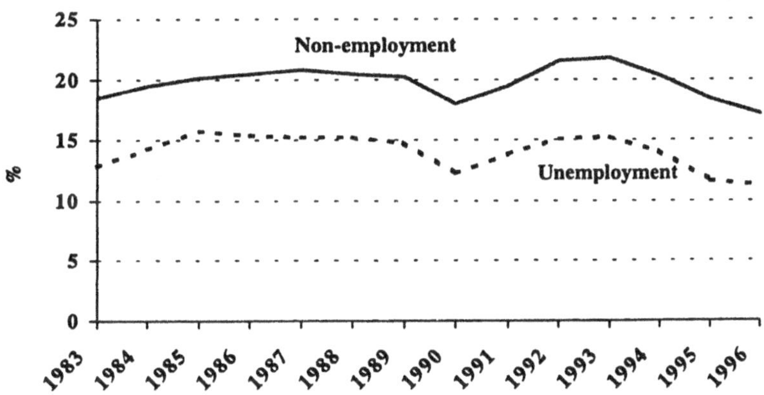

Some obvious reasons may be cited for the falling employment rate among younger and older males. Labour force participation has been falling over the long run among teenagers and young adults due to the rise in educational participation. In the past, a high rate of labour force participation by elderly males was partly a reflection of the high propensity of older farmers to be classified as gainfully occupied and a decline was to be expected as the importance of the farm labour force diminished. It is also likely that the deteriorating earnings prospects facing poorly-educated older workers and wider provision of various "pre-retirement" pension options have also contributed to the fall labour force participation.[7]

To test for the existence of a cyclical discouraged worker effect, we have explored the relationship between the age-specific labour force participation rates and the unemployment rates and a time trend.

Figure 2.8c
Unemployment and non-employment rates, males aged 45-64

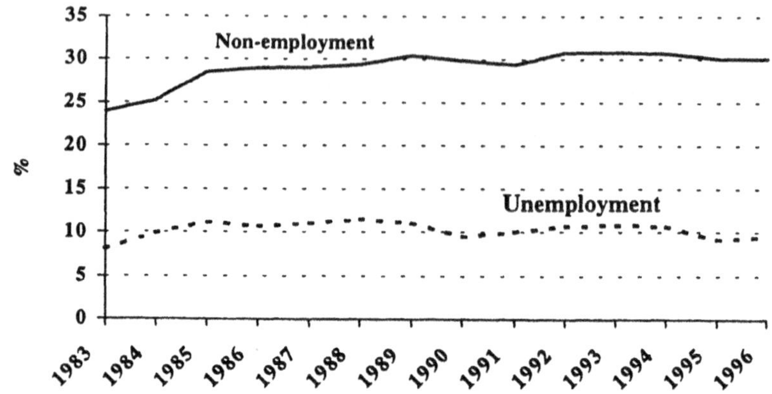

The results in Table 2.2 show a marked non-linear trend in the 15-24 and 45-64 age groups. Having fallen rapidly, participation rates in these age groups are tending to level off. The influence of the unemployment rate is small and not statistically significant, suggesting that cyclical influences on participation are not important. Moreover, the coefficients of the unemployment rate are positive, indicating that if anything, the participation rates vary pro-cyclically (although the effect is not significant in any age group). This is contrary to the generally reported result of counter-cyclical variation in participation rates (Borjas, 1996). The positive coefficients on the unemployment rate could be a reflection of a tendency for reductions in the participation rates to have resulted in lower unemployment rates in the 15-24 and 45-64 age groups. Among males of prime working age, 25-44, there is no evidence of systematic influences on the participation rate, which has remained in a narrow range between 92.3 and 94.8 per cent.

These results do not indicate the existence of a significant level of labour market discouragement in the guise of cyclical variations in the participation rate, but the sharp fall in the participation rate among younger men should be borne in mind in assessing the unemployment rate in this age group.

In Figure 2.9, we show the ILO unemployment rate for married and single males.[8] The cyclicality of the rate for single men is higher than that for married men, and there is a much more pronounced downward trend in the latter. In 1988, the ratio of the single to married unemployment rate was 1.4:1, by 1996 it had risen to 1.85:1. The reasons for the relative increase in the unemployment rate among single men merits further research.[9] Changes in the population structure may be relevant. The ratio of single to married men aged 20-39 rose from 0.9:1 to 1.4:1 over this period. As marriage became a rarer status, it may also have become more selective of characteristics favourable to good labour market outcomes.

Table 2.2
Regression of labour force participation rate *(y)* on unemployment rate *(x)* and trend, log-linear specification, 1983-1996
(absolute *t*-ratios in parentheses)

		Estimated coefficients				
Males aged	*Intercept*	*x*	*Trend*	*Trend squared*	R^2	*D.W.*
15-24	4.14	0.0214	-0.0341	0.00067	0.985	1.78
	(77.8)	(0.64)	(9.1)	(2.7)		
25-44	4.54	0.0005	0.0012	- 0.00014	0.10	1.30
	(63.9)	(0.8)	(0.5)	(0.8)		
45-64	4.40	0.0160	- 0.0148	0.00063	0.91	2.25
	(71.4)	(0.6)	(5.3)	(3.5)		

Note: Unemployment and labour force participation rates on ILO definitions.

In view of the likely greater element of voluntary unemployment among unmarried males, the rate among married males is of particular significance as an indicator of labour market conditions. This had fallen to 8.7 per cent in 1996, indicating that labour market conditions are now much tighter than is suggested by the overall unemployment rate of 11.9 per cent.

Figure 2.9
Unemployment rate by marital status, males

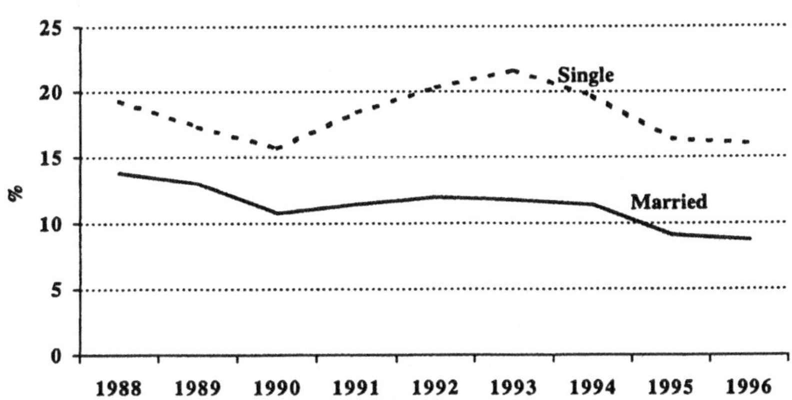

Discouragement and disguised unemployment

We have drawn attention to the existence of a certain number of men who are not economically active according to ILO definitions but who none the less have some attachment to the labour force and may regard themselves as "unemployed". In this section, we explore the reported job search behaviour and some of the characteristics of those in this situation and use these to gauge the extent of the phenomenon of hidden unemployment.

In Table 2.3 we investigate the level of interest in employment among men of prime working age who are classified as ILO inactive in 1993. Only a relatively small minority (13.3 per cent) of those inactive were looking for work,[10] and of these a sizeable minority (38.3 per cent) stated that they could not take up work within two weeks (predominantly because of educational commitments). Thus, only 8.2 per cent of inactive males could be classified as unemployed in the sense of passively seeking work and available for work.

Table 2.3
Attachment to labour force of ILO inactive males aged 20-59

<table>
<tr><td colspan="4">Looking for job?</td></tr>
<tr><td colspan="2">Yes = 13.3%
Could start within two weeks?</td><td colspan="2">No = 86.7%
Want a job?</td></tr>
<tr><td>Yes = 61.7%</td><td>No = 38.3%
(of which
Must complete
education
= 67.8%)</td><td>Yes = 21.9%
(of which
Discouraged = 26.4%)</td><td>No = 78.1%</td></tr>
</table>

Note: "Discouraged" equals not looking for work for one of the following reasons: (i) lack of education/skill/experience; (ii) too young; (iii) could not find any work; or (iv) believe no work available.

The label "discouraged workers" could be applied to ILO inactive males who state that they are interested in employment, even if not currently seeking a job. The LFS asks all of those not looking for work whether they "want a job". A minority (21.9 per cent) of inactive males answered "yes" to this question. Not all of these should be regarded as discouraged workers, however, because some gave reasons such as "in school" or "retired" for not seeking work. We have treated as discouraged workers only those who wanted a job and said they were not looking for work for one of the following reasons:

1 lack education/skill/experience;
2 too young;
3 could not find any work; and
4 believe no work available.

The numbers in these categories constitute 4.9 per cent of ILO inactive males. If this 4.9 per cent of discouraged workers is added to the 8.2 per cent interested in and passively seeking work, we obtain a total of 12.1 per cent of the inactive aged males aged 20-59 who might be classified as in some sense unemployed. Treating those in these categories as "unemployed" raises the rate of unemployment, but not very significantly.[11] In 1993, the conventional ILO unemployment rate among males aged 20-29 was 15.3 per cent; if the individuals defined as discouraged workers in Table 2.3 are added to the numerator and denominator, the unemployment rate rises to 16.8 per cent. This shows that despite the growing proportion of inactive men in the prime working age groups, the extent of disguised unemployment and discouragement appears to be relatively minor.

We have examined some of the characteristics of those falling into the discouraged worker/disguised unemployment categories in 1993 (see Table 2.4). Those in these categories were less well educated than the total population of males of prime working age. On the other hand, those in the first category (not seeking work for reasons of discouragement) were markedly older than both those in the second category (passively looking for work), and than the population as a whole. Those in the second category were less likely to be married. Thus, a picture emerges of two fairly distinct types of discouraged workers: one comprised of somewhat older, poorly educated men who have given up working due to the belief that there are no jobs, presumably suitable, available, or none for which they are qualified; and a second group consisting of younger men, also relatively poorly educated (having regard to their age) who are not actively seeking work, but are interested in a job.

It is possible to use the published LFS data and that contained in Garvey (1988) to study the relationship between an inclusive measure of unemployment with the conventional rate over the period 1983-96. In the published LFS results, the ILO inactive population is broken down into those who are "marginally attached to the labour force" and "others economically inactive". The following sub-categories, which are similar to those we have discussed above, are classified as marginally attached to the labour force in the LFS:

1 discouraged workers (not looking for work due to pessimism about employment prospects);
2 those passively seeking, and available for, work.[12]

Table 2.4
Characteristics of discouraged workers (percentage distribution)

	Males aged 20-59	Discouraged Workers I*	Discouraged Workers II**
		Age	
20 – 24	15.8	10.5	18.7
25 – 29	12.4	9.6	10.0
30 – 34	14.0	7.9	13.2
35 – 39	14.1	13.2	15.6
40 – 44	13.7	16.7	14.5
45 – 49	11.9	11.8	13.2
50 – 54	10.2	14.5	8.2
55 – 59	8.0	15.8	6.6
		Education	
No formal Education	0.6	5.7	1.6
Primary	24.7	66.7	52.8
Inter/Group	28.7	19.3	28.2
Leaving	26.6	5.7	12.1
3rd Level non univ.	9.2	1.8	2.1
3rd Level university	8.3	8.3	2.4
Higher degree	1.8	0.0	0.5
		Marital status	
Single	35.6	34.6	44.1
Married	61.5	58.8	51.7
Divorced	0.9	1.8	0.8
Widowed	2.1	4.8	3.4

Note: * Prime aged males categorised as ILO inactive, wanting to work but not looking due to discouragement as defined in Table 2.3. ** Prime aged males categorised as ILO inactive, looking for work and able to commence within 2 weeks.

The effect of amplifying the definition of unemployment by treating these categories as unemployed rather than inactive is to raise the unemployment rate by about 8 per cent in 1996, from 11.9 to 12.9 per cent. Figure 2.10 shows how the broad and narrow unemployment rates have varied since 1983. It is clear that the same cyclical pattern is present in both series, but there has been a tendency for the gap between them to widen.

Figure 2.10
Male unemployment rate
including and excluding marginally attached workers

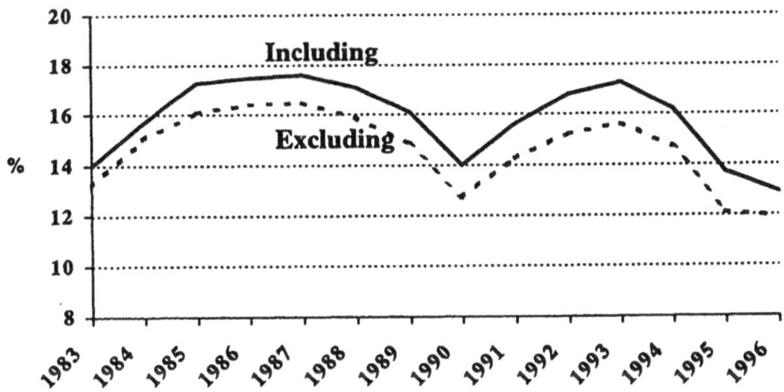

To establish the relationship between the two rates more precisely, we have regressed the log of the inclusive unemployment rate (y) on the log of the conventional unemployment rate (x) and a time trend, for the period 1983-96, with the following result.

$$\hat{y} = \underset{(1.0)}{0.2} + \underset{(17.4)}{0.97x} + \underset{(2.5)}{0.0037Time} \tag{5}$$

D.W. = 1.62
R^2 = 0.96

The elasticity of the inclusive rate with respect to the conventional rate is not significantly different from unity, indicating that the two measures share the same cyclical pattern. The trend variable is statistically significant, however, indicating that the rate of marginal attachment to the labour force has been increasing over time, independently of the rate of unemployment as conventionally measured. This is an important finding, indicating a deterioration in the labour market situation not revealed in the conventional measure of male unemployment. None the less, the general conclusion is still valid, that the rate of "hidden unemployment", although rising, is not very large among Irish men.

Conclusion

In this chapter, we have reviewed the evidence on the level and trend in male unemployment in Ireland since 1983. We showed that the various measures of the unemployment rate that are available - the PES and ILO definitions, and the rate excluding and including those "marginally attached to the labour force" - all display the same general pattern over time. While there is no major discrepancy between these alternative indices of unemployment, the conventional ILO rate is lower than PES rate or the rate which treats men who are marginally attached to the labour force as unemployed. The relative importance of those excluded from the conventional measure of unemployment has been increasing over time. We believe that it makes sense to view the various measures of unemployment as locating individuals on a continuum depending on their attachment to the labour force and the intensity of their job search activity.

The non-employment rate provides a comprehensive measure of the gap between the numbers at work and the total in each demographic group. While the unemployment rate has not drifted upward since 1983, the non-employment rate has shown a positive trend due to the downward trend in labour force participation rates. In the younger age groups, there has been a big increase in the proportions staying on in the educational system, while among older men, early retirement has become increasing common. It is striking that after age 50, the majority of non-employed men are not unemployed but either retired, disabled, or permanently ill. The numbers in these categories have been on a long run upward trend, but do not appear to be cyclically sensitive.

We looked at the characteristics of those who could be classified as constituting the "hidden unemployed" - the men who although not actively seeking work were either passively interested in employment or had given up looking for work because they believed they would not obtain an offer of employment. We showed that there are two distinct groups among the hidden unemployed: one comprised of older men who had given up looking for work because they believed they would not get an offer of a suitable job; the other comprised of younger men who had not yet started seriously to look for a job. Both sub-categories shared many of the characteristics of those who are unemployed according to conventional definitions, in particular low educational levels.

The performance of the Irish labour market in recent years has been impressive. Employment has grown at an unprecedented rate. While women have benefited disproportionately from this boom, there has also been a marked improvement in male labour market indicators, especially since 1993. The rate of unemployment among married men had fallen to 8.7 per cent by 1996. Among older men, however, there has been little decline in either the unemployment or the non-employment rate - the latter has remained close to 30 per cent since the 1980s. The majority of older men who were not working are retired or permanently ill, rather than unemployed.

It is likely that the options of early retirement and/or permanent invalidity will grow in importance relative to overt unemployment among older men. The state benefit system has encouraged those on unemployment benefits or assistance to switch to various pre-retirement schemes. For those with poor educational qualifications, these options are likely to be more attractive than remaining in long term unemployment with little chance of obtaining a job that would significantly increase disposable income. While these inactive men constitute a growing number of workless people dependent mainly on state transfer payments, and enjoying only a modest standard of living, their significance for the measurement of labour market slack is probably not very great. It is unlikely that a significant proportion of them would be drawn back into the employed labour force even under the most favourable economic conditions.

It may be concluded that the rise in non-employment among older Irish men is mainly a reflection of long run structural changes in the economy and society rather than an indication of an increase in the macroeconomic output gap. While the increasing tendency for men to drop out of the labour force before the normal retirement age poses important social and human questions, its economic significance is limited by their lack of skills and weak motivation to seek employment.

Appendix

Table A2.1
Male unemployment rates (%)

Age group	15-64	15-64 Excl. marginally attached	15-64 incl. marginally attached	15-24	25-44	45-64	Single	Married
1983	15.3	13.3	14.0	22.1	12.9	8.1	n.a.	n.a.
1984	17.0	15.0	15.7	24.8	14.3	9.9	n.a.	n.a.
1985	18.8	16.1	17.3	24.8	15.8	11.2	n.a.	n.a.
1986	19.0	16.4	17.5	28.3	15.4	10.7	n.a.	n.a.
1987	19.3	16.6	17.6	27.2	15.3	11.1	n.a.	n.a.
1988	18.6	15.9	17.1	26.0	15.3	11.5	19.2	13.8
1989	17.6	14.8	16.1	22.5	14.8	11.1	17.4	13.0
1990	15.2	12.7	14.0	19.9	12.3	9.6	15.7	10.7
1991	17.3	14.2	15.6	23.3	13.9	10.1	18.3	11.4
1992	18.1	15.2	16.8	24.9	15.1	10.7	20.2	11.9
1993	18.7	15.6	17.3	27.0	15.3	10.9	21.6	11.7
1994	17.7	14.7	16.2	25.4	14.0	10.8	19.5	11.3
1995	15.4	12.1	13.7	20.5	11.6	9.2	16.4	9.1
1996	14.7	11.9	12.9	19.3	11.3	9.6	16.1	8.7

Source: Labour Force Surveys, 1987-96 and Garvey (1988).

Table A2.2
Male labour force

Age group	15-24	25-44	45-64
1983	64.0	92.3	82.8
1984	62.6	93.9	83.0
1985	61.7	94.8	80.6
1986	60.2	93.9	79.5
1987	58.1	93.5	79.7
1988	56.0	93.8	79.6
1989	53.6	93.7	78.1
1990	53.4	93.5	77.5
1991	52.3	93.5	78.4
1992	50.6	92.5	77.5
1993	49.7	92.3	77.6
1994	48.8	92.7	77.7
1995	49.1	92.4	77.0
1996	47.1	93.3	77.3

Source: Labour Force Surveys, 1987-96 and Garvey (1988).

Table A2.3
Age-specific male unemployment rates

Age group	15-19	20-24	25-54
Australia	19.2	15.4	7.5
Belgium	32.5	18.9	6.4
Canada	20.9	17.1	9.5
Denmark	8.5	11.5	6.7
Finland	29.8	32.1	17.4
France	21.9	24.5	9.7
Germany	5.8	9.0	6.9
Greece	20.6	19.5	4.8
Ireland	32.8	24.7	14.4
Italy	33.0	27.8	6.0
Japan	8.3	5.0	2.0
Luxembourg	11.4	7.9	2.5
Netherlands	16.0	12.4	5.6
New Zealand	19.4	13.2	7.0
Norway	12.7	10.7	4.7
Portugal	11.3	12.4	4.8
Spain	39.8	36.4	16.4
Sweden	17.7	19.3	7.9
UK	20.8	18.3	9.8
US	19.0	10.2	4.9

Source: OECD, (1996, Chapter 4).

References

Borjas, G. J. (1996), *Labor Economics,* McGraw-Hill: New York.

Garvey, D. (1988), "What is the Best Measure of Employment and Unemployment in Ireland?", *Journal of the Statistical and Society Inquiry Society of Ireland,* Vol. XX, Part V, pp. 185-236.

IMF (1997), *World Economic Outlook,* Washington, D.C., May.

Juhn, C. (1992), "Decline of Male Labor Market Participation: The Role of Declining Market Opportunities", *The Quarterly Journal of Economics,* (February), pp. 79-121.

Murphy, A. and Walsh, B.M. (1996), "The Incidence of Male Non-Employment in Ireland", *The Economic and Social Review,* Vol. 25, No. 5, pp. 467-490.

Murphy, A. and Walsh, B.M. (1997), *Aspects of Employment and Unemployment in Ireland,* National Economic and Social Forum: Dublin.

OECD (1996), *Employment Outlook,* OECD: Paris.

Royal Statistical Society (1995), "The Measurement of Unemployment in the UK", *Journal of the Royal Statistical Society,* Series A, Part 3, pp. 363-417.

Walsh, B.M. (1993), "Labour Force Participation and the Growth of Women's Employment, Ireland, 1971-1991", *Economic and Social Review,* Vol. 24, pp. 369-400.

Acknowledgements

This paper forms part of the Research Project on Unemployment supported by the Social Science Research Council of the Royal Irish Academy. Support was also received from the Centre for Economic Research, University College Dublin, and IBEC, the Irish Business and Employers Confederation. We wish to acknowledge the Central Statistics Office for making available to us the anomymised 1993 Labour Force Survey data used in this paper and in particular, Donal Garvey and Joe Treacy for their support and help. Valuable research assistance was received from Gavan Conlon.

Notes

1 If E = employment, P = population, and U = unemployment, the employment rate E/P = (1-U/(U+E))x((U+E)/P), that is (1 *minus* the unemployment rate) *times* the participation rate.

2 The Irish Live Register of the unemployed has become an increasingly unreliable guide to the level and trend of unemployment. See Murphy and Walsh (1997) for a discussion of this issue.

3 For a discussion of these measures, see Murphy and Walsh (1997).

4 See Murphy and Walsh (1996) for a detailed discussion of this issue.

5 See OECD (1996) for a review of these developments.

6 As there is virtually no difference between the PES and ILO age-specific non-employment rates, only the ILO rate is shown in Figure 2.5.

7 The numbers in receipt of a state Invalidity Pension increased from 20,849 in 1983 to 40,226 in 1994, while the numbers on the pre-retirement schemes introduced in 1990 had reached 18,000 by 1996.

8 These cannot be calculated for years before 1988 from published data.

9 In our study of the factors affecting participation and unemployment based on the 1993 LFS returns, we found that single men had worse outcomes, *ceteris paribus,* than married men (Murphy and Walsh, 1996).

10 They were not, however, "actively" seeking work, which is the reason they were not classified as unemployed. This means that they did not indicate the use of any of the thirteen possible methods of job search specified in the LFS prompt.

11 If we let E =employed, U= unemployed and D = discouraged workers, the conventional unemployment rate is U/(U+E) and the broader measure is (U+D)/(U+E+D).

12 A small number of lay-offs, who are not looking for work, are also included in this category.

3 A review of the role of active labour market policies in Ireland

Catherine Kavanagh

Introduction

With the persistence of unemployment in many European countries, active labour market policies (henceforth denoted ALMPS) have increasingly moved to the forefront of policy agendas. Creating jobs and combating high unemployment have become a key priority for most countries. This strategy stems from the belief that unemployment has an important structural component, which cannot be tackled by macroeconomic measures alone. A standard recommendation in recent policy documents from both the OECD and EU has been a greater emphasis on ALMPS.[1] This encompasses a shift in labour market expenditures to active measures (as distinct from passive unemployment compensation measures) which mobilise labour supply, enhance labour market access, improve the quality of the labour force, and strengthen the search process in the labour market.

In Ireland, the expansion of ALMPS in the form of education and training policies, direct job creation measures, enterprise schemes, and employment subsidy schemes has been advocated by policy-makers, economists and lobby groups in response to high unemployment levels. NESC (1993, p. 123) was concerned with the "role which education and training policies can play in promoting employment growth and in reducing the extent of unemployment, especially long term unemployment". The Council was of the view that human resource development or manpower policies must be an essential ingredient of any plan to tackle unemployment. The Central Review Committee Progress Report on the PCW (1995, p. 42) urged the "enhancement of skills and aptitudes of the labour force", believing it to be "essential in ensuring Ireland's future prosperity and continuing competitiveness". O'Donnell (1993, p.83) states that "in the very long run, of course, a vibrant productive sector, combined with appropriate manpower and other policies, can ensure low unemployment". Additionally, an expansion of special employment schemes has been advocated as a means of alleviating social exclusion, particularly if they are targeted on the long term unemployed (Gray, 1992; Duggan, 1993a).

Research on the effectiveness of ALMPS in Ireland is limited. A common perception of what works and what does not seem to work is only slowly gaining ground, not least because of the socio-economic context in which labour market policies have to operate remains in constant flux. However, this does not detract from the need to take stock of and critically review, the role of ALMPS. The purpose of this chapter is to review the role of ALMPS in Ireland and the contribution they can make to alleviating unemployment. To do this, the international literature on the possible macroeconomic and microeconomic effects of ALMPS is examined, and this is followed by a survey of Irish studies, which attempt to evaluate the effectiveness of individual programmes. The outline is as follows. First, we review the rationale and objectives of ALMPS. The next section provides a synopsis of the positive and negative effects associated with such schemes. The following section presents a brief overview of the current system of programmes on offer in Ireland, with particular emphasis on FAS schemes. A further section summarises the major studies which have attempted to evaluate particular training and employment programmes. This is followed by a discussion of the implications of the recent mushrooming of different employment generating groups. A final section concludes with a summary of the main points.

Rationale for and objectives of active labour market policies

The term active labour market policies usually encompasses a range of employment policy measures that directly target the unemployed and disadvantaged. The OECD classification consists of five broad categories: (i) job broking, including information, placement, and counselling delivered by a Public Employment Service (PES); (ii) labour market training in order to enhance the skills of the unemployed; (iii) youth measures; (iv) subsidised employment, including direct job creation; and (v) measures for the disabled. The term 'active' is used to distinguish such measures from 'passive' income support for the unemployed. In this respect, ALMPS have the potential to influence both the demand for and the supply of labour. On the one hand, training programmes are aimed at mobilising labour supply, and improving the productivity of the workforce. On the other hand, subsidised employment schemes, direct subsidies to companies, job creation and employment generating activities are aimed at influencing the demand for labour.

Rationale

Government intervention in the Irish labour market is by no means new. Until the early 1970s, unemployment was seen to be caused by insufficient aggregate demand. The role of demand management policies was to "put the unemployed to work" through social public works programmes which would act as a countercylical response to rising unemployment. This was supplemented by manpower policies on the supply-side. However, the rationale for intervention has changed since the mid-1970s. Up to then, the rationale for intervention was one of market failure. Intervention was justified on the basis of imperfections in the labour market. Imperfections manifested themselves in the form of 'mismatch'. The training of manpower to produce a more effective match between the supply and demand for manpower, and bring together jobseekers with known employment opportunities was assumed to promote economic efficiency.

Tarling (1993) suggests the rationale is still one of market failure. However, since the 1970s, traditional labour market policies have been varied and broadened to cope with rising unemployment in Ireland and elsewhere. This was accompanied by the observation that economic growth does not necessarily lead to employment growth, which some interpreted as the failure of traditional macroeconomic policies in reducing unemployment (Dineen, 1984). In addition, as unemployment rose, so also did structural and long term unemployment. Any labour market improvements did not automatically benefit the long term unemployed. As the range of labour market policies grew to include direct employment-creating measures, the rationale for increased labour market intervention has also broadened to include social inclusion and equity, in addition to efficiency.

The change in rationale for more active intervention is evident in both the international and Irish literature. The OECD (1970) suggested that "any move towards economic restraint for the sake of disinflation, which can be expected to create unemployment, should be combined from the outset with preparation of selective counter-action". Active manpower policies figured prominently among the various prescriptions proposed by the Secretariat as a means to halt the worsening inflation-employment trade-off and to break cycles of 'stop-go' which had become prevalent in macroeconomic demand management (OECD, 1990). Dineen (1984) proposed that the introduction of direct employment-generating schemes and employment policies in Ireland during the mid-1970s was an explicit attempt by government to change policy emphasis from indirect employment creation (through incentives offered to the market sector and by accommodating manpower policies to assist private enterprise) to more active interventionalist measures which included training for the unemployed. The schemes were first introduced as a temporary measure, at a time when government remained convinced that the growth-employment relationships of the 1960s were interrupted but for a short period (Dineen, 1984, p.268). The experience of the 1980s and 1990s has ensured that the emphasis on active intervention remains.

Objectives

Although there are many and varied objectives associated with ALMPS, several common themes are evident in the literature. It is generally argued that job broking, labour market training, and direct job creation for the unemployed can serve as methods to reduce the level of unemployment without the same risk of generating inflation as traditional demand policies (OECD, 1990; OECD, 1994; Layard et al, 1991). An informative summary of the objectives of ALMPS is given by Calmfors (1995a, p.1). He sees ALMPS as playing two roles. The first he suggests, is to "keep the unemployed going" in general during a recession, so that the effective aggregate supply of labour is maintained. This view is supported by Layard et al (1991). The second function is to "adjust the structure of supply to demand". This is also the view of Jackman (1994) and the OECD (1990) and is the traditional way of viewing

ALMPS. The argument is that ALMPS facilitate the matching of workers to jobs and keep the unemployed in contact with the labour market while at the same time, improving their skills. The OECD (1994, p.100) suggest that in this way, ALMPS are "particularly appropriate instruments for improving the prospects of poorly qualified job-seekers and the long term unemployed". According to this view, the objective of ALMPS is thus to raise labour market efficiency and equity simultaneously. As Katz and Murphy (1992) note, this argument is particularly relevant for the discussion about shifts in demand from unskilled to skilled labour in the OECD countries because of technological developments, competition from low-wage economies and the relative decline of the manufacturing sector. However, it is not altogether clear how the objectives of efficiency and equity can be met. In addition, the different elements of ALMPS will necessarily produce different results. It is therefore necessary to distinguish the different components of ALMPS.

The objective of training and education is to increase the skills of the workforce. A common held belief is that education and training play a crucial role in international competitiveness as it is seen as investment for the future (NESC, 1993; European Commission, 1994). NESC (1993) note that training has become one of the main anti-unemployment policies in Ireland, as in other European countries. This reflects the view that 'better' training will somehow increase levels of employment. This assumes that there really is a significant mismatch between skill levels and job vacancies and that the economy will benefit in a more general way from having a more highly skilled workforce. Government involvement in training ranges from highly specific, targeted measures (based on the identification of special skill needs and the development of training programmes to meet these needs) to the more general measures to increase skill levels of the population as a whole. While one may expect the former to be successful, the latter may be less so, being based as much on a very generalised belief as on rigorous problem identification.

The objectives of special employment measures such as employment subsidies, direct job creation schemes and enterprise or self-employment schemes are similar. All three aim to maintain employment and achieve an early reduction in the levels of unemployment. Job-creation schemes aim to increase employment opportunities in additional new markets, supported by an 'infant industry' type of argument (Tarling, 1993). Very often, certain programmes focus on marginalised individuals such as the long term unemployed, disadvantaged youths and the disabled with the objective of promoting social inclusion, social cohesion and social equity. However, the ability of these special measures in achieving their objectives, not the least in their effectiveness at reducing unemployment, has been questioned (OECD, 1993; Breen and Halpin, 1988; Breen and Halpin, 1989). Finally, the objectives of employment services are to offer counselling, guidance and placement aid in addition to administering income support. Most European Public Employment Services' (PES's) have as their aim to prevent marginalisation, and reduce the risk of demotivation by ensuring quick identification of employment needs, and offering immediate access to training, thereby limiting the possibilities of drift into long term unemployment.

The effects of ALMPS

In theory, there are several macroeconomic benefits that have been attributed to ALMPS. The benefits of ALMPS are seen to stem from the microeconomic effects of a more efficient, more skilled and productive labour force, leading to increased productivity and an expansion of overall employment in the macroeconomy (OECD, 1993; Calmfors and Lang, 1994). However, ALMPS are also associated with several adverse side effects, which tend to reduce regular employment.

Figure 3. 1
The Beveridge curve

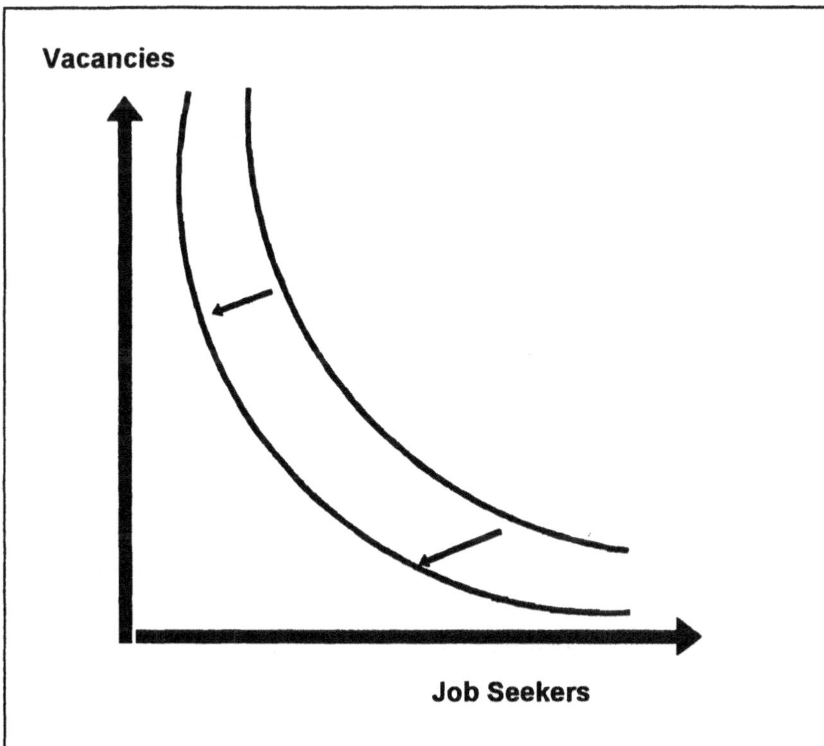

Positive effects of ALMPS

There are five potential benefits generally attributed to ALMPS. Calmfors (1994) suggests that the first most obvious benefit of ALMPS is to raise output (and welfare) in general in society by putting the unemployed to work or letting them invest in human capital. The benefits are seen in increased psychological well-being among programme participants. There exists some support for this argument (Korpi, 1994; O'Keeffe, 1986; Fitzpatrick Associates, 1995; Duggan, 1993b).

A second beneficial effect, associated in particular with PES activities and training programmes, is the increased efficiency of the matching process, so that a given number of job-seekers is associated with fewer vacancies. This can be seen in Figure 3.1 as a backward movement of the Beveridge Curve. Jackman (1994) and Layard et al (1991) argue that the Beveridge relationship has been more favourable in countries with ALMPS.

Figure 3.2
The labour market

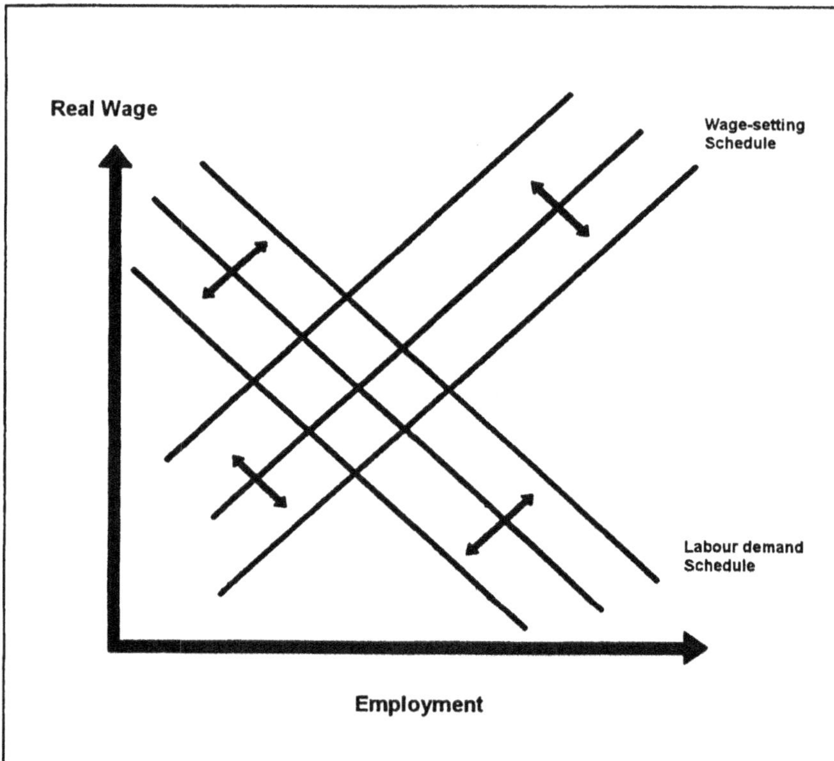

A third effect of ALMPS is to raise the productivity of the labour force, which is in fact an explicit aim of training programmes, but can also result from on-the-job training in special job creation programmes. The macroeconomic effects of a more productive labour force can be seen in Figure 3.2 as an outward shift of the labour demand schedule, raising employment and wages. This is based on the neoclassical assumption that the demand for labour schedule equals the marginal product of labour, and an increase in productivity shifts this schedule to the right, *ceteris paribus*.

A fourth effect of ALMPS is that they help to maintain the size of the effective labour force (Layard et al, 1991). Programmes, by maintaining the skills and search efficiency of the unemployed, reduce the risks of long term unemployment and keep up competition for the available jobs. In this way, wage pressure is reduced, which tends to raise employment. This can be seen as a shift downwards of the wage setting schedule in Figure 3.2.

Figure 3.3
The flows in the labour market

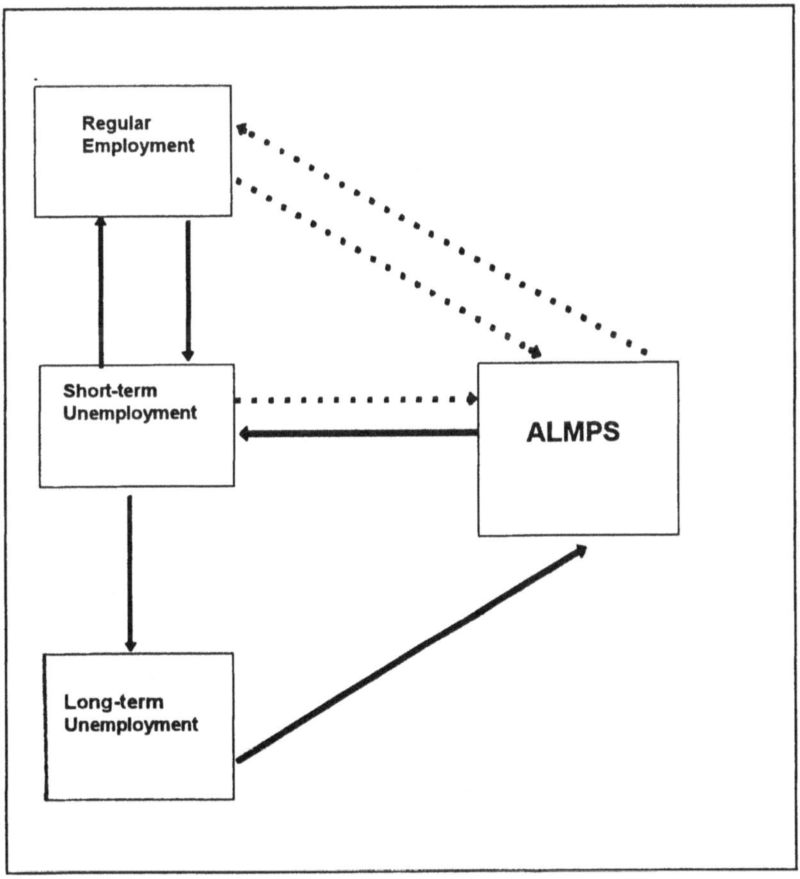

The ability of ALMPS to influence flows into and out of short and long term unemployment is illustrated in Figure 3.3. If ALMPS serve as methods to maintain the search effectiveness and skills of the unemployed, then some of the long term unemployed are lifted back to the same competitive status as the short term unemployed, thus reducing wage pressure (Calmfors, 1995a).

Figure 3.4
Re-allocation of labour

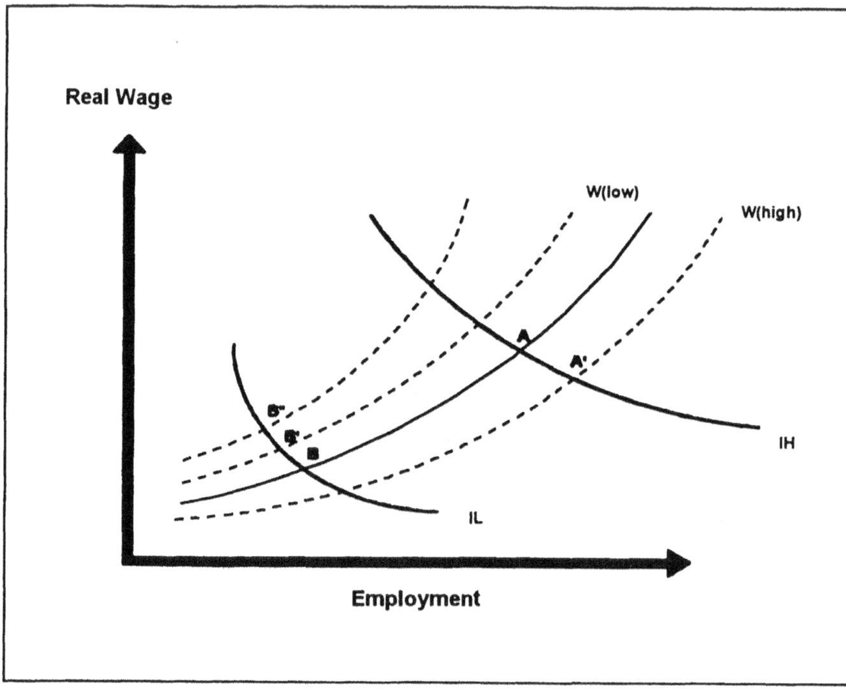

The final effect which results from training and other mobility-enhancing schemes, is the reallocation of labour between different sub-markets. This effect is essentially seen as "cheating the Phillips Curve" (Calmfors, 1995a). By shifting labour from high-unemployment to low-unemployment sectors, and thus exploiting the convexity of the Phillips curve, ALMPS are believed to reduce inflationary pressure at each level of aggregate unemployment (Lindbeck, 1975). Calmfors (1995a) casts this argument in a modern form. If the wage setting schedule in each sector is convex, then a transfer of labour from a low-employment to a high-employment sector ought to lower wages more in the latter sector than they are raised in the former (see Figure 3.4). The wage-setting schedule in Figure 3.4 shifts down in the high wage/high employment sector, W(high), and shifts upwards in the low wage/low employment sector, W(low), so that the equilibria for the two sectors move to A' and B', respectively. Because of the curvature of the wage-setting schedule, Calmfors argues that the consequences should be a net gain in aggregate employment.

Adverse side-effects of ALMPS

There are several negative aspects and costs associated with ALMPS. First, Calmfors and Lang (1993) suggest that ALMPS may actually raise wages and thus crowd out regular employment. They argue that programmes, by reducing the welfare loss from being laid off, may accommodate high wage demands and thus weaken the incentives to wage restraints. The consequence of accommodation is thus to raise wage pressure and thereby reduce regular employment. The crowding-out effect is illustrated in Figure 3.2 as an upward shift of the wage setting schedule.

A second adverse effect of ALMPS relates to deadweight losses, displacement effects, and substitution effects. Deadweight losses are particularly relevant to employment subsidies and occur where many of the subsidised hirings would have been created anyway. Displacement effects arise when some already employed workers are displaced by some of the subsidised hirings. Displacement effects are also associated with enterprise schemes geared at promoting self-employment. This is because those that are encouraged by the scheme to set up their own business are often in competition with existing domestic firms. Finally, substitution effects occur when it becomes profitable for employers to replace one category of workers with another. The substitution effect is associated with subsidised employment and job creation programmes and subsidised employment of various target groups. These effects drive a wedge between the gross and net numbers of jobs created. To the extent that these negative effects are realised, the labour demand curve in Figure 3.2 will shift to the left.

Calmfors (1995b, p.17) states there are also likely to be *locking-in effects* of training and job creation programmes. He states that "even if there are positive *treatment effects* of programme participation once it is completed, search activity is likely to be less during programmes". He notes there is support for this line of reasoning in Sweden. All the displacement and substitution losses associated with job creation schemes and subsidised employment can be minimised by making sure that the subsided jobs are additional, i.e. they would not have been performed otherwise. However, this makes it less likely that programme participants learn skills that raise their competitiveness in the regular job market, a view supported by Duggan (1993a).

ALMPS are also subject to the time-inconsistency problem. This is because it may take a long period of time for participants to build up skills that are perceived in the current period to be desirable in the job market. However, by the time skills are in fact required, they may be redundant in the job market. The time-inconsistency problem is also relevant to government expenditure on programmes. If government is concerned with unemployment, it always has an incentive to use ALMPS, and may end up with too large labour market programmes when it pursues discretionary policy. The analysis here is similar to the Barro-Gordon (1983) analysis of monetary policy.

The above classification of positive and negative effects illustrates that ALMPS can influence both the labour demand schedule and the wage setting schedule.

The current situation in Ireland

ALMPS are well established in Ireland. However, as in other OECD countries, there has been a major expansion of these programmes since the early 1980s. The OECD (1993) show that total expenditure on labour market programmes (including passive measures) is high in Ireland relative to other OECD countries, amounting to 4.29 per cent of GDP in 1990, and surpassed only by Denmark at 5.64 per cent of GDP. The proportion of this expenditure on active measures is also high at 1.51 per cent of GDP. This rose to 1.56 per cent in 1991, and to 1.77 per cent in 1992. Foras Aiseanna Saothair (FAS) is the principal agency for the delivery of labour market programmes in Ireland.[2] To provide an overview of the current programmes on offer by FAS is an ambitious endeavour. A plethora of programmes, targeted at different groups in society, with different aims and objectives has emerged over the last decade. This section has a more modest objective. The aim is to summarise the different programmes by classifying them under the following headings: (i) services for the unemployed; (ii) services for employers; and (iii) services for local communities.

Unemployed initiatives

FAS offers a variety of programmes targeted at the unemployed. It provides a job placement and recruitment service through a network of employment service offices. It also provides training programmes, subsidies to unemployed persons starting enterprises, and opportunities for job-seekers through Community Employment (CE), a direct job-creation scheme.

CE was launched in April 1994, replacing three existing programmes, Teamwork, (TWK), the Social Employment Scheme (SES), and the Community Enterprise Development Programme (CEDP). SES was a major initiative aimed at providing temporary part-time employment for the long term unemployed over 25 years with projects organised by the voluntary or public sectors, with the objective of reintegration in the labour market. However, training in the programme was minimal (Tansey Webster and Associates, 1988; Creedon and Ronayne, 1993). The CEDP was similar to the SES, but differed on eligibility and payment conditions. It also attempted to address the training deficiencies evident in the SES. TWK was aimed at unemployed young people.

According to FAS, the CE programme has three main objectives: (i) providing part-time opportunities for the long term unemployed and those at risk of becoming long term unemployed; (ii) personal development of participants and consequent improvement of their future job prospects; and (iii) delivering economic and social benefits to communities by contributing to local development. At present, CE is the largest single programme provided by FAS. In 1994, it provided part-time employment for approx. 40,000 participants by the year-end (FAS, 1994). In reality, training on CE remains limited, but FAS (1996) has expressed an undertaking to "improve the quality of CE, with particular emphasis on the relevance of these programmes to participants and sponsoring groups".

In addition to the CE, FAS also offers a vast range of programmes aimed at training the unemployed. These include the Specific Skills Training programme (SST), Alternance training, and Foundation Skills (FS). Training courses target different groups, ranging from poorly qualified persons with low educational attainment, to women who wish to re-enter the labour market after a prolonged absence, and to individuals with specific skill deficiencies which may be in demand in local labour markets. Alternance training is designed to reintegrate the long term unemployed over 25 years into the labour market, and allows trainees to alternate between vocational training and employment experience. SST training courses are at a more advanced level than foundation training programmes, and are aimed at providing the participant with an employable skill. FS encompasses basic skills training, including Youthreach, for young school leavers. Re-integration Training (RT) consists of special courses aimed at retraining older experienced workers in returning to the workforce and updating job skills and practices. Other training measures directed at the unemployed are provided by the Vocational Educational Committees (the Vocational Training Opportunity Scheme, VTOS), and administered by the Department of Education, and by the Conference of Religious of Ireland (the Part-Time Job Opportunities scheme, PTJO). VTOS provides opportunities for the long term unemployed to avail of second-level education. PTJO is a pilot programme funded from the CE budget. However, it differs from CE on several grounds. First, participants work variable hours (up to 19.5 hours a week), and are paid the "going rate for the job". Second, spouses of live registrants and persons on Pre-retirement Allowance are eligible to participate, unlike CE. Third, participants may be taken on for the full three year duration of the pilot scheme. The Conference of Religious of Ireland (CORI) have suggested that this programme be made available to people in the 18-20 year age group who are excluded at present. Currently, a significant proportion of the participants on this scheme are long term unemployed (47.1 per cent for over 3 years or more), between the ages of 25-34 years, (33.71 per cent) and predominantly female (67.74 per cent).

In addition to training programmes, and the CE programme, FAS also provides various enterprise and employment subsidy schemes. The Enterprise Scheme (previously the Enterprise Allowance Scheme) aimed at promoting self-employment among the long term unemployed. The Employment Incentive Scheme (EIS) and the Employment Subsidy Scheme (ESS), both had as their objective to reintegrate the long term unemployed in the labour market, by stimulating demand for these workers. In 1994, FAS decided to phase-out the EIS and ES, in the light of the introduction of alternative schemes by government. Several new schemes have come on board in 1996, including Jobstart, and Workplace. Both these schemes are aimed at encouraging employers to take on unemployed persons. Workplace is a 5 week programme designed to give job-seekers and employers the opportunity to see how they might fit together in the long term. Participants must be receiving unemployment compensation for 6 months or over, and while on the programme, retain their normal social welfare status and entitlements. Jobstart, on the other hand, is aimed at individuals who are long term unemployed for three years or longer, including time spent on CE or in vocational training. Employers on Jobstart must provide a full-time job at the going wage rate and will receive £80 for 52 weeks. These programmes, to some extent, replace the EIS and ESS.

Finally, just like the PES in other countries, as an outcome of the government's decisions on the Report of the Task Force on Long-Term Unemployment (1995), a nationwide integrated Local Employment Service (LES) was established in 1996. The aim of the LES is to provide an integrated locally based service for the long term unemployed who will have access to guidance, training, education and employment support. It was introduced on a phased basis, beginning in the twelve established Partnership areas, and in two non-Partnership areas, Kildare and Clare.[3] To augment these services, FAS also provides a range of enhanced core services in its Employment Services Office. To co-ordinate the activities of the LES, FAS established a LES special unit. This unit sets standards for quality of service, provide professional training and accreditation as well as support to the guidance, counselling and active employment placement services.

Community initiatives

FAS provides a variety of initiatives to assist communities in developmental ventures. As well as training of certain disadvantaged groups in the community, these initiatives are aimed at promoting projects in areas such as: tourism and heritage centres; small manufacturing and craft companies; community service companies; and recreational and leisure related enterprises. Other schemes, apart from CE, include Community Training programmes (CT), Community Training Workshops (CTW), Community Youth Training programme (CYT), Community Enterprise Programme (CEP), Travellers Training Workshop (TTW) and the FAS Co-operative Development Unit (CDU). Although many community initiatives are aimed at reintegrating the disadvantaged, some programmes are similar to direct job-creation measures. For example, the CEP provides a package of advice, training and financial assistance to community groups who want to become involved in the creation of economically viable jobs. The primary objective is to help communities provide direct or indirect employment on co-operative or community group projects. The CDU aims to assist and encourage the creation of a commercially viable worker co-operative sector.

Employer initiatives

FAS works with the business community both in the re-training of existing employees and in the provision of skills needed by recruits seeking employment in Irish businesses. Programmes include the Industrial Restructuring Training Programme (IRTP), the Training Support Scheme (TSS), Job Training Scheme (JTS), Standards-Based Apprenticeship, and Levy Grant Scheme (LGS). IRTP is the major vehicle by which FAS assists the retraining requirements of Irish companies. TSS provides assistance to support the retraining of persons in key areas. It is targeted at all existing employees at all levels from operative to management. FAS has the legal responsibility for the organisation and control of apprentice training in certain designated occupations, including the registering of apprentices and monitoring and recording their progress through all phases of the apprenticeship. LGS is aimed at funding training in designated industries, including: textiles; clothing and footwear; electronics sector of the engineering industry; food, drink and tobacco; and chemical and allied products. JTS is a work-based training programme provided by employers in co-operation with FAS. It is aimed at using the training capacity and expertise within the workplace to train potential employees. It provides full-time training for between 13 and 52 weeks, with FAS contributing 75 per cent of the training costs, where trainees have to be unemployed.

Summary of programme evaluations in Ireland

There exists a range of microeconomic evaluations of the effects of different programmes on individual participants in Ireland as elsewhere. However, research on the macroeconomic effects has been limited. For example, there exist few studies on the impact of ALMPS on employment and wages, with the notable exception of OECD (1993) and several studies on the Swedish economy.[4] OECD (1993) argue that the reason macroeconomic evaluations are limited is because of the problems associated with empirical methodology. These problems include (i) simultaneity bias, (the size of ALMPS is likely to be influenced by the amount of unemployment), (ii) the fact the policy stance is endogenous (making it difficult to disentangle the effect of policy on the labour market) and (iii) few observations.

The only macroeconomic effects of ALMPS for Ireland are provided by the OECD (1993). They present cross-country evidence on the wage effects of expenditures on ALMPS by estimating a wage equation over the period 1985-1990, where real wage growth is determined by the gap between actual and structural unemployment (taken to be the unemployment rate that would prevail in equilibrium). Structural unemployment is a function of expenditure on ALMPS as a percentage of the wage bill . Of significance, was the fact that expenditure on ALMPS appeared to have statistically positive wage-raising effects for only two countries, Ireland and Spain. For the majority of countries, expenditure on ALMPS had a beneficial effect in that it reduced structural unemployment by facilitating wage moderation (OECD, 1993, p.51). However, these results should be interpreted with caution, given the problems identified with macroeconomic empirical investigation.

One of the advantages of microeconomic studies is that there exists a large number of observations. But these studies are not without their problems. Calmfors (1995b. p.18) notes that unless controlled experiments can be performed, there is the "uncertainty as to whether selection bias has been adequately controlled for - there will be a negative bias if programmes target problem cases and a positive one if mainly those with the best labour market prospects are admitted". Furthermore, micro studies can only offer partial equilibrium estimates, since the impact on non-participants (such as displacement and accommodation effects) is not taken into account.

The results of microeconomic studies internationally have been diverse. Sometimes positive, usually rather small, effects are found, but very often it has been impossible to detect any such impact at all (see for example, OECD 1993), although smaller programmes which are focused on specific groups with clearly identifiable needs tend to perform better. Calmfors (1995b, p.19) notes that "the conclusion from international microeconomic studies is that is has been surprisingly difficult to establish the expected positive effects on individual participants". In this context, we should be clear what we mean by 'positive'. Tarling (1993, p.4) states that "economic efficiency should demand that eventually the [positive] outcome should be a job". This definition, he contends, can be extended to include improved employability of participants in the short run. Additionally, if a political dimension is added, it can be extended to the point of anything which is not "registered claimant unemployment". On a similar vein, The Council for Social Welfare (1989, p.51) claimed that "the only economic justification for these measures is that they should genuinely enhance a person's capacity to contribute to the economy in the long run. In practice, political considerations as to what meets EC Social Fund criteria, or removes people from the unemployment count, have also played a part".

Most international micro studies tend to evaluate the effectiveness of ALMPS on the basis of economic efficiency, that is, the attainment of regular full-time employment. Alternative quantitative outcome variables such as unemployment and earnings are also measured. OECD (1993) suggests that this type of analysis is partial since it does not include all possible goal variables, and it does not address the issue of how ALMPS work. Similarly, Tarling (1993) makes that case that effectiveness should also include the comprehensiveness of inclusion in the labour market. However, the effectiveness of ALMPS in achieving social inclusion and social cohesion is associated with obvious measurement difficulties. For this reason, most micro studies in Ireland have focused on the analysis of placement rates when individuals have completed a programme or, as in many of the studies commissioned by FAS, focused on identifying the benefits perceived by participants on schemes, and by the co-ordinators and the sponsors, often with little if any quantification and little attempt to value the benefits. The exceptions are independent studies by Lehmann and Walsh (1990) who examine outflow rates from unemployment, and O'Connell (1996) who also examines income from post-programme employment.

Early studies on the effectiveness of ALMPS include those by Geary and Dempsey (1977), Nolan (1978), O'Donnell and Walsh (1978), and Williams et al (1982). Geary and Dempsey found that the relief aspects often tended to conflict with the efficiency objectives. They advocated more immediate supervision, detailed planning well in advance, and close central control. O'Donnell and Walsh examined the effectiveness of the Premium Employment Programme (PEP) which had as its objective to "encourage the re-employment, in agriculture and manufacturing industry, of workers who had lost their jobs due to the recession, and the return to full-time employment of workers in these sectors who were on short-time" (Nolan, 1978, p.86). Little evidence was found by O'Donnell and Walsh to suggest that the PEP had a measurable impact on employment or unemployment during its operation. Williams et al (1982, p.79) evaluated Youth Employment Policies and found that "Irish labour market policy was more demand-orientated than was justified by existing and foreseeable high levels of unemployment". Furthermore, they found that AnCO and the National Manpower Service (replaced by FAS) explicitly aimed to place the most attractive candidates for available job opportunities partly because they were strongly influenced by the "placement success" criteria used to evaluate the programmes and organisations.

More recent studies have evaluated individual employment schemes programmes, (for example, Breen and Halpin, 1988; Breen and Halpin, 1989; Ronayne and Creedon, 1993,) while others have undertaken an evaluation of various training and employment initiatives, (for example, Breen, 1991; Lehmann and Walsh, 1990; McKeown and Smyth, 1990; and O'Connell, 1996). In addition, many of these studies have been directly commissioned by FAS.[5] It is not the aim of this section to evaluate in detail the entire range of existing studies or indeed all of those commissioned by FAS. Rather, a brief summary of these studies with their principal conclusions is offered in Table 3.1.

Just as in the international literature, Table 3.1 highlights the diverse nature of results emerging from these studies. FAS studies appear to give more favourable results regarding the benefits conferred by programmes. However, as shown in the table, analysis in many of these studies has tended to focus on identifying whether the psychological well-being of participants has increased. Little quantification is involved, with no attempt at valuing the supposed benefits. Furthermore, the partial analysis problem arises, and the conclusions must therefore be viewed with caution, because they fail to take account of how participants would have fared in the labour market had they not participated on such schemes. A notable exception here is the evaluation of ALMPS by O'Connell (1996) Because this study employs a more rigorous methodology which incorporates regression analysis to examine the effectiveness of various schemes, I place greater weight on the results emerging from this study.

What does appear to emerge from these studies is the consensus that employment schemes such as the EIS and ESS are associated with significant deadweight and substitution costs. Enterprise schemes such as the EAS and Enterprise programme are prone to high displacement costs and as noted by Breen (1988, p.xi) "the majority of Enterprise firms generate no additional jobs". The argument assumes that success is measured by the number of jobs created. But this line of reasoning ignores the possibility that programmes act as a preventative measure. ALMPS may be viewed as successful if they actually prevent job losses or if job losses are less than would have occurred without the programmes. However, it is difficult to measure the effectiveness and success of programmes in maintaining employment or preventing job losses.

Table 3.1
Summary of major studies on effectiveness of training programmes and employment schemes in Ireland

Authors of study & scheme examined	Conclusions
Breen (1991) *Various training and employment schemes for youths*	While employment schemes were partially effective, training programmes were less so. FAS training improved the chances of an unemployed person immediately by about 20% However, just 1 year after participation, the probability of being in a job showed little or no difference between participants in programmes and similar unemployed non-participants.
Breen and Halpin (1988) *Enterprise Programme (formally the Enterprise Allowance Scheme)*	Based on interviews with 438 individuals who entered the scheme. The high deadweight and displacement losses identified led authors to conclude that the scheme would only make a very modest contribution towards creating additional jobs and reducing unemployment.
Breen and Halpin (1989) *EIS*	Based on interviews with 405 employers who participated in the scheme, and on data relating to their employees. Deadweight losses very high (68%), which diminished the job creation effects. Also high substitution losses (21% of total participation). Authors did not envisage scheme as a major programme in combating unemployment.

Authors of study & scheme examined	Conclusions
CORI (1995) *PTJO*	PTJO Progress Report indicated that this scheme has been successful in employing primarily long term unemployed. 76.7% of all participants in 1995 (967 in total) were in receipt of some type of unemployment payments prior to working on the programme. Of these, 47.1% were unemployed for 3 years or more, and 17.41% for 4 years or more. These figures were as high as 64% in some areas (Finglas, Blanchardstown and Laois). The type of employment generated on the project has ensured there are no major adverse effects.
Creedon and Ronayne (1993) *SES*	A survey of 56 participants on the SES who were asked to identify the benefits of the scheme. Although several benefits were outlined, no attempt was made to value these. Limitations identified included (i) the duality arising between the SES as a labour market intervention on the one hand and as a source of cheap labour for under-funded, voluntary and community-based organisations, on the other hand; (ii) SES does not provide long term unemployed with the range of support needed to realistically improve their employment prospects; (iii) concern was expressed at the manner in which new employees were recruited, and the low level of demand for labour.
Craig and McKeown (1994) *Activities of the Twelve Area-based Partnership Companies*	Identified only the benefits of the scheme (both public and placement). Using interviews with managers of each partnership, qualitative benefits were only identified. Enrolment courses used as a measure of quantitative benefits emanating from partnership involvement in education and training. No attempt made to value these benefits.
DKM (1995) *All FAS training and employment schemes*	An analysis of gross and net exchequer costs. Identified only the financial benefits including savings on social welfare payments and attracting ESF funding from the EU, using participant profiles. Exchequer costs found to be 65% lower than total FAS cost and 58% in the case of CE.
Duggan (1993b) *SES with training*	Identified benefits perceived by participants, sponsors, FAS and by the co-ordinator, using information from FAS files and interviews with beneficiaries. Little quantification and no attempt made to value the benefits.
Fitzpatrick Associates (1990) *CEP*	Highlighted cost-savings and benefits and identified deadweight and displacement costs. Cost-savings included gains and savings to the exchequer and attracting ESF subvention. Benefits included direct employment in community enterprise groups, and psychological benefits to participants. Benefits not valued, gross costs and annual cost per job aided were estimated using various assumptions and taking account of deadweight and displacement costs.
Lehmann and Walsh (1990) *WEP, EIS, EAS, TWK, SES*	An evaluation of the effects of these schemes on the overall outflow rate and age-by-duration outflow rates from unemployment using regression analysis. WEP showed evidence of deadweight and substitution losses. EIS exhibited substantial negative distortive effects. Similarly, authors concluded that TWK and SES have negative effects on their respective targeted group, with TWK taking the best of the young long term unemployed and SES taking the best of the older long term unemployed. Finally, EAS did not appear at all significant, which prompted authors to allude to possible deadweight losses.

Authors of study & scheme examined	Conclusions
Fitzpatrick Associates (1995) *CE*	A cost-benefit analysis of the scheme, rather than an estimation of the net benefits. Five different scenarios incorporating various mixes of assumptions were modelled. Deadweight and displacement effects were also taken into account. In the "most likely" scenario, the cost benefit ratio was almost two to one with the value of benefits around 90% greater than the net exchequer cost of the programme.
McKeown (1993) *CTW*	Analysis of placement of participants in further education or employment. No assessment of other benefits. No attempt to value the benefits. However, author concluded that these schemes were a "valuable national resource for disadvantaged young people".
McKeown and Symth (1990) *Several education and training programmes for the long term unemployed*	Assessment involved interviewing staff to identify the benefits of the programmes and reporting their views. No attempt made to value the benefits. No assessment made of other benefits of programmes.
O'Connell (1996) *Foundation and SST training courses, EIS, ESS, SES and CE*	Using regression analysis, author examined the effectiveness of four different types of training and employment schemes on (i) probability of employment within 2 months, (ii) probability of employment within 18 months after leaving a programme, (iii) the proportion of total post-programme period spent in employment and (iv) income from post-programme employment. These were deemed preferable to an examination of mere placement rates, which take no account of participant qualifications and characteristics, and do not therefore measure effectiveness accurately. Author found that SST and employment subsidy schemes were effective in conferring long term benefits to participants, but direct employment schemes such as the SES and CE, together with foundation skills courses were less successful, conferring only short term benefits. In addition, the income of participants from these two types of programmes was not significantly different to non-participants. Reservations expressed about CE and SES schemes.
O'Connell and Sexton (1993) *Various FAS training programmes*	Authors found that (i) programmes aimed at early school leavers exhibited low rates of progression to further education and training, and were not well integrated with the rest of the education and training system; (ii) VTOS and Alternance programmes exhibited low employment placement rates (only 30% one year after completion of the programme), with only 9% undertaking further education and training; (iii) with regard to the SST, the impact varied but generally, better qualified and experienced participants benefited more in placement terms than other participants.
O'Keeffe (1986) *The SES with training (a pilot initiative)*	Examined the benefits perceived by participants, sponsors, FAS and by the co-ordinator from FAS files and interviews with participants. Findings in relation to labour market benefits compared favourably to other studies. Little quantification and no attempt to value benefits.
Ronayne and Devereux (1993) *SES*	A survey of 5 SES sponsors, 40 current participants and 56 past participants. Each was asked to indicate benefits obtained from scheme from their perspective. No attempt to value benefits. Found that the quality varies greatly, with only a minority of quality schemes in existence. Authors concluded that the key finding was the limited impact that this scheme had as a labour market intervention.

Authors of study and scheme examined	Conclusions
Tansey Webster and Associates (1988) *SES*	An examination of the impact of the programme from a macroeconomic, microeconomic and an exchequer perspective, including identifying costs and benefits. Authors concluded that "the most critical point identified by respondents was that schemes did not benefit participants and did not provide them with either a real job or with access to learning new skills"

Although direct job-creation schemes such as the SES, CEDP and the more recent CE which contain a minimal basic level of training, are not associated with either deadweight or displacement losses, the problems identified with these schemes are that they are temporary and cost more than unemployment assistance (Breen, 1990). There are other negative effects. The low level of training does not provide skills that are in demand in the job market, limiting the employment prospects of participants (Ronayne and Devereux, 1993, Tansey Webster and Associates, 1993). Commenting on the SES, O'Keeffe (1996) notes

> ... the potential value of the scheme in improving the employability of individuals and creating services and assets for the community has not been realised. This means that the maximum benefits are not being received for the money being spent on the scheme. The Department of Labour makes no attempt to systematically analyse the achievements of individual projects against their costs and compare these with other similar projects. There is often no clear picture of what is being achieved on the projects aided. More emphasis is placed on the jobs created than on value for money obtained.

Fitzpatrick and Associates (1995) claim that this conclusion would still appear to be valid for both the SES, and its successors, the CEDP and the CE.

The negative effects of the ALMPS must be balanced against the undoubted positive effects. Several studies have identified these beneficial effects,[6] but valuation of, for example, the personal or labour market benefits to individuals or the value to communities of the work done on CEDP and CE, is associated with obvious measurement difficulties. Fitzpatrick and Associates (1995) note that the output from these projects is typically in non-traded services, which makes it extremely difficult to value them in financial terms. Furthermore, commenting on negative research findings of effects of these schemes, O'Donnell (1993, p.86) suggests that "to look no further than the deadweight effects is to assume that a person who spent a year on a programme has no better job prospects than if he or she were still unemployed...These unavoidably ignore the hysteresis effects and cannot possibly test the possibility that direct hiring, in combination with a range of interventions in the economic and social environment, could produce a permanent effect from temporary schemes". Hysteresis is the tendency for unemployment levels to remain high after an adverse shock, or to remain low after a boom period which has generated employment. Lehmann and

Walsh (1990) provide the only study here who incorporate the hysteresis effect into their argument.

A further argument rests on the cliche that "prevention is better than a cure". Breen (1991) suggests that more attention should be diverted at preventing the problems that the programmes are trying to address. These include preventative measures such as early intervention through counselling and identification of retraining needs, that prevent inflows into unemployment and more importantly, long term unemployment, a view mirrored by NESC (1993), and OECD (1990).

The role of training

It is worth examining and evaluating in more detail the role of training in ALMPS. Training (for the unemployed and employed) is a significant element of ALMPS in Ireland, as elsewhere. In 1992, 0.49 per cent of GDP was spent on this category. NESC (1990) note that training is the solution to unemployment *only* if there is a specific and identifiable skills mismatch between the unemployed and available jobs. However, if as Sheehan (1992) and O'Donnell (1993) propose, that only a fraction of unemployment in Ireland can be said to be due to mismatch, then training will only reduce the level of unemployment if it is accompanied by other policy measures which stimulate the demand for labour of those undergoing training.[7] This has led to calls for training to be accompanied by policy measures which stimulate the demand for the labour being trained (NESC, 1990; Duggan, 1993a). This view is echoed by NESC (1993) who propose that "training policies to combat long term unemployment must be combined with the creation of demand in the labour market specifically targeted on the long term unemployed, if such training policies are to be effective".

Many training programmes have been criticised on the basis that they do not provide skills that are required in the job market. For example, Roche and Tansey (1992, p.54) showed that although Ireland spent a higher proportion of GNP on training than any other European country, "training for those at work is inadequate" since "about 90 per cent of FAS's budget goes on activities which are loosely classifiable as training, but fit better under the heading of unemployment support". They recommended that "a greater proportion of FAS resources and activities should be allocated to industry-relevant training directed towards those at work and preparing for work" (Roche and Tansey, 1992, p.52). On a similar vein, Duggan (1993a, p.6) notes that while there are attempts to provide training on such programmes as the CEDP and community development strategies, "the type of skills provided while not untransferable to the wider labour market, are nevertheless not widely in demand".

O'Donnell (1993) argues that training of the long term unemployed which merely redistributes job chances, might be worthwhile. This is the case if the objectives of such training programmes include social inclusion. However, this reinforces the need to target the schemes on particularly disadvantaged groups. According to NESC (1993), an ALMP which includes intervention through counselling and identification of retraining needs, at the moment of job loss, enhances training as an instrument in fighting unemployment.

Much of these findings on the effectiveness of training programmes in Ireland are also evident in other countries. The OECD (1990, p.34), states that "[training] will be of little avail unless it actually leads to work. Training programmes must therefore reflect both short term and long term considerations". Similarly, the OECD (1993), in their evaluation of the effectiveness of ALMPS concluded that broadly targeted training programmes were largely ineffective at reducing unemployment levels although many programmes targeted at specific disadvantaged groups were found to be effective.

There does appear to be a consensus in the literature however that properly designed programmes of appropriate size should be able to make a contribution in the fight against unemployment.[8] Much of what constitutes properly designed ALMPS includes a greater emphasis on targeting the disadvantaged, determining optimal timing of policy interventions, setting compensation levels as close as possible to unemployment benefits, refining eligibility criteria, and co-ordinating the interaction between ALMPS and the unemployment insurance system as well as the appropriate length of programmes. Calmfors and Lang (1993) also highlight the importance of targeting, claiming that if it is insufficient, then wage-raising effects may dominate with crowding-out effects on regular employment as the result. This is because programmes in this case serve not only to improve the job prospects of outsiders (the unemployed) but to improve the alternative employment opportunities of insiders as well. The less targeting there is, the more important it is that compensation in programmes is not too high, if adverse wage-setting effects are to be avoided. There is support for much of this reasoning in the Irish literature. Lehmann and Walsh (1990) argue that not all long term unemployed are disadvantaged, and schemes which target *all* the long term unemployed tend to take the best from the target group, thereby failing to reintegrate the truly disadvantaged. They call for more refined selection criteria so that the truly disadvantaged are targeted, a recommendation supported by OECD (1993).

Some recent developments

There appears to be a continuous stream of new policy initiatives in the field, reflecting to some extent the commitment on the part of the European Commission and the Government to a more locally based approach to the issue of unemployment and local development. Initiatives include the Leader Programme, the Poverty Programmes, the Integrated Rural Development Programme, the Twelve Area-based Partnership companies, the County Enterprise Boards and the recent Local Employment Service. Commitment to local development is also emphasised in the National Development Plan. The mushrooming of these different groups should be viewed with caution. There is the danger that policy initiatives emerge as an attempt by politicians to persuade the general public that something is being done about unemployment, rather than being based on any real evaluations of the needs of the disadvantaged in the labour market and the demands of the community. When something does not produce the desired results, there is rapid feedback in the form of additional or alternative policies. Furthermore, it becomes politically unpopular to phase out programmes that are found to be inefficient. So the question arises: where does it all stop?

Obviously, co-ordination of the various groups is required. In view of this, it is surprising that procedures have not been established for regular evaluations of the various programmes on offer, and regular assessments of the objectives and aims of the groups to ensure that no conflicting strategies emerge. This may require an independent government body which is given the task of monitoring the activities of the various groups. In addition, it is important to ensure effective co-ordination between departments and between national or regional authorities and other relevant actors.

It must be said that Government is still groping with little understanding of which policies will work and which will have little or no impact. NESC (1990) noted that Ireland already has a broad range of schemes targeted on the long term unemployed and that these are undersubscribed to, despite high levels of unemployment. One possible recommendation is to imitate the Swedish system which links unemployment payments and participation on labour market programmes. However, Calmfors (1995a) is strongly critical of this approach. He argues that with such a use of ALMPS, the incentives to strive for maximum efficiency in terms of enhancing re-employment probabilities are likely to be seriously weakened as the marginal utility from re-employment should fall to the extent that programme participation is expected to generate a future stream of unemployment benefits. Calmfors (1994) provides some evidence that this may have occurred in both Denmark and Sweden.

Conclusion

The purpose of this chapter was to examine the role of ALMPS in Ireland. To do this, a review of the rationale and objectives of these policies, together with the macroeconomic and microeconomic benefits and costs described in the international literature, was presented. An examination of Irish microeconomic studies revealed little support for the effectiveness of ALMPS in reducing unemployment. This is a cause of concern, given that Irish governments have committed themselves to substantial increases in programmes directed at the unemployed. Additionally, the recent developments of other employment generating institutions indicate the further expansion in the quantity of provision of such programmes, rather than an improvement in the quality of existing programmes.

ALMPS need to be effective in order to justify increased expenditure on them. Effectiveness should not just be judged solely on economic grounds but should also include social considerations, and the ability of programmes to act as preventative measures. Success in this context is more difficult to measure and little work has been done in this area. However, some general conclusions are possible. First, careful targeting is important if the truly disadvantaged in society are to benefit. In Ireland, the establishment of the Local Employment Service should help in addressing this issue. Second, management and administration should be efficient. Close monitoring and regular evaluations should be standard practice. Third, close interaction between labour market policies and economic policies is essential to ensure the sustained growth of output and employment. After all, ALMPS are only one element in a wide range of factors that impact on unemployment. Other policies include measures which stimulate the demand for labour, which would result in greater participation on programmes if participants believed there was a real chance of a job in the wider labour market, on completion of a programme.

Finally, we should not rule out other policy options. These include some controversial measures that may add to labour market flexibility, such as shorter benefit duration, less strict employment protection legislation, and measures affecting the relative bargaining position of unions and the scope of collective bargaining. As Calmfors (1995b) points out, the very existence of ALMPS does not imply that other labour market institutions need not change. It should not be automatically assumed that ALMPS are a quick and easy solution to unemployment. The discussion in this chapter has highlighted the need for further investigation to identify the proper role of ALMPS in combating unemployment.

References

Barro, R.J. and Gordon, D.B. (1983), "A Positive theory of Monetary Policy in a Natural Rate Model", *Journal of Political Economy*, Vol. 91, pp. 589-600.

Breen, R. (1990), "Unemployment Policy and Unemployment in Ireland", in *Work, Unemployment and Job Creation*, Conference of Major Religious Superiors: Dublin.

Breen, R. (1991), *Education, Employment and Training in the Youth Labour Market*, General Research Series, Paper No. 152, ESRI: Dublin.

Breen, R. and Halpin, B. (1988), *Self-Employment and The Unemployed*, General Research Series, Paper No. 140, ESRI: Dublin.

Breen, R. and Halpin, B. (1988), *Subsidising Jobs: An Evaluation of the Employment Incentive Scheme*, General Research Series, Paper No. 144, ESRI: Dublin.

Calmfors, L. (1991), "What Can We Learn from the Macroeconomic Experience of Sweden?", Seminar Paper No. 482, Institute for International Economic Studies: Stockholm.

Calmfors, L. (1994), "Active Labour Market Policy and Unemployment - A Framework for the Analysis of Crucial Design Features", *OECD Economic Studies*, No. 22, OECD: Paris.

Calmfors, L. (1995a), "Labour Market Policy and Unemployment", *European Economic Review*, Vol. 39.

Calmfors, L. (1995b), "What Can We Expect From Active Labour Market Policy?", Seminar Paper No. 546, Institute for International Economic Studies: Stockholm.

Calmfors, L. and Lang, H. (1995), "Macroeconomic Effects of Active Labour Market Programmes in a Union Wage-Setting Model", *The Economic Journal*, Vol. 105, pp. 601-619.

CORI (1995), *Part Time Job Opportunities: Progress Report*, Conference of Religious of Ireland: Dublin.

Council for Social Welfare (1989), *Unemployment, Jobs and the 1990s*, The Council for Social Welfare: Dublin.

Craig, S. and McKeown, K. (1994), *Final Evaluation Report on the Twelve Pilot Area-based Partnership Companies, 1991-1993*, Combat Poverty Agency: Dublin.

Creedon, M. and Ronayne, T. (1993), *To Whose Benefit? A Study of the Experiences and Views of Participants on the Social Employment Scheme in Tallaght*, Tallaght Centre for the Unemployment Ltd: Dublin.

Davy Kelleher McCarthy (1995), *Gross and Net Exchequer Costs of FAS Training Programmes and Employment Schemes*, FAS: Dublin.

Dineen, D. A. (1984), "Anti-Unemployment Policies in Ireland Since 1970", in Henning R., and Richardson, J. (eds.), *Unemployment - Policy Responses of Western Democracies*, SAGE Publications: London.

Duggan, C. (1993a), "Employment Programmes: Prospects and Issues", paper presented at conference on Employment Programmes in a Changing Labour Market, November 15th & 16th, Dublin Castle, Dublin.

Duggan, C. (1993b), *Moving in a New Direction: An Evaluation of a Pilot Scheme to Build Training into the Social Employment Scheme*, report prepared by WRC Social and Economic Consultants for the Tallaght Centre for the Unemployed: Dublin.

European Commission: (1994), "European Social Policy - A Way Forward for the Union", White Paper, European Commission: Luxembourg.

European Parliament (1993), "The European Employment Initiative", Party of European Socialists, Declaration of the Party Leaders' Conference, December 9th:Brussels.

FAS (1994), *FAS Annual Report and Financial Statements,* FAS:Dublin.

FAS (1996), *FAS South West Regional Plan,* FAS: Dublin.

Fitzpatrick Associates (1990), *Evaluation of the Community Enterprise Programme*, FAS: Dublin.

Fitzpatrick Associates (1995), *Cost-Benefit Analysis of the FAS Community Employment Programme*, FAS: Dublin.

Geary, R.C. and Dempsey, M. (1977), *A Study of Schemes for the Relief of Unemployment in Ireland*, Broadsheet No. 14, ESRI: Dublin.

Gray, A. (1992), "Expanding Employment - The Need for Improved Policy Responses", in Gray, A. (ed.) *Responses to Irish Unemployment - The Views of Four Economists*, Indecon: Dublin.

Henning R. and Richardson, J. (1984), *Unemployment - Policy Responses of Western Democracies*, SAGE Publications: London.

Jackman, R. (1994), "What Can Active Labour Market Policy Do?", *Swedish Economic Policy Review*, no. 1.

Katz, L. F and Murphy, K. (1992), "Changes in Relative Wages 1963-87: Supply and Demand Factors", *Quarterly Journal of Economics*, Vol. 107.

Korpi, T. (1994), *Escaping Unemployment*, Swedish Institute for Social Research, Stockholm University: Stockholm.

Layard, R., Jackman, R. and Nickell, S. (1991), *Unemployment*, Oxford University Press: Oxford.

Lehmann, H. and Walsh, P. (1990), "Employment Schemes in Ireland: An Evaluation", *The Economic and Social Review*, Vol. 22, No. 1.

Lindbeck, A. (1975), *Swedish Economic Policy*, Macmillan Press: London.

McKeown, K. and Smyth, E. (1990), *Continuing Education and Training for the Long term Unemployed in the European Community: Ireland.* Limited Circulation,

European Centre for the Development of Vocational Training (CEDEFOP), Berlin. [Published in summary form by CEDEFOP in 1992, Berlin].
NESC (1990), *A Strategy for the Nineties*, Government Stationary Office: Dublin.
NESC (1992), *The Relationship Between Employment and Growth in Ireland*, Government Stationary Office: Dublin.
NESC (1993), *A Strategy for Competitiveness, Growth and Employment*, Government Stationary Office: Dublin.
Nolan, B. (1978), "An Examination of the Premium Employment Programme", *Central Bank of Ireland Annual Report,* Central Bank of Ireland: Dublin.
O'Connell, P.J. (1996), "The Effects of Active Labour Market Programmes on Employment in Ireland", Working Paper No. 72, ESRI: Dublin.
O'Connell, P.J. and Sexton, J.J. (1993), *Evaluation of the Operational Programme for the Occupational Integration of Young People in Ireland: Objective 4 of the Community Support Framework*, ESRI Report to the Department of Labour and the European Commission, DG5.
O'Donnell, R. (1993), *Ireland and Europe: Challenges for a New Century*, Policy Research, Paper No. 17, ESRI: Dublin.
O'Donnell, R. and Walsh, B. 1978), *Survey of the Premium Employment Programme*, ESRI: Dublin.
OECD (1970), *Inflation. The Present Problem*, OECD: Paris.
OECD (1990), *Labour Market Policies for the 1990s,* OECD: Paris.
OECD (1993), *Employment Outlook*, OECD: Paris.
OECD (1994), *The OECD Jobs Study: Evidence and Explanation Part 11, The Adjustment Potential of the Labour Marke*t, OECD: Paris.
O'Keeffe, D. (1986), *Review of the Social Employment Scheme*, Department of Finance: Dublin.
Roche, F, and Tansey. P. (1992), *Industrial Training in Ireland: Report to the Industrial Policy Review Group*, Government Stationary Office: Dublin.
Ronayne, T. Devereax, E. (1993), *Labour Market Provision for the Long-term Unemployed: The Social Employment Scheme*, PAUL Partnership: Limerick.
Sheehan, J. (1992), "Education, Training and the Culliton Report", Policy Paper No. PP92/5, Department of Economics, University College Dublin.
Tansey Webster and Associates (1988), *Review of the Social Employment Scheme*, FAS: Dublin.
Tarling, R., (1993), "The Role and Potential of Employment Schemes in Combating Unemployment and Social Exclusion", paper presented at conference on Employment Programmes in a Changing Labour Market, November 15th & 16th, Dublin Castle, Dublin.
Williams, S, Scharpf, F. and Spring, W. (1982), *Review of Youth Employment Policies in Ireland*, OECD: Paris.

Notes

1 See for example, OECD (1990), European Parliament (1993) and OECD (1994).

2 FAS has a network of over 50 employment service offices and 20 Training Centres throughout the country.

3 In early 1997, the government extended the LES to four additional areas.

4 See for example, Calmfors (1991).

5 For a complete summary of the evaluations of programmes commissioned by FAS, see Fitzpatrick Associates Report to FAS, *Cost-Benefit Analysis of the Community Employment Programme*, 1995.

6 See also, *Community Employment – Participant Perceptions*, a report by FAS and the Dept. of Psychology, U.C.C., FAS South West Region, 1995.

7 While a skill mismatch or skill shortage may not be a major cause of concern, Roche and Tansey (1992) argue that there is a high degree of complacency about the adequacy of skills in Ireland, in that they are not on a par with best practice competitor countries. This view is echoed by the Industrial Policy Review Group.

8 For example, OECD (1993, 1994), NESC (1993), Calmfors (1995b) and O'Connell (1996).

4 Comment

Francis O'Toole

This chapter provides commentary on the following four presentations which were made during the morning session of the conference: *Irish Unemployment in a Historical Perspective* (J.J. Lee); *Unemployment in Ireland: A Post-Keynesian-Institutionalist Perspective* (C.Clark); *Unemployment, Non-Participation and Labour Market Slack among Irish Males* (A.Murphy and B.Walsh); and *A Review of the Role of Active Labour Market Policies in Ireland* (C.Kavanagh). Disproportional space is dedicated to Clark's paper owing to its rather novel, at least in an Irish context, approach to unemployment but it should not be inferred that the other three papers are of lesser important.

Irish unemployment in a historical perspective

Lee's energetic presentation provided an excellent introduction to the conference. In providing a historical perspective to Irish unemployment, Lee highlighted three issues of specific importance to Ireland: (i) values and vested interests; (ii) unavailability of information; and (iii) long term unemployment and culture of poverty. Either through coincidence or collusion these three issues provided the themes for the remaining three papers (Chapter 1-3, this volume) in the morning session.

Clark's paper questions the values implicit within neoclassical economics and highlights the presence of implicit, as well as explicit, vested interests among the supporters of neoclassical economics. The myth of neoclassical economics is supported, propagated and perpetuated by these supporters as well as by trained neoclassical economists.[1] More generally, Lee highlighted the presence of strong cultural, economic, political and social vested interests in Ireland and suggested a link between these interests and the apparent willingness of the Irish to accept unemployment.

In his presentation, Lee used the example of differing unemployment statistics to illustrate unavailability of information. The differences between the two most widely used statistics for unemployment in Ireland - the Live Register and the Labour Force Survey - also provide some of the background to Murphy and Walsh's paper and it is hoped that Murphy and Walsh's research programme will allow an improved targeting of unemployment policies. Lee's final theme of the connection between a culture of poverty and the growth in long term unemployment in Ireland provides a link with Kavanagh's paper which discusses active labour market policies. Kavanagh's paper highlights the importance of local-based initiatives in tackling long term unemployment and over-coming a culture of poverty.

Unemployment in Ireland: a post-Keynesian/institutionalist perspective

According to Clark, there are two underlying explanations for the relatively high levels of Irish unemployment: (i) labour slack (a concept broader than the standard neoclassical measures of unemployment) which is inherent in "advanced" capitalist systems; and (ii) Keynesian-type demand deficiency factors specific to the Irish economy. Clark is particularly comprehensive and challenging in his exposition of labour slack and the failings of neoclassical economics but could be accused of being slightly less than comprehensive in his analysis of the unemployment problem specific to Ireland.

Neoclassical economics and post-Keynesian/institutionalist economics

Unemployment is examined in the context of a contrast between the neoclassical and post-Keynesian/institutionalist (PKI) approaches to the functioning of labour markets. The neoclassical model is built upon the assumption of rational (in a narrow instrumentalist sense, of course) self-interest seeking individuals operating in a single market-clearing equilibrium labour market environment; the unique and stable equilibrium being supported by marginal productivity theory - to each according to contribution, from each according to (the given) utility function. Labour demand and supply are functions of the real wage rate; demand (supply) being a decreasing (increasing) function of the real wage rate.[2]

Clark claims that the PKI approach to unemployment differs from the neoclassical approach in that the former accepts the existence of labour markets as opposed to a single labour market and the former also sees labour demand and supply as being primarily dependent upon social and cultural norms as opposed to the real wage level. The initial contribution of Clark's treatment of the PKI approach to unemployment is in the replacement of standard measures of unemployment with a measure of generalised labour slack. As Clark points out, the standard definition of unemployment ignores discouraged workers, involuntary part-time workers and workers "employed below their productive capacities". Under the broader definition of labour slack, which incorporates discouraged workers and involuntary part-time workers, the average rate of unemployment in the OECD for 1993 increases from 9.5

per cent to 12.2 per cent (see Table 1.1). If the definition of unemployment is broadened further to account for the influence of the non-availability of welfare on the level of disguised unemployment, the average unemployment figure for the G7 countries for 1990 increases from the published figure of 6.7 per cent to 14.9 per cent (see Table 1.2). By broadening the measure of unemployment, the relatively poor performance of Ireland with respect to unemployment is lessened somewhat in each case.[3]

The post-Keynesian part of the PKI label stems from an emphasis on demand deficiency as being the most important factor in explaining unemployment. Demand deficiency stems from two sources: (i) policy-makers' (neoclassical in their economic orientation) fixation with the eradication of inflation via high interest rates and consequently low levels of investment; and (ii) capitalism's inherent inability to sustain sufficient levels of demand. This latter point, according to Clark, is particularly relevant in the post-cold war world when advertising and conspicuous consumption can not be expected to fill the demand void created by the decline in the military industrial complex.

The PKI approach to lowering unemployment focuses attention on four related factors: (i) a move away from restrictive economic policies; (ii) the creation of a Bretton Woods type institutional international agreement; (iii) a move away from financial speculation and a move towards productive investments; and (iv) a move away from increasing levels of income inequality. Commentary on each point is left to the following section on Ireland.

Unemployment in Ireland

The PKI approach outlines extensively the causes of high levels of unemployment in the capitalist system(s) of the OECD but Clark's PKI treatment of possible solutions to Ireland's relatively high level of unemployment is implicit rather than explicit; the reader is left to extrapolate from causes to solutions. The predominant cause of Irish unemployment is identified as sustained decreases in aggregate demand during the 1980-92 period. Table 1.4 contrasts the 1970-1979 period with the 1980-1992 period. The former period exhibits an average annual growth rate in total domestic demand of 5.4 per cent while the latter period exhibits a 0.3 per cent growth rate. Similar stark comparisons are made for private consumption, public consumption and gross fixed investment. The average unemployment rate in the former period was 7.34 per cent compared to 14.57 per cent in the latter period. The cause of (solution for) unemployment appears obvious - decreased (increase) aggregate demand.

There is, however, something missing from this account of Ireland's recent unemployment experience, surprisingly so given the institutionalist economist's attention to historical influences and data. Table 1.4 would have benefited greatly from the inclusion of some data on the state of the Irish public finances. Given the inclusion of this data, an alternative explanation might present itself. Within the Irish institutional environment, unemployment remained artificially low in the former period owing to an excessive increase in aggregate demand which was sustained by an explosion in Ireland's internal and external debt. It is important to note that the PKI's general approach to an explanation for Ireland's unemployment level is not being questioned here, merely the unquestioning adoption of a "reverse the process" approach to solving this problem. Clark signals his awareness of the position of Ireland as a small open economy when he suggests that lowering the level of income inequality may have the undesired effect in respect of the level of domestic demand, of increasing imports rather than increasing the level of domestic demand. It seems strange that Clark does not identify this same problem in the context of the implicit proposal to increase aggregate demand in order to address the unemployment problem.

The return to a Bretton Woods type accord is beyond the scope of Irish domestic policy but it would have been interesting to hear the PKI's view of European Monetary Union and its effect on Irish unemployment. On the one hand, the pooling of monetary policies across countries would appear to reduce risks and uncertainties and hence lower interest rates and increase aggregate demand, but on the other hand a European Central Bank is likely to be dominated by conservative (i.e. inflation-averse) central bankers. It would also have been interesting to hear suggested policy responses to the problems of increasing capital mobility and speculation. Clark finishes on a high point by noting some of the major contributions of the PKI perspective to the debate on unemployment: the need for neoclassical economics to rethink its attitude towards the nature of work and social participation.

Unemployment, non-participation and labour market slack among Irish males

Murphy and Walsh's paper addresses the decreased rate of market employment of Irish prime age males. Surprisingly, this is a new area of research in Ireland owing to the previous existence of data restrictions. The authors note that important policy implications could flow from the decomposition of non-employment among males into non-participation and unemployment.

Most of the analysis centres on the 1993 Labour Force Survey (LFS) and two definitions of unemployment are utilised: (i) the International Labour Office (ILO) definition which tends to be relatively narrow; and (ii) the Principal Economic Status (PES) definition which tends to be relatively wide.[4] In the authors' words, "[i]t is notable that up to 23 years of age and after age 50, a majority of those who are not employed are in categories other than 'unemployed': 'at school' or 'students' in the case of the younger males and 'disabled/permanently ill' or 'retired' among older males." Data in the paper also show that between the years 1979 and 1993, there has been almost no fall in the participation rate of males aged between 25 and 54; obviously the experiences of "younger" males and "older" males should be distinguished from the experience of "intermediate" males.

The econometric analysis centres on the influence of various independent variables on the average male's likely labour market status, in particular on probabilities of participation and employment. In summary, the analysis suggests that unemployment is less likely to affect older well-educated married males with a mortgage and a small number of children living in Dublin. Participation probabilities are similar in nature to employment probabilities apart from the age variable, with increasing age leading to increased participation initially but decreased participation subsequently. The analysis and commentary signals the importance of networks (providing for fruitful job search experience) and "dove-tailing" whereby married couples find themselves either both employed or both unemployed. This latter point highlights the importance of social welfare legislation.

The econometric analysis is exemplary. For example, where possible the authors have ruled out reverse causation. At this stage, however, the authors' analysis has only been carried out with data from the 1990s (and perhaps can only be carried out with data from the 1990s owing to data restrictions) and it would be very valuable from a policy perspective to repeat the analysis with data from, say, the 1970s. Without such an analysis and comparison of results, it may be precipitous to implement policy implications stemming from the above analysis, as alternative "explanations" for the Irish experience of male unemployment also suggest themselves. For example, Strobl and Walsh's paper (Chapter 6) suggests that heterogeneity in the unemployment inflow during the 1980s caused by the changing occupational structure of employment led to the build-up of long term male unemployment. Interested readers are also directed to Barry and Hannon's paper (Chapter 5) which provides some complementary evidence.

A review of the role of active labour market policies in Ireland

The presence of structural and frictional unemployment signals the need for a micro-based policy response to unemployment. Kavanagh reviews active labour market policies (ALMPS) as opposed to passive policies commonly associated with tampering with the social security safety net.[5] Micro-based policies are directed at the economy's AS (aggregate supply) curve whereas macro-based polices tend to be directed at the economy's AD curve (aggregate demand). As such, Kavanagh's paper may be contrasted with Clark's paper which argues for AD-enhancing policies. These policies could, of course, be seen as complementary rather than in conflict.

Kavanagh charts the recent evolution of ALMPS in Ireland. Micro-based policies in the 1970s tended to be directed at narrowly defined market failures involving a significant private dimension, e.g. specific job training, whereas micro-based policies in the 1980s and 1990s have widened the concept of market failure and decreased the private dimension. In particular, ALMPS have progressed to encompass non-specific job training, job brokering, subsidised employment schemes and schemes specifically aimed at youth unemployment. The growing importance of ALMPS is probably related to increased globalisation of the labour market and the need for improved job flexibility.

Kavanagh outlines both the positive and negative effects commonly ascribed to ALMPS. On the positive side: improved labour matching which may also allow the economy to "cheat" the Phillips' Curve; increased productivity of the labour force and increased labour force. On the negative side: the dead-weight loss (as some jobs would have been created anyway); the displacement of old jobs with "new" jobs; the replacement (substitution) of non-subsidised employees with subsidised employees; and the locking-in effect (the unemployed cannot take employment offers if locked into a training course). This latter effect is unlikely to be a problem in the Irish context and it could also be argued that the substitution effect could decrease long term unemployment even if it has no effect on total unemployment. Ireland's expenditure on both active policies (1.51 per cent of GDP) and passive policies (2.78 per cent of GDP) are relatively high by international standards.

Kavanagh divides ALMPS into three categories: (i) initiatives for the unemployed - for example, Community Employment (CE), which provides limited training for the long term unemployed (40,000 participants); (ii) community initiatives - for example, the Community Enterprise Program (CEP), which provides advice in the creation of economically viable community jobs; and (iii) employer initiatives - for example, Jobstart which offers the employer 80 pounds per week per employee for 52 weeks.

After a fairly comprehensive overview of these ALMPS, Kavanagh reviews the literature which has evaluated ALMPS in Ireland. The methodological problems underlying macro-based evaluations are known to be very severe; wage-equation models very tentatively suggest that ALMPS in only Ireland and Spain (within the OECD) lead to wage increases. Micro-based evaluations also have their methodological problems. For example, participants who remain unemployed are treated as equivalent to non-participants while the positive effects of social inclusion are ignored. The evaluations suggest the presence of significant dead-weight and substitution effects with smaller programs focused on small groups (not surprisingly) performing better. Kavanagh highlights the trade-off between targeted and non-targeted training: targeted training may benefit (or at least not adversely affect) non-participants as well as participants and limit adverse wage-increasing effects whereas non-targeted training serves the purpose of social inclusion.

Overall, Kavanagh is somewhat skeptical of the ad-hoc mushrooming of different groups and programmes which attempt to address unemployment and calls for increased co-ordination. It could, however, also be argued that this apparent lack of institutional legitimacy has allowed scope for considerable, and much needed, innovation through the establishment of local development initiatives. This latter view is supported in a recent OECD publication - *Ireland: Local Partnerships and Social Innovation* (1996). An area-based approach encourages wider participation, the use of local expertise and resources, and the addressing of local needs. This relatively new form of public and private local co-ordination, at least in an Irish context, is represented by 38 area-based partnerships which are, in part, supported by European Union structural funds. These partnerships represent unplanned "democratic experimentation" and the OECD report argues that they mirror the movement within the market economy away from the old firm based on economies of scale and towards the new firm based on partnership with an equal emphasis being placed on flexibility and participation. Obviously, in line with Kavanagh's argument, there needs to be some increase in the accountability of these area-based partnerships in the future, not least so as to reap the benefits, in terms of informational feedback, of social partnership. The difficulty stems from a severe democratic deficit in local government in Ireland. "Excessive" liberties allowed the area-based partnerships to avoid excessive bureaucracy and innovate. In particular, as argued by NESC (1996, p.51) the OECD report "... challenges us to develop more effective systems of 'learning by monitoring'."

References

Expert Working Group Report (1996), *Integrating Tax and Social Welfare*, Stationery Office: Dublin.

NESC (1996), *Strategy into the 21st Century: Conclusions and Recommendations,* Report No.98, NESC: Dublin.

OECD (1994), *The OECD Jobs Study; Evidence and Explanations, Part I,* OECD: Paris.

OECD (1994), *The OECD Jobs Study; Evidence and Explanations, Part II,* OECD: Paris.

OECD (1996), *Territorial Development, Ireland: Local Partnerships and Social Innovation* (prepared by Professor Charles Sabel and the LEED Programme), OECD:Paris.

Notes

1 Having invested much time and some effort in training (presumably of a neoclassical rather than a post-Keynesian/institutionalist nature) to be an economist, the present author admits the possibility of vested interests.

2 Neoclassical economics identifies labour market flexibility, combined with increasing competition from low-wage countries, as the underlying cause of unemployment in the OECD. In his presentation, Clark demonstrated using data from the OECD Jobs Study (1994), however, that there were no significant simple correlations between either high wages and standard measures of unemployment 1or, more interestingly, measures of labour "inflexibility" and standard measures of unemployment; the empirical evidence is not particularly supportive of this neoclassical approach to unemployment.

3 Clark claims that the adoption of broader measures of unemployment does not lead to a significant relationship being established between measures of social spending and unemployment. This seems somewhat surprising given that the unemployment figures for the G7 countries increase significantly when account is taken of the non-availability of comprehensive welfare systems.

4 The Live Register unemployment figure is relatively wide compared with both of the LFS definitions.

5 For a review of passive policies in Ireland, see the Expert Working Group Report (1996).

5 Education, deprivation, hysteresis, unemployment

Frank Barry

Aoife Hannan

"If poorly qualified you are more likely to be poor and unemployed; if poor and unemployed your children are more likely to receive poor qualifications".

Introduction

The strong growth in output and employment experienced in Ireland over the last ten years has had little impact on the numbers of long term unemployed. This results from a combination of factors: the extreme openness of the Irish labour market, the poor educational and skill levels of the long term unemployed, and the fact that their reservation wages are at or close to their floor (since otherwise they would be able to undercut the wage demands of more highly-skilled competitors). The importance throughout Europe of such high levels of long term unemployment has given rise to much discussion of "hysteresis", whereby temporary adverse shocks, if sufficiently long-lasting, have permanent adverse effects.

Traditionally, economists thought of high unemployment as a cyclical phenomenon; unemployment would eventually moderate wage demands and thereby open up new employment opportunities. Hysteresis suggests however that workers who become long term unemployed find it extremely difficult, if not impossible, to break back into the labour market. We argue that hysteresis is bound up with the strong shift in demand away from poorly skilled workers that has occurred in recent decades. For the most part, however, we are concerned with a more profound form of hysteresis, and one that has attracted less attention from economists; by this we mean the likelihood that today's early school-leavers contain disproportionate numbers of the children of those who are currently long term unemployed, and that these will become the long term unemployed of the future. Deprivation in this way is handed down from generation to generation through differential access to, and participation in, the education system. This appears to us to be one of the most profound issues facing Irish society today.

Our chapter proceeds as follows. In the next section, we review the findings of a number of papers in the Irish economics literature that demonstrate that poor educational qualifications increase the chances of being unemployed and reduce the level of income associated with whatever employment can be found. The following section then reviews the sociology literature, focusing on educational participation as the mechanism through which inequality is transmitted from generation to generation. To state our argument bluntly: "if you are poorly qualified you tend to be poor, and, if poor, your children tend to receive poor qualifications". The subsequent section argues that higher educational qualifications have become even more important in recent years, which will cause income distribution to become even more unequal.[1] In the next section, we review some aspects of the Irish education system that contribute to the cycle of deprivation. A final section summarises and concludes.

Educational qualifications and income and employment opportunities
("if you are poorly qualified you tend to be poor")

Evidence on the relationship between education and unemployment is available from a number of recent studies. Murphy and Walsh (1996) for example show that the chance of an individual being unemployed declines as their educational qualifications increase. For men between the ages of 20 and 59, for example, someone with an Intermediate Certificate has 13 per cent less chance of being unemployed than someone without school qualifications; a person with a Leaving Cert has 20 per cent less chance of being unemployed, while someone with a University Degree has 28 per cent less chance. (The equivalent figure for a non-Degree third level qualification is 21 percent). McCoy and Whelan (1996) show that among 1995 school leavers in the labour force, "the unemployment rate among those with the Leaving Certificate was over 40 percentage points lower than among those without qualifications". Comparing these results with those of Murphy and Walsh (1996), we see that possession of a Leaving Certificate is more important for younger age groups in terms of finding a job than was the case for older age groups.

Evidence on how wages are related to educational qualifications comes from Callan and Harmon (1996). Their study uses the 1987 Survey of Income Distribution, Poverty and Usage of State Services, conducted by the Economic and Social Research Institute, to estimate the impact of various factors on employee earnings. Focusing on males aged 18 to 64, they find that higher educational qualifications are consistently associated with higher wage rates. For example, the gross hourly wage for an individual with a Group Certificate is 15 per cent higher than for an individual with just a primary school education. Compared to the same base, the wage for an individual with an Intermediate Certificate is 19 per cent higher; a Leaving Cert leads to a wage 35 per cent higher than if one has only primary school qualifications; a sub-degree third level qualification is worth 46 per cent more, and a university degree a full 74 per cent more. Splitting the sample into three age groups of male workers, those aged 18 to 32, those aged 33 to 49, and those aged 50 and above, reveals that years spent in education is more important as an earnings determinant for the younger grouping. This corroborates the implication of the unemployment data discussed above, that those who drop out of the education system early today will suffer more from this than their parents might have done.

The studies we have cited so far focus only on qualifications achieved. A recent study by Breen, Hannan and O'Leary (1995), however, points to the fact that the grades achieved in public examinations are also important. Focusing on labour market experiences one year after leaving school, they find that grade point scores have significant effects on both the probability of employment and on the gross hourly wage achieved by those with jobs.

Educational participation and the cycle of deprivation
("the children of the poor tend to receive poor qualifications")

A number of recent sociological studies have highlighted the difficulty faced by individuals in Ireland in extricating themselves from positions of relative poverty; while the offspring of people in the middle-income ranges are reasonably mobile on the income-distribution ladder, the offspring of the poor tend to stay on the bottom rung. Studies from the early 1970s, for example, showed a lower degree of outflow from working class status in Ireland than in the UK, and more recent studies suggest that the mobility process has not altered significantly since then (Breen et al, 1990, p. 66). Breen and Whelan (1996) draw particular attention to the extremely low levels of inter-generational *upward* mobility seen in the Irish data compared to that emerging for other (Central and Eastern as well as Western) European countries (Ibid. p. 29). For example, only 11 per cent of those of industrial working class origins were to be found in the professional, administrative and managerial class in Ireland (in both the 1973 and 1987 samples) compared to 18 per cent in England, 21 per cent in Poland and 22 per cent in both Sweden and West Germany. Increasingly, of course, as we move from the 1970s into the era of higher unemployment, it becomes important to distinguish between "working class" and "unemployed". Data from 1982 show that "men from manual backgrounds are three times more likely to be unemployed than are those from professional and managerial backgrounds" (Breen et al, 1990, p. 66).

These various statistics, then, suggest a relatively low degree of upward social mobility out of the working class in Ireland. Since the proportion of the population deriving their income from inherited property (particularly family farms) has declined, now more than ever before the way in which access to the fruits of society is passed on is through differential access to, and participation in, the educational system. The evidence indicates that upward mobility in Ireland is low as a consequence of the poor access to, and low participation of, poorer children in the Irish education system.

Some evidence on educational participation categorised by parental social class is presented in Table 5.1 below.

Table 5.1
Percentage of entrants to second level reaching Leaving Cert and Third Level (1980/81 estimates)

	Leaving Cert		*Third Level*	
	Boys	Girls	Boys	Girls
Upper non-manual	97	100	50	35
Lower non-manual	59	71	26	16
Skilled manual	32	74	10	11
Semi/unskilled manual	16	41	4	7
All	50	69	21	16

Source: Breen et al (1990, p. 132, Table 6.2B).

The table shows that amongst this cohort group, boys whose fathers were executives, managers or professionals were at least six times more likely to sit for the Leaving Certificate than those from an unskilled or semi-skilled labouring family, and almost thirteen times more likely to enter third level.

A purely meritocratic educational system would imply that the differences in participation rates shown in the table above could be accounted for by equivalent differences in ability across social classes. As we will discuss later, however, a range of studies have shown that, even allowing for differences in ability, class origins exert a significant influence in determining how far a pupil progresses within post-primary education (Ibid. p. 133). Breen (1984) reports similar findings in the case of third-level education, with class origins exerting an influence over and above Leaving Certificate results in determining a pupil's likelihood of entering third-level education. Nor, of course, are Leaving Certificate results an unbiased measure of ability, since working class boys in particular are bunched together in vocational schools "in a pupil environment which does little to encourage educational attainment".

Crucially, these class differences in educational participation do not appear to be changing much over time. Breen and Whelan (1996, chapter 6) analyse the experiences of three age cohorts, those born between 1922 and 1936, those born between 1937 and 1949 and those born between 1950 and 1962. They find that while education participation and education qualifications increase monotonically from the oldest to the youngest cohort, the class differences between outcomes vary hardly at all.

Industrial change: are higher educational qualifications becoming increasingly advantageous?

The sociologists we have been citing point to the declining impact of educational credentials in promoting social mobility. Breen and Whelan (1996, p. 122) for example conclude that "the relative advantage associated with a higher level of education has declined over time as the number possessing such qualifications increases". Economists focus of course on the purchasing power of individuals rather than on fluidity between social classes. A number of international studies suggest that the economic return to individuals of (at least higher, but also perhaps more basic) educational qualifications has increased rather than decreased since the late 1970s, notwithstanding the huge increase in numbers possessing such qualifications. This shows up along two dimensions: (i) the rate of unemployment has increased substantially since the 1970s, and unemployment affects disproportionately those with poor educational qualifications; and (ii) for those with jobs, the returns to particular types of education have increased over the course of the 1980s.

We discussed earlier one of the findings of the Callan and Harmon (1996) study which suggested that today's early school leavers will be more disadvantaged than their parents would have been. When we come to look at qualifications achieved, however, rather than just at the number of years spent in education, their results require more careful interpretation. They find for example that the return from completing the Leaving Certificate (as well as sub-degree and sub-Leaving Certificate qualifications) rises as we move through the age cohorts from youngest to oldest, suggesting that these qualifications are a more important determinant of earnings for older groups, amongst whom, of course, they are scarcer. They take this as evidence of "qualifications inflation". This is open to debate however, since their study looks only at those currently employed. Since the length of time spent unemployed is strongly determined by an individual's educational qualifications, it is possible that in terms of overall expected returns to education, measured by expected earnings weighted by the expected probability of having a job, these qualifications may in fact convey higher benefits now than heretofore, relative to having no qualifications.[2] This is still the subject of controversy however, bearing as it does on the "human capital" versus "signalling" argument on the role of education in the labour market. This result does emerge clearly for university degree qualifications, however, even from the Callan and Harmon (1996) study. The marginal benefit in earnings terms of completing degree courses is higher for the younger generation than for the older, the much greater scarcity value of these qualifications amongst the older groups notwithstanding.

The trend, furthermore, of higher education contributing more today to one's earning power (compared to those with less qualifications), has occurred right across the industrialised world over the course of the 1980s. Typically, most has been written about the US case, so we will look at those numbers first. The college/high-school differential measured across all experience levels rose from 40 per cent in 1963 to 48 per cent in 1971, and reached 58 per cent in 1989. Measured over the first ten years of experience only, the change during the 1980s was from 28 per cent at the beginning of the decade to an end point where college graduates earned 69 per cent more per hour than high-school graduates (Murphy and Welch, 1992). Equivalent data for thirteen other countries, nine advanced and four middle-income economies, are presented by Davis (1992). He shows that among the advanced economies, the 1970s saw widespread declines in education differentials, but the pattern changed around 1980 to one of flat or rising education differentials in all the sample countries (the US, Japan, UK, France, Sweden, Canada, West Germany, Australia and the Netherlands) except the Netherlands. Table 5.2 below replicates part of Davis' Table 3.

Table 5.2
Changes in education differentials during the 1970s and 1980s

Country	Educ.group ratio	Year	Ratio Value	Year	Ratio Value
US	College/HS	1979	1.37	1987	1.52
Japan	College/Upper HS	1979	1.26	1987	1.26
UK	Univ/no qual	1980	1.53	1988	1.65
Canada	Univ/HS	1980	1.40	1985	1.43
Sweden	Univ/post-sec	1981	1.16	1986	1.19
Netherlands	Univ/sec	1983	1.43	1987	1.23
W.Germany	(14-18)/(11-13)	1981	1.36	1984	1.42

Source: Davis (1992).

It is clear from the table that earnings differentials between higher and more basic educational qualifications increased in virtually all of these countries over the course of the 1980s. In some countries this was associated with a fall in the real wage of workers with poor qualifications. In the US for example, the purchasing power of the wage earned by a worker with 12 years schooling or less fell by one-fifth between 1979 and 1993. In Europe, with its more comprehensive social welfare nets, the real wages of the low skilled were prevented from falling. The real wages earned by more skilled workers rose right across the industrialised world however, indicating that the relative demand for more highly skilled workers has been increasing more rapidly than the supply.[3]

A good deal of research energy has gone into attempting to account for these developments. The main competing explanations put forward for the strong growth in the relative demand for more highly skilled workers have been (i) increased trade with developing countries, and (ii) skill-biased technical change. We will consider each of these briefly. The trade with developing countries view is associated primarily with Wood (1994), who argues that imports of goods which use less-skilled labour have displaced less-educated workers in the West. There are a number of developments though which are not fully consistent with this view. Among these are the fact that, contrary to the conventional model upon which Wood's analysis rests, the proportion of skilled to unskilled workers has been rising across all sectors of the Western economy. (If this were due just to increased supply, though, it should occur through a fall in the education differential, which is of course the opposite of what needs to be explained). Furthermore, and again in contrast to Wood's model, the greatest increases in skill-intensity have been in the more highly skilled segments of OECD industry.[4]

These latter developments are however consistent with the alternative view that skill-biased technical change is at the heart of the matter.[5] Prais (1995) argues that recent technical change entails automation, as opposed to the period of mechanisation that prevailed previously. Automation, he argues, displaces unskilled operators while increasing the demand for technicians, supervisors and maintenance engineers. Mechanisation, by contrast, entailed the replacement of skilled craftsmen by machines operated by unskilled or semi-skilled labour.

Returning to the Irish case, we have seen that it is not yet clear whether demand increases have outstripped supply for all educational qualifications, though the case that this has occurred for some qualifications seems incontrovertible. Further evidence supporting an increase in the relative return to more highly skilled labour comes from Kearney's (1997) study of changes in the Irish manufacturing sector. In line with international usage, Kearney defines salaried Administrative and Technical Staff as skilled workers, and Industrial Workers (comprising Supervisors, Operatives and Apprentices) as less skilled.

Table 5.3
Wage rates as a proportion of Admin./Tech. wages in Irish manufacturing

Occupation	1979	1990
Supervisors	0.79	0.78
Apprentices	0.30	0.29
Operatives	0.57	0.54
All industrial workers	0.57	0.54
Clerical	0.57	0.63

Source: Kearney (1997).

For our purposes, the terms "highly educated" and "less well educated" seem more appropriate. Kearney leaves clerical workers as a separate category, since computerisation has arguably increased substantially the required educational levels of this group of workers. Table 5.3 below shows the wage rates of each of these groups as a proportion of the wage rates of Administrative and Technical Staff in 1979 and 1990. It is clear that the wages of all categories of industrial workers have fallen relative to those of "white collar" workers over the course of the 1980s, while the relative wages of clerical workers have risen. Even if we were to count clerical workers amongst the ranks of the less well educated however, the relative wages of the less well educated would still have fallen, since clerical workers comprise around 10 per cent of the manufacturing workforce, compared to the more than 76 per cent accounted for by industrial workers.

Aspects of the educational system that contribute to the cycle of deprivation

The shift in demand against low-skilled labour has turned the poorly educated in the US into "the working poor". In Europe, with its more comprehensive social welfare systems, the poorly educated have become social-welfare dependents instead. This might lead us to believe that high unemployment of low-skill workers might prevail in countries in which the ratio of high-to-low skill wages is not very great. Some countries have avoided the dilemma of having to choose between the routes of high unemployment or substantial numbers of the "working poor" however. Nickell and Bell (1996) point out that in Germany, the Netherlands and Sweden, wage differentials are not as great as in the US or the UK (as may be seen in Table 5.2 above), while the unemployment rate among the low-skilled is no higher than in the US. They note for example that German men in the bottom wage decile earn more than twice as much as American men in a similar position, and yet are hardly more likely to be unemployed. They ascribe these successes to the national education and training systems, arguing that the successful systems produce a much more compressed distribution of outcomes than the British or American systems. The most important factor determining the success of these systems is the strong emphasis placed on sustaining a high level of performance on the part of the bottom half of the ability range.

Prais (1995) ascribes this to the strong grounding in the basics of reading, writing and arithmetic imparted to everyone in the early years of compulsory schooling in the successful systems (the precise details of which he analyses), alongside much greater attention being devoted to vocational education. He points out, for example: (i) that in the successful systems, learning objectives during the period of full-time education are focused more on providing the majority with attainments suited for subsequent skilled vocational training rather than on the preparation of the minority entering academic university courses; (ii) for early school leavers in the successful systems, part-time attendance at vocational college is frequently mandatory; and (iii) in the successful systems, intermediate vocational qualifications are much more prevalent than in the UK. Furthermore, these represent industry-specific rather than firm-specific knowledge, with written tests as an essential adjunct to workshop experience. These qualifications then represent "an open door" to higher qualification levels including university degrees.

In many of these respects, clearly, Ireland is closer to the British system than it is to those of the successful Continental countries. A number of studies have pointed to the high variability of standards across the Irish primary and post-primary educational system, for example. Thus, the 1995 OECD Economic Survey of Ireland notes that "the performance of Irish schools is much more uneven than in other countries", and suggests that "the variability of school performance may be one explanation for the large differences in student performance according to the social status of their parents" (OECD, 1995, p. 80).

A comprehensive analysis of the performance of the second-level system in Ireland is provided by Hannan et al (1996), who focus on the factors determining how well pupils of different abilities do at school. Amongst their findings are that, even controlling for pupils' individual ability and individual family background, having a high proportion of peers from an unskilled manual background leads to significantly lower Junior Cert and Leaving Cert grades. Thus the point made in *Understanding Contemporary Ireland* (Breen et al, 1990, p.140) that working class boys are overrepresented in the vocational schools system, which contains "substantially greater proportions of children with numeracy and literacy problems", while middle class children are overrepresented in secondary schools, is of considerable practical significance. Hannan et al (1996) criticise also the "streaming" of pupils by ability in school. Along with other educationalists, they find that this worsens the performance of low-ability pupils by more than it improves the performance of those of high-ability. They comment also on the process of transition from school to work, training and further education, pointing out that the process has become increasingly dependent on academic grades, or "points", to the neglect of alternative certification arrangements or appropriate subject specialisations. This further acts to the detriment of those with vocational or practical rather than academic skills.[6] Nor does the Irish training system appear to be successful in overcoming the obstacles facing early school leavers. Thus, O'Connell (1996) finds that, amongst graduates of FAS courses, those with educational qualifications find jobs more easily, and at higher rates of pay, than do those without Junior or Leaving Certificates.

Conclusions

This chapter contains a sobering message. Economists have traditionally thought of high unemployment as a cyclical phenomenon; unemployment eventually moderates wage demands thus opening up new employment opportunities. Recently however, theories of "hysteresis" have gained widespread acceptance; i.e. that workers who become long term unemployed may not exert a wage-moderation effect. We suspect that hysteresis may be bound up with the strong shift in demand away from unskilled (or deskilled) workers that we have discussed in this chapter. We also discussed another, ultimately more virulent, form of hysteresis; this arises if the children of the long term unemployed drop out of school with little or no educational qualifications. Given recent trends in industrialised-economy labour markets, this means these children will grow up to be the long term unemployed of the future. The only way to prevent these developments, with their implications for the growth of the underclass and of crime, is to break the link between poor parental income levels, poor school performance and early school-leaving behaviour on the part of children.

References

Barrett, A., Callan, T. and Nolan, B. (1997), "The Earnings Distribution and Returns to Education in Ireland, 1987-1994", Paper No. 1679, Centre for Economic Policy Research: London.

Barry, F. (1996), "Has Trade with the South increased Income Inequality in the North?", *Trocaire Development Review*, pp. 51-63.

Barry, F. and Hannan., A. (1996), "Education, Industrial Change and Unemployment in Ireland", Paper No. 96/18, Centre for Economic Research : UCD.

Breen, R. (1984), *Education and the Labour Market: Work and Unemployment among Recent Cohorts of Irish School Leavers,* Paper no. 119, ESRI: Dublin.

Breen, R., Hannan, D. and O'Leary, R. (1995), "Returns to Education: Taking Account of Employers' Perceptions and Use of Educational Credentials", *European Sociological Review*, Vol. 11, No.1, pp. 59-73.

Breen, R., Hannan, D., Rottman, D. and Whelan, C. (1990), *Understanding Contemporary Ireland*, Gill and Macmillan: Dublin.

Breen, R., and Whelan, C. (1996), *Social Mobility and Social Class in Ireland*, Gill and Macmillan: Dublin.

Callan, T. (1993), "Returns to Educational Investment: New Evidence for Ireland", in *The CSF 1989-1993: Evaluation and Recommendations for the 1994-1997 Framework*, Final Report to the Department of Finance, ESRI: Dublin.

Callan, T. and Harmon, C. (1996), "The Structure of Earnings: New Evidence for Ireland", work in progress.

Davis, S. (1992), "Cross-Country Patterns of Change in Relative Wages", *National Bureau of Economic Research Macroeconomics Annual*, pp. 239-300.

Hannan, D., Smyth, E., McCullagh, J., O'Leary, R., and McMahon, D. (1996), *Coeducation and Gender Equality: Exam Performance, Stress and Personal Development*, Oak Tree Press in association with the Economic and Social Research Institute: Dublin.

Katz, L., and Murphy, K. (1992), "Changes in Relative Wages 1963-87: Supply and Demand Factors", *Quarterly Journal of Economics*, Vol. 107, pp. 35-78.

Kearney, I. (1997), "Changes in the Demand for Skilled Labour in Irish Manufacturing, 1979-90", unpublished manuscript, ESRI: Dublin.

Kellaghan, T., Weir, S., ó hUallacháin, S. and Morgan, M. (1995), *Educational Disadvantage in Ireland*, Department of Education, Combat Poverty Agency and Educational Research Centre: Dublin.

McCoy, S. and Whelan, B. (1996), *The Economic Status of School Leavers 1993-95: Results of the School Leavers' Surveys*, ESRI: Dublin.

Murphy, A., and Walsh, B. (1996), "Labour Force Participation and Unemployment in Ireland: A Microeconometric Study", paper presented to the Annual Conference of the Irish Economic Association, Dromoland Castle, Co. Clare.

Murphy, K., and Welch, F. (1992), "The Structure of Wages", *Quarterly Journal of Economics*, Vol. 107, pp. 285-326.

Nickell, S., and Bell, B. (1996), "Changes in the Distribution of Wages and Unemployment in OECD Countries", *American Economic Review*, Papers and Proceedings, Vol. 86, No. 2, pp. 302-308.

O'Connell, P. (1996), "The Effects of Active Labour Market Programmes on Employment in Ireland", Paper no. 72, ESRI: Dublin.

OECD (1995), *Economic Surveys - Ireland*, OECD: Paris.

Prais, S.J. (1995), *Productivity, Education and Training*, Cambridge University Press: Cambridge.

Walsh, B., and Whelan, B. (1976), "A Micro-Economic Study of Earnings in Ireland", *Economic and Social Review*, Vol. 7, No. 2, pp. 199-219.

Wood, A. (1994), *North-South Trade, Employment and Inequality: Changing Fortunes in a Skill-Driven World*, Clarendon Press: Oxford.

Acknowledgements

We thank Damian Hannan, Colm Harmon, Morgan Kelly and Chris Whelan for helpful comments.

Notes

1 Barrett, Callan and Nolan (1997) find that a substantial proportion of the increase in earnings dispersion in Ireland between 1987 and 1994 can be explained by the increased returns to education.

2 Compare also the returns to basic education in 1972 identified by Walsh and Whelan (1976) with those for 1987 reported by Callan and Harmon (1996).

3 The decline in education differentials for the US in the 1970s combined with its increase in the 1980s is rguably due to the fact that, for the US, the relative supply of highly educated workers grew more rapidly in the earlier decade than in the later one (Katz and Murphy, 1992).

4 Barry and Hannan (1996) find that this occurred in Ireland also.

5 See Barry (1996) for an overview of the debate between these competing hypotheses.

6 On the whole area of educational disadvantage in Ireland, see Kellaghan et al (1995).

6 Male long-term unemployment and structural employment changes in Ireland

Eric A. Strobl

Patrick P. Walsh

Introduction

Since the 1980s, Ireland has experienced a large and persistent increase in male Long term Unemployment (LTU), i.e., those who have been unemployed for more than a year. This leads one to ask the following questions. Who are the long term unemployed in Ireland? And, why did the males that entered the unemployment pool, particularly during the 1980s, remain there for very long durations? One popular explanation is based on the unemployment state dependence thesis (see for example Layard et al, 1991). Accordingly, a downturn in the business cycle increases the flow of workers into the unemployment state. As the spell of unemployment increases, an individual's human capital, or perceived human capital, can depreciate. A pro-longed recession can lead to disenfranchising individuals from the labour force by extending the duration of their unemployment spell. This creates an ineffective portion of labour supply which in turn creates wage pressure in a recovery period and causes unemployment to persist.

Another competing theory is based on the heterogeneity of the unemployed. Specifically, those that remain in the unemployment pool for long durations are inherently different from those that experience short spells. One possible cause of heterogeneity in the characteristics of individuals that flow into unemployment are changes in the structure of employment. Institutional changes, the globalisation of trade and technology advancement can induce important structural changes in the sectoral composition and the occupational structure of employment which can lead to the separation of older, unskilled individuals, with few or no educational qualifications, from the state of employment. These individuals would tend to have much lower re-employment probabilities than many others flowing into unemployment. The sunk costs associated with the re-training of their older human capital and the limited duration of return in the investment may lead firms to exclude them from the effective labour force even if, as a consequence, they incur higher wage costs. Thus, under this scenario, human capital is not unemployment but employment state dependent. In other words, it is not the duration of the unemployment spell but the nature of the prior employment spell that creates an ineffective portion of labour supply. In addition, it is not the business cycle *per se* but structural changes in employment over the business cycle that causes LTU.

Both of the theories described above suggest that LTU spells are not voluntary. It is however also popular to argue that, while business cycles and structural changes do increase the unemployment inflow, it is the generosity of the Irish welfare system and the high taxation of employment that induces many individuals to become part of an unemployment culture. Given the degree of welfare compensation and their employment possibilities, these individuals, in contrast, choose to stay long term unemployed. Due to the lack of studies on the causes of LTU, the relative importance of these theories in the Irish context is not clear. While the characteristics of the long term unemployed are well documented (see for example, the Department of Enterprise and Employment, 1996), the origin of the long term unemployed is not. Studies like Breen and Honohan (1991) and Harrison and Walsh (1994) assume a homogenous inflow of workers in their analysis of LTU. Both of these papers find relatively constant duration specific hazard rates over the 1980s. This would suggest that the aggregate trends in LTU are pushed by increases in the unemployment inflow and not changes in the conditional hazard rates. However, neither of these papers allows for unemployment heterogeneity in their analysis. O'Mahony (1983), on the other hand, rejects heterogeneity in terms of age, skill level and area of residence as the prevalent cause of long term unemployment in the 1970s.

In this chapter, we investigate the build-up of male LTU by allowing for heterogeneity both in the unemployment inflow and conditional survival rates.[1] Specifically, we construct a consistent semi-annual series of the male flows into and out of the Irish Live Register for the period 1967 to 1995. Utilising the information embodied in the inflows and information embodied in the duration specific stocks of the Live Register, we also develop a methodology that allows us to decompose the unemployment inflow by age and unemployment scheme and the unemployment outflow by duration of spell, age and unemployment scheme. Our results in conjunction with other evidence, presented in the next section, indicate heterogeneity in the unemployment inflow to be a cause of the build-up of LTU. In the following section, we use the results of the unemployment flow decomposition and evidence from other studies to argue that it was heterogeneity in the unemployment inflow caused by the changing occupational structure of employment that caused the persistence in LTU. We state our conclusions in the subsequent section. All data construction methodologies can be found in the appendix.

Semi-annual male unemployment flows

Information on the flows of individuals into and out of the Irish Live Register is not available from official data sources before 1983. Thus, we use an approach similar to that of Harrison and Walsh (1994) to construct a consistent semi-annual series of male unemployment flow data, details of which are provided in the appendix. The stock of unemployment and the constructed overall semi-annual inflows and derived outflows are plotted in Figure 6.1.

Figure 6.1
Irish semi-annual male unemployment inflow, outflow & stock
(3 pt. mov. avg)

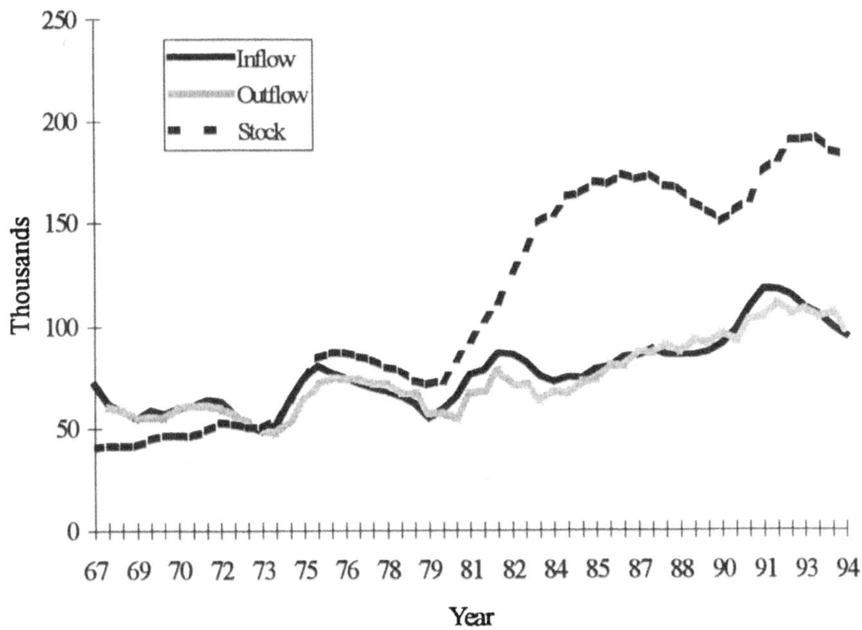

It must be realised at this point that the stock is a measure which can accumulate over time while the inflow and outflow are period specific. Any change in the semi-annual unemployment stock level arises when the inflow does not equal the outflow over any six month interval. Since the late 1960s, the stock has mainly been on an upward trend except for three year periods in the late 1970s and in the late 1980s. This resulted from flow activity in which inflows were generally greater than outflows. The flows in the late 1960s and early 1970s consisted of approximately 60,000 entries and 60,000 exits over each six month interval. The flow activity from 1980 onward has almost persistently increased. By the early 1990s the flows, approximately 110,000 entries and 110,000 exits over each six-month interval, were three times the flows in the early 1970s. The trends in the stock and the flows highlight the fact that the incidence of completed and uncompleted spells of unemployment has generally increased for males over time. It is apparent from Figure 6.1 that the turnover (i.e., the sum of the inflow and outflow) has been quite substantial over the entire sample period, especially in periods where there was a large build-up in the stock. In Figure 6.2, we depict the minimum number of unemployment compensation state transitions necessary to induce the changes in the total stock, which is just the absolute value of the change in the unemployment stock versus the actual number of unemployment compensation state transitions taking place, which is the sum of entries and exits to the unemployment compensation state. Accordingly, the gap between the actual versus the minimum number of unemployment compensation state transitions has increased substantially since the late 1960s.

Figure 6.2
Net change in male unemployment stock vs. male unemployment turnover

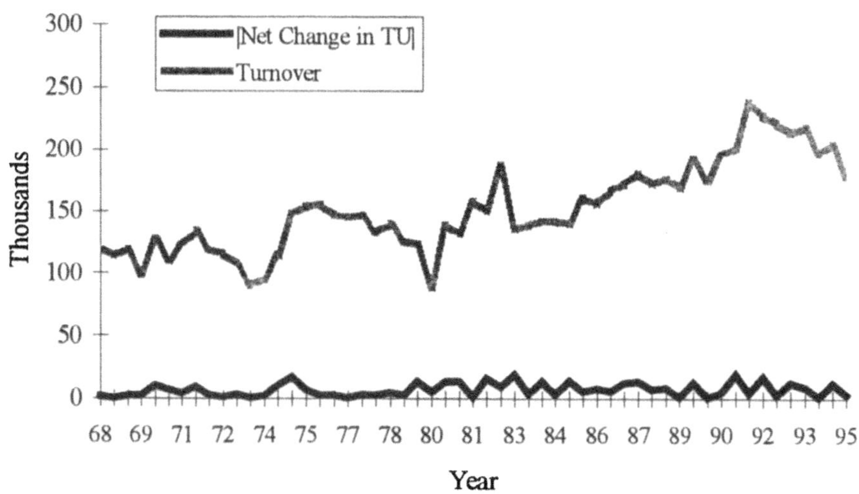

The observed turnover can of course be either due to a small number of males experiencing many unemployment compensation state transitions within a six month period or consist of different males entering and exiting the unemployment pool. Due to the absence of information on recurrent spells within a six month period, we can only calculate the upper and lower bound of the number of different individuals experiencing unemployment compensation state transitions; our methodology for such can be found in the appendix. We plot the upper and lower bound of the number of different males experiencing these transitions in Figure 6.3. This reveals that even when we account for the maximum number of recurrent spells, a substantial proportion of the unemployment dynamics within a six-month interval, is determined by a large number of different males. Over the 1980s for instance, the number of male individuals involved in the turnover was at least 30,000, but could have been up to 110,000 over any six month interval.

Figure 6.3
Upper and lower bound of male unemployment transitions

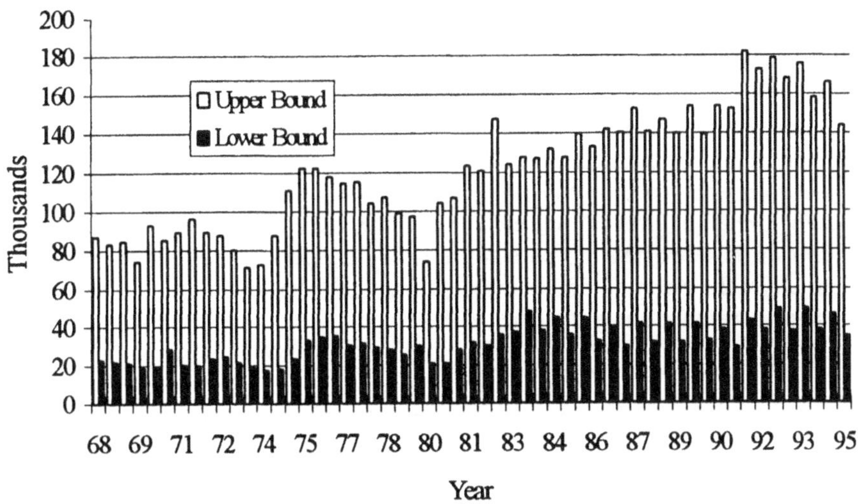

Some interesting features of Irish unemployment have thus far arisen from our analysis. Since the 1960s, the male unemployment stock, inflows and outflows have increased substantially. We find that the number of transitions have increased radically with the build-up in the stock and that these are due to a substantial number of different individuals making transitions to and from unemployment within six-month intervals. Moreover, as noted in the introduction, most of the build-up in the stock is due to a build-up of the long term unemployed. This suggests that, particularly since the 1980s, there may be differences between those that enter and exit and those that remain in the unemployment pool. In order to investigate this, we construct the male unemployment outflows from the Live Register conditional upon being of a particular duration spell, age and unemployment scheme over time, as detailed in the appendix. The methodology employed also allows us to compare the characteristics of males in the stocks with those in the flows and trace the dynamics behind the trends in the overall stock of unemployment and the stock of LTU. The only exception is posed in the decomposition by unemployment scheme, which can only be undertaken for duration spells under a year. This arises from the fact that when individuals flow into LTU on an Unemployment Benefit (UB) scheme, there is the possibility that they may switch over to receiving Unemployment Assistance (UA) during their spell in LTU when the duration of their receipt of benefits is completed.[2]

In order to provide a comparison between duration-specific stocks and outflows, we first plot the duration analysis of the stock of the unemployed in Figure 6.4. In the late 1960s and early 1970s, about 60 per cent of the total stock were short term unemployed males. This suggests the dominance of multiple short spells in the total unemployment pool in this period. This assertion is verified by Figure 6.5 which shows that over 60 per cent of the total outflows were from the short term pool and over 80 per cent of the total outflows were from duration categories under a year, as derived using our methodology described above. In the latter half of the 1970s, one witnesses a growing share of long term unemployed males and a declining share of short term unemployed males in the total stock. In contrast, still over 80 per cent of total outflows for males were from durations under a year. By the 1990s, the share of long term unemployment in the total stock reached over 50 per cent. However, over the entire period close to 80 per cent of those exiting did so from duration categories under a year. Thus the gap between the duration of a completed spell and that of an incomplete spell has persistently widened since the late 1970s.

Figure 6.4
Male unemployment stock decomposition

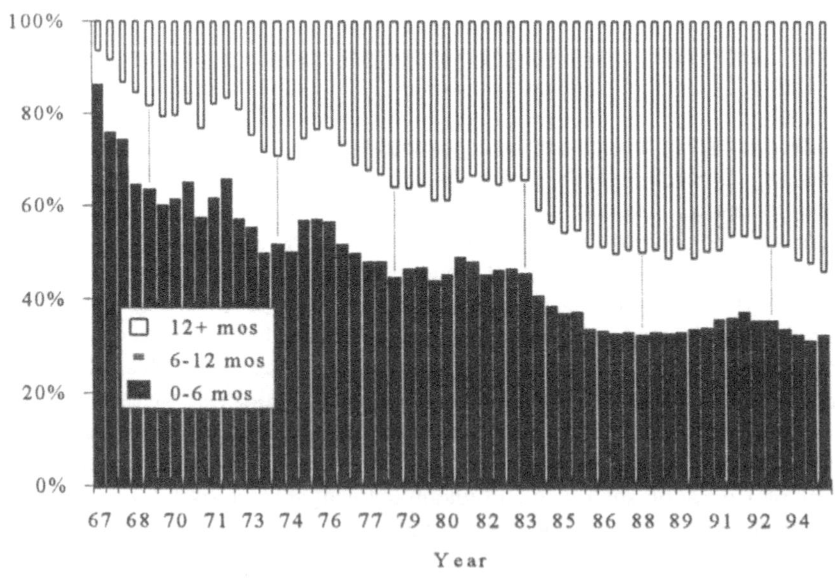

Figure 6.5
Male unemployment outflow decomposition

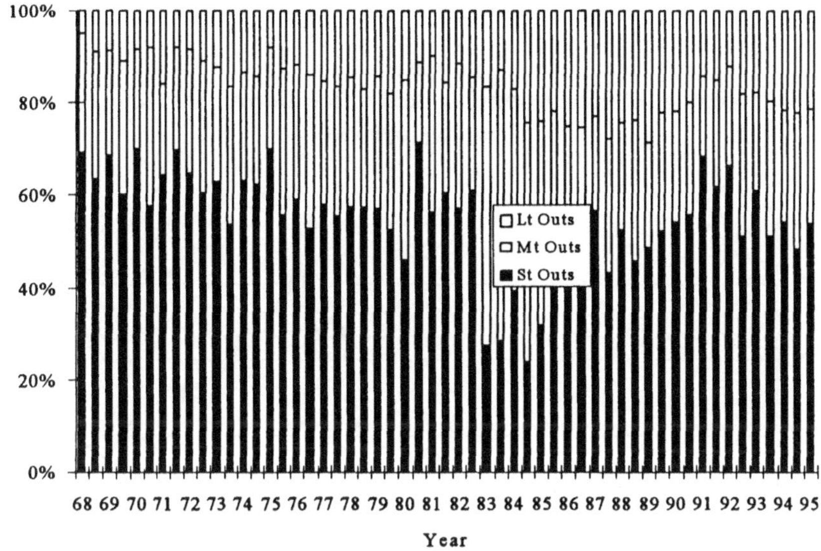

Our methodology also allows us to calculate the percentage of the initial inflow into the Live Register that flows into the LTU pool one year after entry. We depict this series in Figure 6.6. In the late 1960s, any male had, on average, a 90 per cent probability of exiting unemployment within a year. This probability gradually fell to below 70 per cent by the mid-1980s. From that point, it rose to 80 per cent and has remained relatively stable since 1988. Thus, even though there has been a substantial increase in the stock of LTU since 1980, the flows into LTU were only a small fraction of the initial inflow over the entire period. However, the increasing level of inflows into the Live Register ensured that a substantial number of individuals became long term unemployed. Figure 6.6 suggests that the under a year hazard rate did not remain constant over our sample period. Thus, in contrast to the results of Breen and Honohan (1991) and Harrison and Walsh (1994), we find that the trends in LTU have not been solely determined by trends in the level of newcomers to the Live Register.

The inflow, outflow and stock of the long term unemployment are shown in Figure 6.7. From Figure 6.1 and Figure 6.6 we know that the increasing magnitude of newcomers to the Live Register and the proportions of these flowing into LTU generated increasing flows into LTU up to 1988. The general excess of long term inflow over outflow, particularly in the period 1980 to 1988, led to the build-up in the stock of LTU, as is apparent from Figure 6.7. Since 1988, one witnesses declining proportions of newcomers flowing into LTU which resulted in a decline in the stock of LTU in the late 1980s. However, an increase in the magnitude of newcomers to the Live Register caused LTU to grow again thereafter.

Figure 6.6
Percentage of male unemployment inflow flowing into long term unemployment

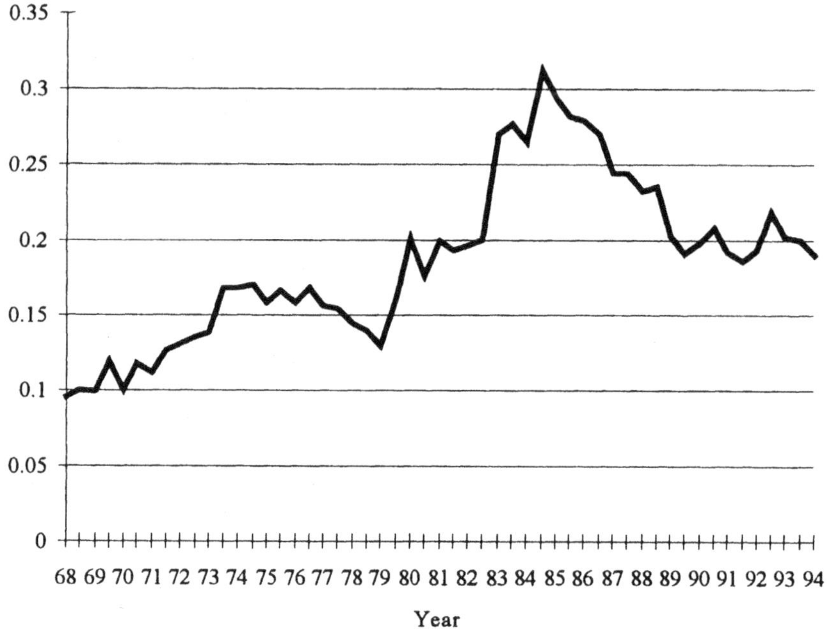

In Figures 6.8, we plot the number of LTU pool transitions as a ratio of the number of transitions in the unemployment pool under a year. This reveals a lack of activity within the long term pool relative to the activity in the under a year unemployment pool. Relative activity increased in the LTU pool between 1980 to 1988 and was mainly driven by large inflows into the LTU pool. The relative activity in the LTU pool has declined since the late 1980s.

Our analysis thus far indicates that there may be a dual structure in the unemployment pool in that there exists a very dynamic under a year and a sluggish LTU pool. Of the large amount of newcomers entering unemployment over six month intervals, only a small fraction experience LTU. One explanation for such a dual structure is heterogeneity among the unemployed, i.e., the cohorts of individuals that flow into LTU have different characteristics than those in the under a year turnover. We now turn to examining the flows and stocks by age and unemployment scheme to seek evidence for this hypothesis.

Figure 6.7
Male long term unemployment stock, inflow & outflow

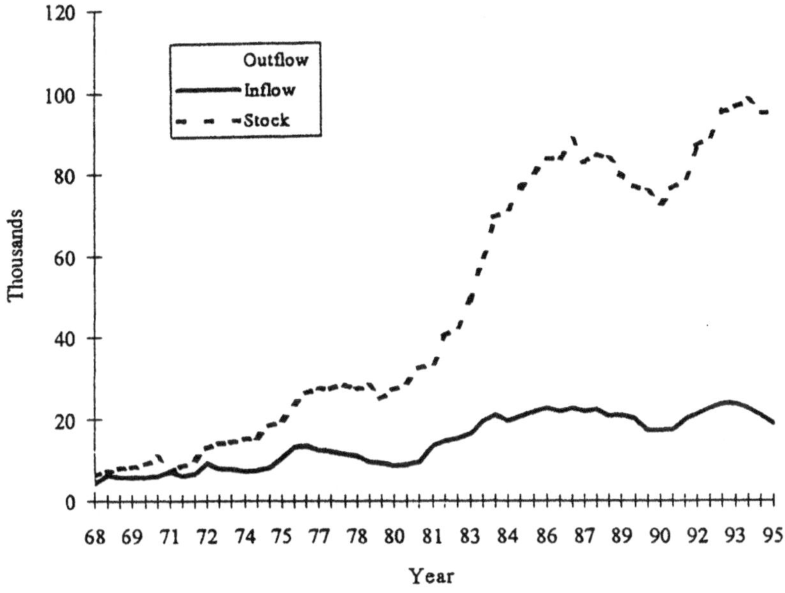

Figure 6.8
Ratio of male long term to under a year unemployment turnover

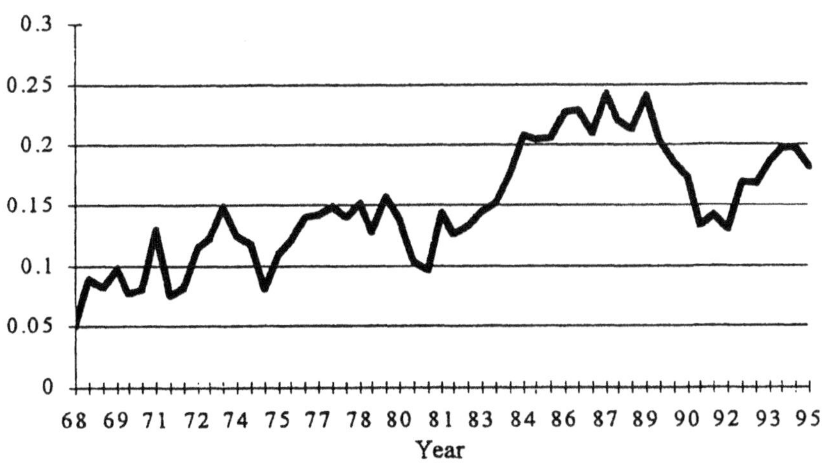

In Figure 6.9, we graph our decomposition of the overall inflow by unemployment scheme up to 1979 and age and unemployment scheme thereafter. From the late 1960s, the share of males entering on UA gradually rises from about 20 to over 40 per cent by 1988, and increases rapidly to over 60 per cent by the mid-1990s. Given that the qualifying conditions for UB were that no less than 26 employment contributions had to be paid from the beginning of the benefit year in which the claim for UB is made,[3] one can assume that those flowing into unemployment on the UB scheme are generally coming from the employment state. The trend witnessed in Figure 6.9 thus implies that flows from the state of employment gradually lost their dominance in the total unemployment inflow over time.

Figure 6.9
Irish male inflow decomposition

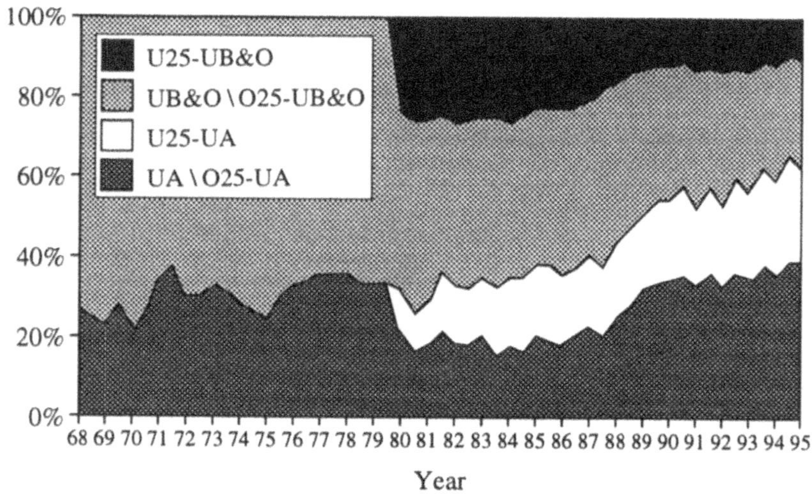

The percentages of the unemployment inflow of males on UA and UB that flow into LTU a year after entry are depicted in Figure 6.10. The survival rate of males on UB rose from 7 per cent in 1968 to 13 per cent in 1975 and fell to 10 per cent in 1979.[4] The survival rates for males on UA in this period were higher but followed similar trends, starting at 15 per cent in 1968, increasing to 30 per cent by 1975 and declining to 20 per cent by 1979. The greater share of males on UB in the inflow of newcomers ensured their dominance in the inflow into LTU despite lower survival rates. In the period since 1980, the survival rate for males on UB increased again from 12 to 27 per cent by 1985, subsequently decreased to 15 per cent in 1988, and has remained stable since. The survival rate for males on UA moved from 20 per cent in 1980 to over 30 per cent in 1985, decreased to just below 25 per cent by 1988, and has remained relatively stable since. Due to the dominance of males on UB in the flows of newcomers up to 1988, the majority of flows into LTU were, as argued above, males that came from the state of employment a year earlier. Since 1988, males on UA (i.e., flows most likely from non-activity or from employment of those that did not qualify them for UB) began to dominate the inflow into LTU due to both their dominance in the flows of newcomers to unemployment and their relatively higher survival rates.

Figure 6.10
Percentage of unemployment inflow flowing into long term unemployment

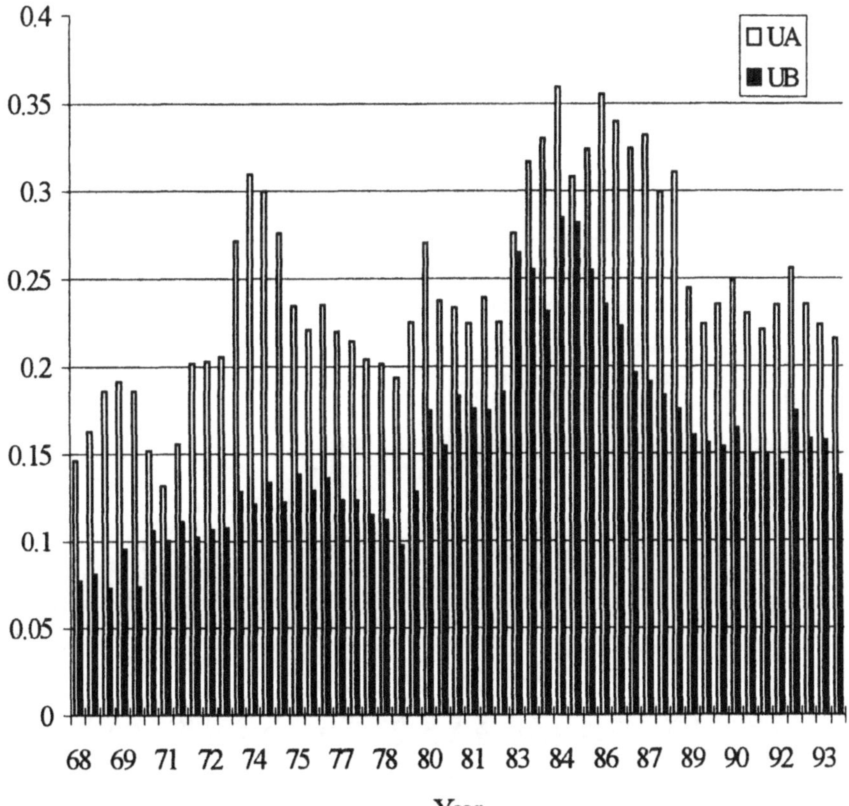

Using the Live Register stock data set, O'Connell and Sexton (1994) have noted that LTU is much more prevalent among the older age classes. Age therefore, may be another important determinant of Irish unemployment dynamics. From Figure 6.9, we know that between 1980 and 1988, younger and older males on UB dominated the inflows. It is also evident that older males had a greater share of the inflow than younger males. From 1988 onwards, the share of males on UB for both age groups gradually declined. In Figures 6.11 and 6.12, we graph the percentage of the initial inflow of males under- and over- 25 on UA and UB, respectively, that flow into LTU a year after entry. Accordingly, the survival rates for older males have been more volatile than those of younger males. In the early 1980s, 20 per cent of the older men on UB remained unemployed after a year. This increased to above 30 per cent by the mid-1980s and gradually declined to around 15 per cent by 1988, remaining relatively stable thereafter. The trends in the survival rates for older men on UA were similar even though the survival rates were generally 10 per cent higher. In contrast, the survival rates for younger males were much lower than older males up to 1988. Since 1988, the survival rates for younger and older males on both UB and UA have nearly converged.

Figure 6.11
Percentage of UB inflow flowing into long term unemployment

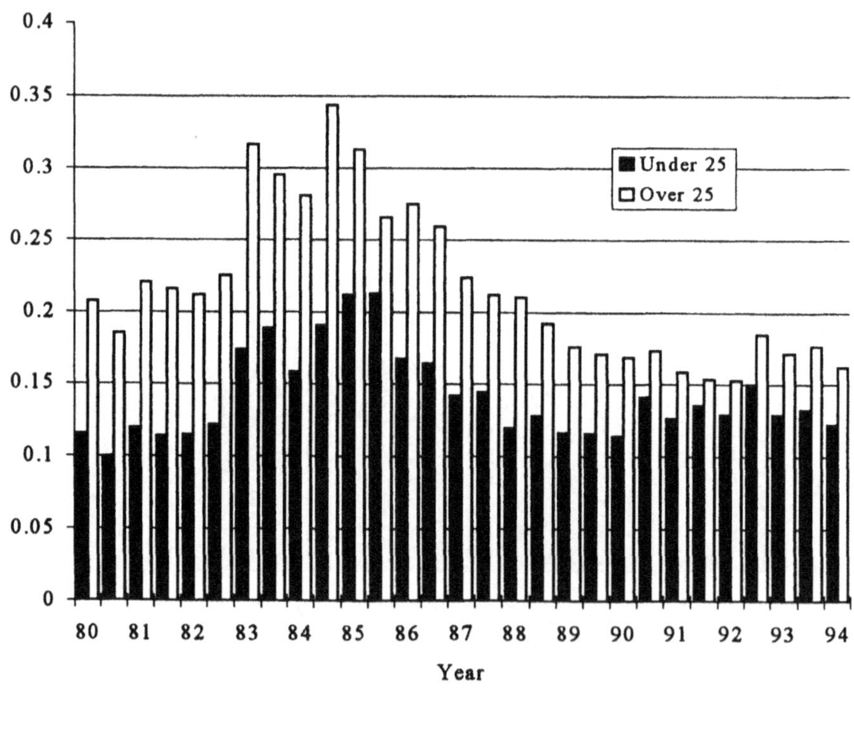

Considering Figures 6.9, 6.11 and 6.12 together allows one to draw a more general picture. Between 1980 and 1988, entries on UB were dominant in the unemployment inflow. In particular, in multiplying the number of older newcomers times their long term survival rate, one will find that older males, particularly those on UB, were responsible for the rising inflows into LTU. Between 1988 and 1995, the survival rates for all male groups fell and the numbers of older entries on UB have been on a declining trend. Even though the inflows into LTU have not superseded their 1988 level, LTU still increased in the 1990s due to low levels of outflows from this pool.

Figure 6.12
Percentage of UA inflow flowing into long term unemployment

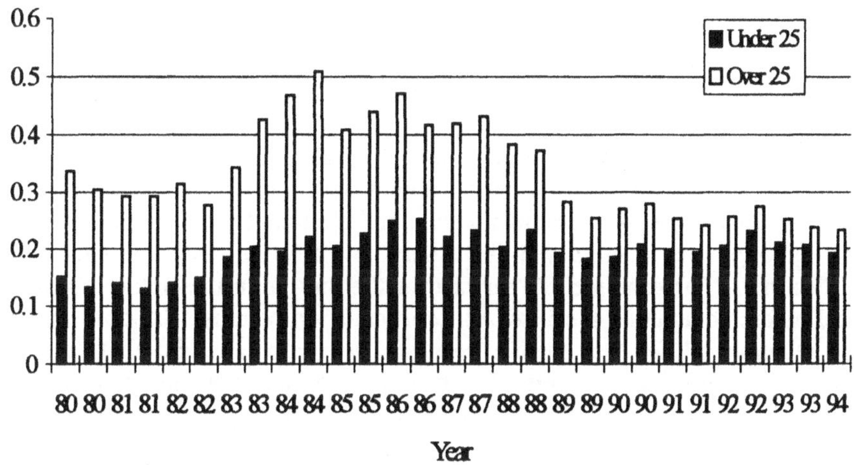

One alarming feature to note is the dominance of claimants of unemployment assistance, particularly older individuals, in the total and long term unemployment inflow since the 1980s. Are these males coming from non-activity or are they males coming from employment who are unable to satisfy the eligibility criteria for unemployment benefit? Given the information available to us, it is difficult to disentangle what is driving this feature. The increasing divergence of the number of unemployed as measured by the Labour Force Survey and the Live Register since 1987 certainly indicates that many of these are not genuinely unemployed, as defined by the ILO. One legislative change that may have played a role is the introduction of the Pre-Retirement Allowance Scheme and Pre-Retirement Credit Scheme in 1990. As pointed out by O'Reilly (1995), recipients on unemployment assistance aged 60 years[5] and over could receive early retirement payments under these schemes if they declared themselves to have retired from the labour market and thus were excluded from the Live Register. While this may have had the immediate effect of reducing the number of older long term unemployed and thus reducing the average age of long term unemployment, it may have also acted as an incentive for those in non-activity near the age of 60 to claim unemployment assistance so as to qualify for these two schemes when they become of age, thereby in the long-run increasing the number of older males and consequently the average age in long term unemployment as measured by the Live Register.

There were also a number of other legislative changes that may have increased the number of younger males flowing into and staying on unemployment assistance. In particular, individuals living in their parents' home are now eligible for a minimum rate of unemployment assistance given that they pass a means test that is independent of their parents' income. Also, the ceiling on the value of board and lodgings, as a percentage of the net parental income, has increased. O'Reilly (1995) argues that this not only increased the family income ceiling below which a person living at the parental home is eligible for UA, but also raised the amount payable to those whose family income is below the ceiling.

Due to data constraints, we are unable to decompose the outflow from LTU into its different age and unemployment scheme components. However, as pointed out earlier, O'Connell and Sexton (1994) found, using stock data, that long term unemployment is distinctly more prevalent among older age groups. The Department of Enterprise and Employment (1996), in comparing the employed, unemployed for less than a year, and the long term unemployed, found that the long term unemployed have very low relative levels of educational qualifications. For example, 82 per cent of the long term unemployed have left school before completing the Leaving Certificate. In contrast, the skill levels of those unemployed for less than a year are not drastically different from the employed. Similar results were already found for the unemployed in 1991 by Sexton and O'Connell (1993). Moreover, Snessens (1995), in linking skill mismatch to unemployment persistence in 14 OECD countries, shows that Ireland has the highest indicator of skill mismatch as measured by the gap between the unemployment rate of skilled and unskilled workers defined on the basis of the educational level and proportion of long term unemployed. All of these factors hint at the theory of heterogeneity among the unemployed as a plausible, at least partial, explanation for the build-up in long term unemployment. Moreover, our analysis above indicates considerable heterogeneity within the newcomers to the Live Register. Only small fractions of each cohort of newcomers flow into LTU. The magnitude of these flows, their compositions by age and unemployment scheme and the corresponding long term survival rates changed over time and are significantly different in the period 1980 to 1988 compared to the period 1988 to 1995. The dominant group in the inflow into LTU in the period 1980 to 1988 was older males coming from the state of employment a year earlier. This is the also the period in which there was a substantial build-up in the LTU stock, increasing from 30,000 to 90,000. In contrast, in the 1970s in which flows from employment were also the dominant force in the unemployment inflow, a similar accumulation in the long term pool did not occur. Since 1988, entries of older males flowing from the state of non-activity have been the driving force of the inflow into LTU. The LTU stock consequently decreased to 70,000 by 1991 and then increased again to just reach under 100,000 long term unemployed males. However, clearly the key period for the build-up of the long term stock was the 1980s.

Structural changes in employment

We noted in the first section that there are a number of theories, such as that of unemployment culture and that of state dependence, that could explain the strong incidence of long term unemployment and its build-up over the 1980s in Ireland. Our analysis from the previous section show that it is older, relatively uneducated males coming from the state of employment that accumulated in long term unemployment while many younger and more educated individuals experienced short spells of unemployment. In contrast, from the late 1980s onwards, we find that the probability of younger and older males flowing into long term unemployment on both UA and UB have converged. These facts suggest that heterogeneity in the unemployment inflow over the 1980s may be the key theory in explaining Irish long term unemployment. If true, the question that remains to be answered is what caused these older, relatively unskilled males to flow into and remain in the unemployment pool for long durations.

The strong incidence of long term unemployment is a feature found in most countries in Europe but not in the US. The OECD (1996) highlight the fact that, compared to the US, a substantial amount of employment adjustment in Europe seems to take place within or between firms resulting in vacancies being filled by workers from inside the firm or from other firms. The workers who do become unemployed in Europe then seem, unlike those in the US, to have difficulty leaving unemployment and can experience long durations in the unemployment compensation state. Thus, as suggested by the OECD (1996), it may be the nature rather than the lack of employment adjustment in the European labour market that causes LTU. As a matter of fact, structural changes in labour demand have been put forth as the prevalent cause for the European unemployment problem (Heylen et al, 1996). Basically, it is argued that there has been a fundamental shift in the occupational structure of labour demand from unskilled towards skilled labour, primarily taking place over the 1980s. As pointed out by Heylen et al (1996), there are a number of, not necessarily mutually exclusive, reasons for this development. Specifically, movements in production from blue-collar to white-collar industries; the introduction of new, more capital intensive, technology; the expansion of trade with developing countries with a comparative advantage in the production of goods that utilise more unskilled labour; and the net outflow of foreign direct investment, can explain this shift in labour demand.

In the Irish case, the fact that the older, relatively uneducated individuals that accummulated in the long term unemployment pool over the 1980s mostly came from the state of employment makes the story of structural employment changes as a cause for the Irish unemployment problem quite plausible. Using Labour Force Survey data, Corcoran et al (1992) studied occupational trends for the period 1971 to 1991 and we reproduce these in Table 6.1. Accordingly there were large shifts between occupational employment over the period. Moreover, it becomes apparent from this breakdown that most of these shifts took place over the 1980s. Whereas in the 1970s only agricultural workers and labourers experienced a decline in employment, over the 1980s occupations such as clerical workers, skilled maintenance, semi-skilled workers, operatives and foremen were subject to employment contractions, while others expanded.

Table 6.1
Annual average (%) changes in occupational employment

Occupation	1971-81	1981-86	1986-90
Agricultural Workers	-3.6	-2.4	-0.1
Managers / Proprietors	3.5	0.3	2.9
Professionals	3.6	1.9	3.7
Associate Professionals	5.0	1.2	2.6
Clerical Workers	3.0	-0.4	-0.5
Skilled Maintenance	4.0	-0.2	-0.8
Other Skilled Workers	0.3	-3.8	3.1
Semi-Skilled and Operatives	1.5	-2.9	1.0
Foremen	2.1	-3.5	-4.9
Transport Workers	0.3	-2.1	1.1
Sales Workers	1.2	1.5	0.0
Security Workers	4.6	2.3	-2.9
Personal Service Workers	0.8	1.7	1.4
Labourers and Others	-1.9	-4.6	-3.8
Total Employment	0.8	-0.8	0.3

Source: Corcoran et al (1992).

The occpational changes may have caused employment adjustments both across and within sectors. As pointed out by O'Connell and Sexton (1994), there have been substantial changes in the sectoral composition of employment in Ireland. Specifically, a decline of agriculture and traditional manufacturing was coupled with a rise in services and modern manufacturing employment. There are also likely to have been changes in the occupational structure of labour demand within sectors. The changing skill structure of employment has been documented for the US manufacturing sector by Berman, Machin and Bound (1995), for France and Germany by Sneessens (1995), and for the UK by Machin, Ryan and Van Reenan

(1996). All these studies indicate that the decline of unskilled employment is mainly explained by restructuring within and not between sectors. While Corcoran et al (1992) argue that between sector adjustments are likely to be the driving factor of the changing occupational structure in Ireland, other evidence indicates that, similar to the countries studied above, movements in the share of occupations within at least the manufacturing sector is of greater importance. For instance, Kearney (1996) finds that in almost 80 per cent of 72 sub-sectors of Irish manufacturing, the ratio of skilled to unskilled employment levels rose for the period 1979 to 1991. Using a shift-share analysis, Barry and Hannan's paper (Chapter 5) confirms the importance of within sector skill structure changes by showing that for the same period, these caused over 70 per cent of the increase in the proportion of skilled workers. While the lack of data availability does not allow us to discriminate between the importance of between and within sector occupational changes for unemployment, the CSO *Industrial Analysis of the Live Register* does classify the stock of insured individuals by their previous sector employment up until 1988. We depict the growth of unemployment for several broad sectors in Table 6.2. It is apparent from these calculations that practically all sectors experienced growth in unemployment over the 1980s. This suggests that there are likely to have been factors affecting all sectors, such as within sector occupational employment structure changes, that had a significant role in the increase in unemployment over the 1980s.

Table 6.2
Sectoral unemployment growth rates, 1979-1988

Sector	1979-88
Traditional Manufacturing	140.5
High-Tech Manufacturing	130.9
Building & Construction	111.8
Gas, Electricity & Water	259.1
Transport & Communications	18.4
Distributive Trades	198.7
Finance	262.5
Public Administration	354.7
Professions	242.9
Personal Services	237.2
Entertainment & Sports	128.3
Other Industries & Services	117.1
Agriculture	-30.0
Fishing	164.3

Thus far, we have discussed and provided evidence on how certain structural changes in employment coincided with the build-up of long term unemployment in the 1980s. However, it still needs to be explained why unemployment caused by such employment adjustments would persist as it does in Ireland. In a standard neoclassical framework, price and quantity adjustments would tend to reallocate those who lost their jobs to new employment over time. It has been argued that the fact that unemployment persists in Europe, but not in the US, is due to labour market rigidities. In particular, European countries tend to be characterised by more extensive employment protection legislation, greater union power, higher minimum wages, and greater unemployment compensation generosity (Heylen et al, 1996). This, of course, may also have been the case in Ireland. However, we argue for another explanation. Until Ireland's entry into the EC, many sectors of the economy were traditionally protected from external competition and it is likely that prior to this and for some time thereafter, the human capital of workers in many occupations was not sufficiently up-dated and the introduction of new technology was resisted by workers due to a fear of layoffs and new conditions of employment. When the institutional environment changed and all sectors of the economy became increasingly exposed to the gobalisation of trade and new technology, inefficient human capital inevitably had to be shed. The deep recession in the early 1980s presented sectors with the ideal opportunity to undertake such changes. The market, from the demand or supply side, subsequently probably had little incentive to re-build the human capital of these older and unskilled workers. Could a relative wage adjustment not have moved this human capital to employment? New levels of skills were required in all sectors of the economy. The sunk costs associated with the re-training of older human capital and the limited duration of return of such an investment may have led firms to exclude these individuals from the effective labour force even if, as a consequence, they incurred higher wage costs. Moreover, competition from younger and skilled new entrants for the jobs available would have re-inforced the lack of incentives to re-build older, inefficient human capital.

Conclusion

In this chapter, we have decomposed the semi-annual Irish male unemployment inflow into its components of age and unemployment compensation scheme and the semi-annual Irish male unemployment outflow by length of duration spell, age and unemployment compensation scheme. These disaggregations allowed us to investigate the evolutionary path and characteristics of those individuals that became long term unemployed. Our results and other evidence lead us to conclude that the build-up in the long term unemployment stock in the 1980s was primarily due to older, unskilled males. Given that these entered unemployment from the state of employment, we make the argument that it was structural changes in employment, due to changing occupational structures between and within industries, that caused extensive shedding of inefficient human capital over the

1980s that were the root of this phenomena. Moreover, it is likely that the degree of protection of industries and the resistance of workers to new technology prior to the 1980s has amplified the degree of skill mismatch and incidence of long term unemployment in Ireland relative to other European countries

In the face of skill mismatch, the natural response for a government, as a social planner, would seem to attempt to retrain the long term unemployed in order to re-integrate them into the effective labour force. This stance seems to have driven much of the Irish policies, such as a number of employment schemes, as a remedy for the long term unemployment problem. If however, as argued above, the human capital deficiencies of those shed in the 1980s are extensive, then one must ask whether, from an economic efficiency point of view, the costs of training may not outweigh the benefits. As for the future, the introduction of competition into the protected public utilities and private services in the non-traded sector of the economy over the next few years, could again create restructuring of employment that will lead to substantial flows of older males with redundant human capital into the unemployment pool. Thus, another phase of LTU may lie ahead.

Appendix

Construction of semi-annual unemployment flows

Fundamental to the construction methodology is the following equation

$$TU_{t+1} = TU_t + I_{t\rightarrow t+1} - O_{t\rightarrow t+1} \qquad (1)$$

which relates the stock of unemployed at time t+1 (TU_{t+1}) to the stock of unemployed at time t (TU_t), the total number of entries to the Live Register ($I_{t\rightarrow t+1}$) and the total exits from the Live Register ($O_{t\rightarrow t+1}$) during the intervening period. The time points used are the last Friday of May and November of each year up to 1979 and the second to last Friday of April and October in each year from 1980 to 1995. Given the overall inflows, $I_{t\rightarrow t+1}$, into the Live Register during each of these six months intervals, and a five month interval in the case of the period November 1979 to April 1980, the outflows can be derived via equation (1). Thus, our attention focuses on the construction of a consistent semi-annual series for $I_{t\rightarrow t+1}$, commencing in November 1966 and ending in April 1995.

The gender specific count of newcomers to the Live Register has been published by the Central Statistics Office (CSO) on a monthly basis since January 1983. The counts for this series were undertaken on the second Friday of each month up to 1989. As such, they underestimate the total inflow into the Live Register since some newly unemployed individuals have up to the full month, and others as little as one day, to leave the Register and thus may not be present in the count. Since 1989, the counts for this series were undertaken on the last Friday of each week and newly unemployed individuals would have up to a week to leave the Register. Nevertheless, we feel that the majority of the monthly inflows is well captured by the CSO figures for the period 1983 to 1995. To construct a semi-annual series for the inflows in the Live Register which corresponds to the time-points of the stock of unemployment data in April and October, we assume that the monthly inflows accumulate at a uniform weekly rate. The CSO monthly figures can then be aggregated and the appropriate adjustments made for the weeks at the beginning and end of each six-month interval as defined by the unemployment stocks.

Construction of the required inflows for the earlier part of our sample is more problematic as no CSO monthly inflow data are available. Indeed, due to constraints relating to raw data availability, our method of construction had to be modified for two earlier sub-periods, namely, the periods November 1966 to November 1979 and November 1979 to April 1983. For the former period, we made use of the CSO's quarterly unemployment duration analysis, excluding those aged 65 years and over. This analysis is based on duration specific stock data collected on the last Friday of February, May, August and November in each of the relevant years. We assume that the under-five-weeks unemployment duration categories in August and November of each year are representative of the same category in June and July, and September and October, respectively, of the same year. The semi-annual inflow for the period from the end of May to the end of November in each year was constructed as the sum of 25 times the number of males unemployed in the under-five-weeks unemployment duration category in August and November. Similarly, the semi-annual inflow for the period from the end of November to the end of May of the following year was constructed by summing 25 times the number of males unemployed in the under-five-weeks unemployment duration category in February and May of that period.[6]

For the remaining sub-period in the sample, namely, the bridging period November 1979 to April 1983, only semi-annual duration analysis is available from CSO sources. We assume that the under-five-weeks unemployment duration category in October and April of each year is representative of the same category in the other five months of the six-month intervals of April to October and of October to April, respectively. The semi-annual inflow for these periods in each year was constructed as 6.5 times the number of males unemployed in the under-five-weeks unemployment duration category of the respective representative months. The one exception to this rule was the five-month period between November 1979 to April 1980, where the under-five-weeks duration category in April 1980 was only multiplied by 5.5. While our procedure of construction for the period 1966 to 1983 will produce errors in the estimation of the exact number of newcomers, the general trends and levels should be representative of the true inflows and the series should be consistent with the estimates of newcomers to the Live Register for the period April 1983 to April 1995.

Construction of upper and lower bound of individuals in the unemployment flows

We define the upper bound, $Max_{t\rightarrow t+1}$, as the following

$$Max_{t\rightarrow t+1} = I_{t\rightarrow t+1} + O_{t\rightarrow t+1} - O^{NC}_{t\rightarrow t+1} \quad (2)$$

where $O^{NC}_{t\rightarrow t+1}$, the newcomer outflow, is the outflow of individuals who entered unemployment in the period t to t+1 and is calculated via the following identity

$$O^{NC}_{t\rightarrow t+1} = I_{t\rightarrow t+1} - S_{t+1} \quad (3)$$

where S_{t+1} is the stock of those unemployed for under six months at the end of the six month period.

$Max_{t\rightarrow t+1}$ serves as an upper bound by implicitly assuming that those in the gross outflows do not re-enter unemployment over the same six month interval and thus would not be present in $I_{t\rightarrow t+1}$, and by realising that a newcomer entry and exit together must account for a single individual. In order to calculate the lower bound, we assume the maximum possible number of recurrent spells. Thus the lower bound of the number of different individuals experiencing unemployment compensation state transitions, $Min_{t\rightarrow t+1}$, is defined by the following

$$Min_{t\rightarrow t+1} = O_{t\rightarrow t+1} - O^{NC}_{t\rightarrow t+1} = O^{IN}_{t\rightarrow t+1}. \qquad \text{if } O_{t\rightarrow t+1} \geq I_{t\rightarrow t+1}$$

$$Min_{t\rightarrow t+1} = I_{t\rightarrow t+1} - O^{NC}_{t\rightarrow t+1} - O^{IN}_{t\rightarrow t+1} + O^{IN}_{t\rightarrow t+1} = S_{t+1} \qquad \text{if } O_{t\rightarrow t+1} < I_{t\rightarrow t+1} \quad (4)$$

where we define the total outflows net of newcomer outflows as incumbent outflows, $O^{IN}_{t\rightarrow t+1}$, i.e., the exits from unemployment over the six month interval t to t+1 of individuals who entered unemployment prior to this interval. When total outflows are greater than total inflows, then the minimum number of individuals that can account for the unemployment compensation transitions is equal to the incumbent outflow as all inflows could potentially be recurrent spells of just these individuals. If, however, outflows are less than inflows, then the minimum number of individuals accounting for the unemployment compensation transitions is greater than the number of individuals as represented by the incumbent outflow, $O^{IN}_{t\rightarrow t+1}$. The minimum number of individuals in this scenario is the sum of the inflow in excess of total outflow and the incumbent outflow, which, by definition, leaves us with the short term stock taken at t+1, S_{t+1}.

Decomposition of unemployment flows by age and unemployment compensation scheme

The inflows into the Live Register, either as provided by the CSO or as constructed earlier in this chapter, are only given as totals. However, the duration specific stocks of the CSO Live Register set are broken down both by age and unemployment scheme and thus we use these to estimate the proportion of the inflows over each six-month interval that is due to particular age and unemployment scheme groups. The duration specific stocks of the CSO data set are decomposed into those individuals on Unemployment Assistance (UA), those on Unemployment Benefit (UB) and those on the Live Register registered for neither scheme, i.e., those classified as "Other". We choose to group those in the "Other" category with those on UB because many of these would essentially be 'signing on' so as to qualify for UB later. For convenience sake, we will refer to the sum of these two groups as UB. The methodology we employ for decomposing the overall inflow into its components by unemployment compensation scheme rests on the simple assumption that the proportions of these groups in the refined duration specific stock categories of our sample months reflect closely the shares of these groups in the overall inflow for the six month interval in question. More precisely, in order to estimate the components of the total inflow on either UA or UB we, for the six-month intervals starting on the last Friday of November in 1966 up to the last Friday of November in 1979, weighted the semi-annual inflow by the proportions of each unemployment scheme in the under-five-weeks category in the representative months used in the construction of the total inflow. Similarly, in the six month intervals starting in November 1979 up to the last Friday of October 1988 we used the proportions of each unemployment scheme in the under five weeks duration category stock in April and October. Finally, in the six month intervals starting in October 1988, up to the last Friday of April 1995, we used proportions of each unemployment scheme in the under-three-months duration category stock in April and October.[7]

In seeking to decompose the unemployment inflows by age, we are constrained by the fact that the age decomposition in the duration analysis data set was only initiated in 1980. As with the decomposition by unemployment scheme, the decomposition of the total unemployment inflow by age for the period April 1980 to April 1995 also rests on the simple assumption that the proportions of these groups in the refined duration specific stock categories of our sample months reflect closely the shares of these groups in the overall inflow for the six-month interval in question. Up to the last Friday of October 1988, we used the over- and under- 25 years of age proportions of the under-five-weeks duration category stock in April and October to weight the overall male inflows. For reasons given above, we used the over- and under- 25 years of age proportions in the under three months duration stock in April and October to weight the inflows for the remainder of our sample period. We can similarly decompose the total inflow by both age and unemployment scheme from 1980 onwards.

Construction of duration specific unemployment flows

To construct the duration specific flows, we make use of two sources of information, the semi-annual inflows into the Live Register and the corresponding duration specific stocks. The former are derived as outlined above, and the latter are available as part of the Live Register data set.

For expositional ease, we only outline how to decompose the total outflow into the outflow from the under six months duration category, S_t, the short term unemployed, from the between six and twelve months duration category, M_t, the medium term unemployed, and the over twelve months duration category, L_t, the long term unemployed, without further decomposition by age and/or unemployment scheme. However, this methodology can easily be extended to characteristic specific outflows by using the corresponding characteristic specific duration stocks and inflow.

Over any six-month interval t to t+1, we distinguish between two cohorts of individuals that can potentially outflow from the short term unemployment pool. First, all newcomers to the Live Register in the interval t to t+1, ($I_{t\rightarrow t+1}$), may outflow over the six month interval. Since we know that any individual in the short term stock S_{t+1} must have been part of $I_{t\rightarrow t+1}$,[8] this newcomer outflow, $O^{NC}_{t\rightarrow t+1}$, is calculated as in equation (3).

In addition to the newcomers, those incumbent to the short term pool as captured by the short term unemployment stock at the start of the six-month interval, S_t, can also potentially outflow from this pool prior to t+1 and prior to spilling over into the medium term unemployment pool. The construction of this part of the short term outflow however is more problematic. The duration specific stocks of the Live Register allows one to calculate those of this incumbent cohort that remain at t+1 as portrayed by the difference between S_t and M_{t+1}. The difficulty arises when one wishes to calculate the fraction of these leaving the Live Register conditional upon being short term unemployed. In constructing the short term unemployment incumbent outflow, we do know that it will be some fraction of the original stock, S_t. We thus define the outflows from short term unemployment over the time interval t to t+1 as the following

$$O^{S}_{t\rightarrow t+1} = (I_{t\rightarrow t+1} - S_{t+1}) + \lambda_t S_t \qquad (5)$$

where the term in the parentheses on the right hand side is the outflow of newcomers from short term unemployment over the six-month interval, $O^{NC}_{t\rightarrow t+1}$. The second term, $\lambda_t S_t$, is the fraction of the incumbent stock, S_t, that outflowed over the interval t to t+1 while still in the short term pool. The average probability of outflowing from the short term pool as an incumbent, λ_t, is unknown but we proxy it as follows. Since we know that the average probability of outflowing from the short term pool as a newcomer, $\theta_t = (I_{t+1} - S_{t+1})/ I_{t\rightarrow t+1}$, during the same period, we make the assumption that the incumbent's average probability of outflow, λ_t, is proportional to θ_t. However, because the incumbents S_t essentially already had at least some chance, some up to six months and others as little as a day, to outflow over the prior period t-1 to t and failed to do so, one might expect the probability of outflowing from the short term pool to be lower for incumbents. To correct for this potential bias in levels, θ_t is weighted by the ratio of the subset of those who remained incumbent to the newcomers in the prior six month interval, $S_t / I_{t-1\rightarrow t}$. Hence, we take account of the evolutionary path of the unemployed and also allow for period specific conditions to have an effect. If, for example, newcomers to the Live Register over t-1 to t remained for longer durations in short term unemployment, then a larger proportion of the newcomers will be accounted for at t and the level of the newcomer hazard rate over t to t+1 will more accurately reflect the level of hazard rate for incumbents. Thus we estimate the percentage of S_t exiting unemployment from the short term unemployment pool over the six-month interval t to t+1 as the following

$$\lambda_t \approx \theta_t \,.\, (1 - \theta_{t-1}) \tag{6}$$

which makes equation (4) operational.

One can construct the outflow from the medium term unemployment pool in a similar manner to that from the short term unemployment pool. The medium term outflow over any interval t to t+1 can again come from two different cohorts of individuals: the newcomers to the medium term unemployment pool; and those already incumbent to the medium term pool at the beginning of the time interval as the medium term stock, M_t. The group of newcomers to the pool over the interval t to t+1 is simply the proportion of S_t that are estimated to have failed to outflow from the short term pool:

$$I^M_{t\rightarrow t+1} \approx (1 - \lambda_t) \,.\, S_t \tag{7}$$

We estimate the total outflow from the medium term pool over the interval $t\rightarrow t+1$ to be the following

$$O^M_{t\rightarrow t+1} = (I^M_{t\rightarrow t+1} - M_{t+1}) + \lambda^*_t M_t \tag{8}$$

where $(I^M_{t\rightarrow t+1} - M_{t+1})$ is the estimated outflow of newcomers and $\lambda^*_t M_t$ is the estimated outflow of incumbents in the medium term pool that flow out while classified as medium term unemployed. The probability of an incumbent outflowing from the medium term pool before the end of the interval t to t+1, λ^*_t, is expected to be proportional to the average probability of a medium term newcomer outflowing before the end of the interval, $\theta^*_t = (I^M_{t\rightarrow t+1} - M_{t+1}) / I^M_{t\rightarrow t+1}$. To correct for an expected bias in levels we, in line with the reasoning given above for the short term unemployed, weight θ^*_t by the ratio of those remaining from the medium term newcomers of the previous period, $M_t / I^M_{t-1\rightarrow t}$. Thus, we estimate the percentage of M_t expected to outflow from the medium term unemployment pool over the six-month interval t to t+1 as the following:

$$\lambda^*_t \approx \theta^*_t (1 - \theta^*_{t-1}) \tag{9}$$

Since the long term unemployment pool does not empty out over six-month intervals by definition, we are not able to distinguish between long term unemployment newcomer and incumbent outflow. Rather then, we construct long term outflow with the standard flow-stock relationship equation:[9]

$$O^L_{t\rightarrow t+1} = I^L_{t\rightarrow t+1} - \Delta LTU \tag{10}$$

where $\Delta LTU = L_{t+1} - L_t$ is defined as the change in the long term unemployment stock over the six-month interval and the inflow of newcomers to long term unemployment is estimated as:

$$I^L_{t\rightarrow t+1} \approx (1-\lambda^*_t)M_t \tag{11}$$

Given the semi-annual inflows into unemployment and the semi-annual duration stocks, which can also be defined by age and/or unemployment scheme, one can use equations (5) through (11) to conduct a duration spell analysis of outflows from the Live Register.

References

Bartholomew, D., Moore, P., Smith, F. and Allin, P. (1995), "The Measurement of Unemployment in the UK", *Journal of the Royal Statistical Society – Series A*, 158, pp. 363-417.

Berman, E., Bound, J. and Grichiles, Z. (1994), "Changes in the Demand for Skilled Labor within US Manufacturing: Evidence from the Annual Survey of Manufactures", *Quarterly Journal of Economics*, Vol. 109, pp. 367-397.

Berman, E., Machin, S. and Bound, J. (1995), "Implications of Skill Biased Technological Change: International Evidence", mimeograph, National Bureau of Economic Research.

Breen, R., and Honohan, P. (1991), "Trends in the Share of Long term Unemployment in Ireland", *The Economic and Social Review*, Vol. 22, pp. 253-286.

Corcoran, T., Sexton, J.J. and O'Donoghue, D. (1992), "A Review of Trends in the Occupational Pattern of Employment in Ireland 1971-1990", Manpower Forecasting Studies, Paper No. 2, FAS/ESRI: Dublin.

Department of Enterprise and Employment (1996), *Growing and Sharing our Employment*, Department of Enterprise and Employment: Dublin.

Eatwell, J. (1995), "Disguised Unemployment: The G7 Experience", UNCTAD Discussion paper.

Harrison, M.J., Strobl, E. and Walsh. P.P. (1995), "The Impact of Discriminatory

Legislation on Irish Female Unemployment Flows", Trinity Economic Papers, Technical Paper No. 3, Department of Economics, University of Dublin (Trinity College): Dublin.

Harrison, M.J., and Walsh, P.P. (1994), "A Flow Analysis of the Irish Live Register", *The Economic and Social Review*, Vol. 26, pp. 45-58.

Harrison, M.J., and Walsh, P.P. (1995), "Unemployment Dynamics in the Small Open Irish Labour Market", mimeograph, Department of Economics, University of Dublin (Trinity College): Dublin.

Heylen, F, Coubert, L., and Omey, E. (1996), "Unemployment in Europe: A Problem of Relative or Aggregate Demand for Labour?", *International Labour Review*, Vol. 135, pp. 17-36.

Hughes, G. and Walsh, B.M. (1983), "Unemployment Duration, Aggregate Demand and Unemployment Insurance: A Study of Irish Live Register Survival Probabilities, 1967-1978", *The Economic and Social Review*, Vol. 14, pp. 93-118.

Kearney, I. (1996), "Sectoral Shifts in the Demand for Skilled and Unskilled Labour in the Irish Manufacturing Sector 1979-90: A Panel Data Study", paper presented to the Annual Conference of the Irish Economic Association, Dromoland Castle, Co. Limmerick.

Layard, R., Nickell, S. and Jackman, R. (1991), *Unemployment: Macroeconomic Performance and the Labour Market*, Oxford University Press: Oxford.

Lehmann, H. (1993), "The Effectiveness of the Restart Programme and the Enterprise Allowance Scheme", Discussion Paper No. 139, Centre for Economic Performance, London School of Economics: London.

Machin, S., Ryan, A. and Van Reenan, J. (1996), "Technology and Changes in Skill Structure: Evidence From an International Panel of Industries", Discussion Paper No. 297, Centre for Economic Performance, London School of Economics: London.

Nickell, S. (1996), "Sectoral Structural Change and The State of The Labour Market in Great Britain", The Labour Market Consequences of Technical and Structural Change: Discussion Paper Series No 2, Centre for Economic Performance, The London School of Economics: London.

OECD, (1996), "Employment Dynamics in Firms: Their Impact on Labour Markets", Working Paper, DEELSA/ELSA/WP5(96)5, OECD: Paris.

O'Connell, P.J. and Sexton, J.J. (1994), "Labour Market Developments in Ireland, 1971-1993", in Cantillon, S., Curtis, J. and Fitz Gerald, J. (eds.), *Economic Perspectives for the Medium Term*, ESRI: Dublin.

O'Mahony, M. (1983), "The Length of Spells of Unemployment in Ireland", *The Economic and Social Review*, Vol. 14, pp. 119-136.

O'Reilly, A. (1995), "An Analysis of the Changes made to the Live Register since 1970", mimeograph, Department of Economics, University College Dublin: Dublin.

Sexton, J.J. and O'Connell, P. (1993), "Evaluation of Operational Programme to Combat Long term Unemployment Among Adults in Ireland: Objective 3 of the Community Support Framework", ESRI: Dublin.

Sneessens, H., (1995), "Asymmetric Growth Effects, Skill Mismatch and Unemployment Persistence", Discussion Paper no 9525, IRES, Université Catholique de Louvain: Louvain.
Walsh, B.M. (1993), "Labour Force Participation and the Growth of Women's Employment, Ireland , 1971-1991", *The Economic and Social Review*, Vol. 24, pp. 369-400.

Acknowledgements

This research is part of a project on "Who are the Unemployed in Ireland?" funded by the Royal Irish Academcy, Social Science Research Council.

Notes

1 Even though females are playing an ever increasing role in the build-up of long term unemployment, the fact that they were subject to different institutional and legislative settings would make a separate analysis necessary. For an analysis of the impact of the legislative setting on female unemployment flows, see Harrison et al (1995).

2 Up until April 1975, the duration of receipt of unemployment benefit was 12 months, and 15 months thereafter for most groups of recipients. A switch-over is only possible if the individual satisfies a means test. Thus, individuals that remain on the Live Register on UB have no incentive to switch over to UA, assuming that they qualify, until after the full duration of receipt of UB, i.e., once they have been already qualified. Those individuals that do switch over to UA would then be classified as long term unemployed on UA.

3 Employment contributions required to receive UB were increased to 39 in May 1987.

4 Hughes and Walsh (1983) find that in the period 1967 to 1978, changes in the replacement ratio, the real value of transfer payments and the duration of receipt of unemployment benefit, increased the duration of unemployment.

5 Over the following two years the qualifying age was reduced to 55 years for both schemes.

6 No count was available for May 1970, February 1971, May 1979 and August 1979. To estimate the inflow for the six-month intervals affected, the count of individuals in the under-five-weeks unemployment duration

category of the other relevant month, that was available, was multiplied by 6.5.

7 We were limited to this less refined weighting as the Live Register data set changed to no longer include duration categories below that of under-three-months.

8 Any individual who was part of the S_t stock would, if still unemployed, be in the medium term unemployment pool since the short and medium term pools empty out over time by definition.

9 Alternatively we could have constructed long term outflow by solving for:

$O^{Total}_{t \rightarrow t+1} = O^{L}_{t \rightarrow t+1} + O^{M}_{t \rightarrow t+1} + O^{S}_{t \rightarrow t+1}$

$O^{Total}_{t \rightarrow t+1} = I_{t \rightarrow t+1} - \Delta TU$

where $\Delta TU = TU_{t+1} - TU_t$

7 Irish unemployment in a European context

Kieran A. Kennedy

The total level of employment in Ireland is not much higher now than it was over 70 years ago at the time independence was achieved. No other country in Europe has had an experience remotely comparable. It is not surprising therefore that Ireland has had an endemic unemployment problem, though unemployment is not the only manifestation of the deeper malaise of inadequate job opportunities, which was also associated with massive emigration and low labour force participation. Neither is it surprising that the world-wide rise in unemployment since the first oil crisis in 1973 produced acute problems for Ireland.

Historical pattern of unemployment

Remarkably, however, the rise in unemployment in Ireland was comparatively muted up to 1980, despite reduced emigration and a substantial increase in the labour force. Accordingly in 1980, the unemployment rate in Ireland, although it had risen, was not much out of line with the rates then prevailing in the EU, US and UK (see Table 7.1). This achievement, however, was purchased at the cost of unsustainable increases in the balance of payments and in national debt. The inevitable corrective measures had to be set in train at a bad time - just as the world was grappling with the consequences of the second oil crisis. Ireland experienced a traumatic rise in unemployment in the first half of the 1980s, and by 1985 the unemployment rate was nearly double the EU rate, which itself was by then much higher than in either the US or Japan.

During the world-wide economic recovery in the second half of the 1980s, most countries, including Ireland, experienced a moderate fall in unemployment. These gains were largely reversed, however, in the downturn in the early 1990s. The recovery that followed has brought little reduction in unemployment in the EU as a whole, so that the EU unemployment rate is now nearly double the US rate, which is back to its normal long-term floor of about 5½ per cent. In some EU countries, the unemployment situation continues to deteriorate. The deterioration is particularly marked in Germany, the only large European country to sustain a better record in regard to unemployment than the US for most of the period since the first oil shock. Unemployment in Germany is forecast to go on rising at least up to 1997, by which time the forecast rate of 9.4 per cent will be approaching the EU average.

Table 7.1
Unemployment rates for selected years, 1960-1996

	EU	Ireland	UK	US	Japan
1960	2.5	5.5	1.6	5.4	1.7
1973	2.6	5.7	3.0	4.8	1.3
1980	6.4	7.3	6.4	7.0	2.0
1985	10.5	17.0	11.2	7.1	2.6
1990	8.1	13.3	6.9	5.4	2.1
1991	8.2	14.7	8.8	6.6	2.1
1992	9.3	15.5	10.1	7.3	2.2
1993	10.9	15.6	10.4	6.7	2.5
1994	11.3	14.1	9.5	6.0	2.9
1995	10.9	12.3	8.4	5.6	3.1
1996	10.9	11.7	8.2	5.7	3.4

Sources: EC, *Economic Forecasts 1996-1997*, Spring 1996, and OECD *Economic Outlook*, various issues. The EU figures up to and including 1990 refer to the EU 12, excluding East Germany, while the figures for 1991 onwards relate to EU 15, including East Germany. Figures for Ireland for recent years are taken from the latest ESRI *Quarterly Economic Commentary*.

Germany of course has had to cope with the formidable challenge of reunification. But even the star performer among European countries, Sweden, which has not had to face a challenge similar to that of Germany, and where unemployment up to the early 1990s was generally kept below 3 per cent, has not been exempt from a substantial rise to nearly 10 per cent in 1994.

Against this European background, the Irish achievement of the past three years has been all the more remarkable. The Irish unemployment rate has fallen by four percentage points since 1993, and if this progress could be sustained, would be down to the EU average by 1998. Moreover, unlike the fall which took place in the second half of the 1980s, the current decline is not due to a resumption of emigration. It is not without significance for us that the only other major European country experiencing a fall in unemployment is the UK, which traditionally exerted a strong influence on Irish unemployment. To the extent that this influence was exerted through the pull of emigration, however, it has not been operative on this occasion. Accordingly, the improvement in the Irish unemployment rate relative to the EU has been achieved despite a substantially higher growth in the labour force here.

This improvement in the Irish labour market has not been so obvious to the general public because of the heavy concentration on the Live Register figures, which have shown little decline and still stand close to 300,000. There is a large and growing disparity between the numbers on the Live Register and the unemployment measures based on Labour Force Surveys that would be regarded by experts and relevant international agencies as appropriate and comparable across countries. I do not need to go into the reasons for these differences here, since they were outlined in a paper by the Central Statistics Office for the National Economic and Social Forum in January 1996. Subsequently, the results of the special study undertaken by the CSO in conjunction with the April 1996 Labour Force Survey and published on 18 September 1996, confirm that many persons not statistically classified as unemployed in the LFS are included in the monthly Live Register total. It is abundantly clear that the Live Register can no longer be taken as a suitable measure of either the level or trend of unemployment.

There is, of course, no room for complacency about our position - for two important reasons. First, it is not satisfactory merely to reach the general level of EU unemployment, given that that rate itself is unacceptably high. Second, and even more important, sustaining recent progress is not automatic: it will be influenced strongly by the policies and decisions we follow. Before addressing the latter point, it is essential to look at the growth performance underlying Ireland's relative improvement (see Table 7.2).

Comparative growth rates

There has been so much talk about "jobless growth" that it is important to emphasise that the rise in unemployment in the EU since 1973 was not due to a reduction in the employment intensity of growth. The most striking feature of the post-1973 experience in the EU was the decline in output growth, which more than halved from 4.7 per cent per annum from 1960-73 to 2.1 per cent from 1973-96.

Table 7.2
Average annual growth rates of output and employment since 1960, various sub-periods

	GDP	Employment	Productivity	Labour Force
1960-73	4.7	0.3	4.4	0.3
1973-85	2.0	0.0	2.0	0.7
1985-90	3.3	1.3	1.9	0.9
1990-93	0.7	-1.0	1.7	-0.2
1993-96	2.3	0.2	2.1	0.3
Ireland				
1960-73	4.5 (4.4)	0.1	4.4 (4.3)	0.0
1973-85	3.5 (2.4)	0.1	3.4 (2.3)	1.2
1985-90	4.6 (3.9)	1.0	3.6 (2.9)	0.0
1990-93	3.1 (2.8)	0.4	2.7 (2.4)	1.6
1993-96	7.8 (6.7)	3.4	4.3 (3.2)	1.7
UK				
1960-73	3.1	0.3	2.9	0.3
1973-85	1.4	-0.2	1.6	0.7
1985-90	3.3	1.8	1.5	0.6
1990-93	-0.1	-2.1	2.1	-0.4
1993-96	2.9	0.5	2.4	-0.2
US				
1960-73	3.9	1.9	1.9	1.9
1973-85	2.3	1.8	0.5	2.1
1985-90	2.8	2.1	0.6	1.6
1990-93	1.8	0.2	1.6	0.8
1993-96	2.5	1.7	0.8	1.5
Japan				
1960-73	9.6	1.3	8.1	1.3
1973-85	3.6	0.7	3.0	0.9
1985-90	4.5	1.5	3.0	1.4
1990-93	1.7	1.2	0.5	1.2
1993-96	1.4	0.3	1.1	0.4

Sources: As in Table 7.1. Figures for Ireland in parentheses in Columns (1) and (3) relate to GNP and GNP per worker, respectively.

Furthermore, practically all of this decline in output growth was reflected in reduced productivity growth (from 4.4 per cent per annum over the period 1960-73 to 2.0 per cent per annum over the period 1973-96), so that the employment intensity of growth has actually risen in the EU since 1973.

The EU was an area of very low employment growth even before the first oil crisis. This did not matter at that time, however, since labour force growth was also low. Unemployment remained steady at a rate of only about 2½ per cent, while the high productivity growth enabled European living standards to converge rapidly towards the US level. After 1973, despite the huge fall in output growth, the rise in the employment intensity of growth was nearly enough to maintain the previous (low) growth of employment. But this low growth of employment was now a problem because the labour force was growing faster due to demographic factors, and the EU experienced a substantial rise in unemployment.

If we look at the EU figures over the last ten years or so, they provide further evidence that employment growth does respond strongly to output growth. Thus over the period 1985-90 when the EU growth rate recovered to an average of 3.3 per cent per annum, the EU experienced an unprecedented growth in employment of 1.3 per cent per annum. The recession in the early 1990s led to a big fall in employment while the moderate recovery since 1993 has been accompanied by a small growth in employment. There is no basis in EU experience for doubting that if rapid output growth resumed, it would induce strong growth in employment.

The US as well experienced a huge drop in the growth rate of output after 1973, which was also reflected mainly in a decline in the growth rate of productivity. The employment intensity of growth was much higher than in Europe in the 1960s, and it rose sufficiently after 1973 to sustain a continued high growth rate of employment - about enough to match the high growth of the US labour force. The drop in output growth in the US did not therefore induce any long term rise in unemployment in the US. It has brought other problems, however, in that the low rate of US productivity growth implies slow progress in living standards, and indeed the real wages of unskilled workers have been falling.

Japan also experienced a great fall in output growth after 1973, and again this was chiefly reflected in a fall in the rate of productivity growth. Japan faced a growth in its labour force intermediate between the rapid US rate and the slow EU rate. It has managed to sustain a rate of employment growth roughly comparable to its labour force growth, so that its unemployment rate, which was less than 2 per cent in 1973, rose little. In the last four years, however, Japanese unemployment has been creeping up, though at the current level of 3½ per cent, it is still uniquely low among the large developed countries of the world.

In this setting, Ireland is exceptional in that apart from the first half of the 1980s it has experienced no prolonged decline in the growth of real GDP, and the average rate over the period 1973-96 (4.2 per cent per annum) is only slightly below that for 1960-73 (4.5 per cent). It is generally accepted, however, that the GDP measure exaggerates Ireland's comparative growth performance since the early 1970s, but even in terms of the more suitable GNP measure, the decline in real growth in Ireland has been much less than in the EU. The growth rate of real GNP in Ireland fell from 4.4 per cent per annum from 1960-73 to 3.3 per cent per annum from 1973-96, whereas the decline in the EU rate was from 4.7 to 2.0 per cent per annum. Productivity growth has also fallen in Ireland compared with the 1960s, but still has been higher generally than in the EU, as it needs to be if Irish living standards are to converge to EU levels. The really heartening factor, however, is that in the 1990s Ireland's rate of economic growth has been such that it has also given rise to an employment performance consistently much better than that of the EU, and in the past three years has been high enough to ensure a significant fall in unemployment, notwithstanding a high growth in the labour force.

Why has Ireland been doing so well, notwithstanding the fact that, while its rapid expansion has been primed by export growth, 75 per cent of its exports are to the rest of the EU, and the EU has not been particularly buoyant? I think an important reason is that, for once, we have capitalised on the advantages of smallness. As is well known, the small size of a country has many disadvantages, but it also has some advantages. An important one of these is that even in stagnant world market conditions, a small country need not be constrained by lack of demand if it is sufficiently competitive and innovative to win increased market share. A large or even a medium sized country would find this much more difficult to accomplish simply because it already possesses a sizeable market share. Similarly, large countries could not expect to attract foreign direct investment on the same relative scale as Ireland, simply because the pool of such investment is not large enough to meet all demands. Ireland has done much to enhance its competitive position since the second half of the 1980s through national agreements and generally sensible government policies. A few years ago, claims that the "economic fundamentals" (e.g. inflation, the balance of payments and the public finances) were in good order tended to evoke a certain derision, given our bad unemployment situation. But we are now getting the pay-off in terms of output and employment growth for having put the economic fundamentals right. We are also deriving the pay-off for the large investment in education that was initiated 30 years ago with the introduction of free second-level education, which has made possible a structured shift from a low skill to a high skill economy. The EU Structural Funds have undoubtedly helped, especially since overall they have been used reasonably sensibly.

EU policy

In attempting to develop a co-ordinated EU approach to the unemployment problem, the European Commission operates under two major constraints. The first constraint is the limited role of the Community in many areas of economic and social policy. The Community institutions do not constitute a federal government, and most of the key powers to influence unemployment remain with member states. The second constraint is the difficulty in securing a political consensus among the member states on appropriate policies, and indeed the lack of conviction that there is any set of generally acceptable policies capable of restoring full employment.

The European Commission's (1993) White Paper, *Growth, Competitiveness, Employment* (generally known as the Delors White Paper) sought to establish a basis for a new coordinated approach. While implementation has been spotty, and progress on the ground less than anticipated, the document still provides the framework for the Commission's thinking on how the EU should address the unemployment problem.

The White Paper recommended that the Community set itself the objective of creating an additional 15 million net new jobs by the year 2000 (a growth rate in employment of nearly 2 per cent per annum from 1995 to 2000) so as to reduce the EU unemployment rate by half. It was argued that this growth in employment required a combination of somewhat stronger output growth (GDP volume growth of 3.4 per cent per annum) and somewhat higher employment intensity. In regard to output growth, it was emphasised that it was not simply the *actual* rate that needed to be raised but also the *potential* rate, i.e. the rate that could be sustained without overheating. To secure this increase in growth potential, the investment share of GDP would have to rise over a number of years by about five percentage points. This would have to be supported by increased saving, primarily through reduced government deficits, and by policies to sustain business confidence and enhance investment profitability.

Policies regarded by the White Paper as *inappropriate* included protectionism, inflationary monetary or fiscal policy, generalised reductions in working hours or job-sharing, a basic income for all regardless of labour market availability, and drastic cuts in wages. Instead it proposed a strategy comprising three inter-linked elements: the creation and maintenance of an appropriate macroeconomic framework (including the progression of incomes); the improvement of European competitiveness; and structural changes in the labour market.

The appropriate macroeconomic environment, according to the White Paper, is one with a stable monetary policy consistent with inflation of not more than 2-3 per cent per annum. Fiscal policy should initially be geared towards the Maastricht criteria for general government deficits (less than 3 per cent of GDP), but in the longer term, budgetary policy would need to adjust to the higher required level of national saving, implying zero budgetary deficit or even a small surplus. As regards incomes policy, the need to increase the profitability of investment required that, in the medium term, average real wages should increase by one percentage point less than the growth rate of productivity. Given the target growth rate of productivity of 1½ per cent per annum, this would imply very little increase in real incomes, with nominal incomes rising at little more than 2-3 per cent, the target rate of inflation. Once the budgetary policy and wage behaviour were in place, interest rates could fall and this was seen as the chief means of boosting demand through its influence on confidence, competitiveness and the profitability of investment. The merits of maintaining exchange rate stability and the EMU perspective were stressed, both on their own account and as a means of reinforcing the stability of the macroeconomic framework.

A many-sided strategy, involving cooperation between government and business, was proposed in order to enhance the competitiveness of European industry in global markets. Particular stress was laid on the knowledge-based industries and the 'first mover' advantages to be gained from development of environmentally-friendly products. Government intervention in industry should be re-focused on growth markets where Europe has a strong development potential, such as health, the environment, bio-technologies, multi-media activities and culture. Top priority should be given to nonphysical knowledge-based investment, including training. Stress was laid on improving the organisational capacity of firms, on clustered development and on partnerships between large firms and sub-suppliers. To provide the infrastructural underpinning for these initiatives, the White Paper proposed a commitment to developing trans-European networks in telecommunications, transport, energy, and the environment, involving investment of close to ECU 600 billion up to the year 2000, about one-fifth of which would be funded at Community level.

In regard to the labour market, three themes were highlighted: education and training; labour market practices; and statutory charges on labour. It was argued that education and training could help in two ways. It would boost growth by improving competitiveness generally. In addition it could also ensure a greater take up of potential jobs through better matching of supply and demand, and by equipping particularly deprived groups - such as the young, the long term unemployed and the technologically redundant - to compete effectively in the labour market. The White Paper stressed the need to develop systematic lifelong learning and continuing training - to be achieved not so much by extra public funding, but rather by reorganising educational resources in association with the employment services. The latter would involve, inter alia, re-allocating a significant proportion of unemployment compensation to training measures, especially for the long term unemployed and unskilled young people.

In regard to the second theme, labour market practices, the White Paper rejected outright reliance on the free market but advocated a range of measures in order to remove disincentives to hiring less-skilled workers; to facilitate voluntary choices for a shorter working week, career breaks etc.; to stimulate job creation in SMEs and in new economic, environmental and social activities; and to target specific disadvantaged groups so as to provide them with clearer stepping stones into the formal labour market. Concerns about the extent and structure of statutory charges on labour prompted the recommendation that member states adopt a target of reducing them by an amount equal to between 1 and 2 per cent of GDP, which would have to be compensated by increases in other taxes, given the need to maintain low budget deficits. The maximum result would be achieved by targeting the cut on social security contributions in low wage jobs, and by restoring the tax loss through a carbon tax on energy rather than increased VAT.

At this stage, I would have to express some scepticism as to whether the EU would be likely to attain an employment growth rate of nearly 2 per cent per annum with an output growth rate of only 3.4 per cent per annum. It would imply a fall in the rate of growth of labour productivity to 1½ per cent per annum - a low rate by European standards, especially at a time when the rate of technological progress is rapid. The White Paper itself stated that labour productivity in Community manufacturing still lags well behind that of the US and Japan, and needs to be increased; and, furthermore, it stressed the need to improve productivity in services. The White Paper was not oblivious to the potential conflict involved, but it saw "no contradiction between calls for increased productivity growth in all sectors open to international competition and at the same time calling for measures which increase the weight of sectors where productivity increases are low". Essentially, then, the proposed model is one in which productivity growth in the exposed sectors may even have to accelerate, but a greater share of the increased resources than in the past would be channelled, in one way or another, towards the production of labour-intensive products (mainly non-traded services), with the increased weight of the latter giving rise overall to a lower rate of growth of productivity. Such a structured shift towards low productivity activities would be difficult to accomplish at a time when many existing low productivity industries are under pressure from competition from low wage countries outside the EU. Moreover, the small average real wage increases implied in the strategy would make it very difficult to maintain the type of incomes policies seen as necessary to underpin the strategy.

The Essen European Council meeting of December 1994 reached agreement on five priorities for employment policy, which represents the principal plan of action for implementing the Delors White Paper. These priories, which were strongly focused on structural reform of the labour market, were as follows.

1 Promotion of investment in vocational training.

2 Increasing the employment intensity of growth (through flexible organisation of work, wage restraint to encourage and provide room for job creating investment, and local initiatives).

3 Reducing the non-wage costs of labour (especially social security charges).

4 Re-designing income support policies to increase work incentives.

5 Concentration on groups particularly hard hit by employment (the long term unemployed, early school leavers, women and older workers).

In a progress report a year later (Commission of the European Communities 1995) on the implementation of these priorities, the Commission noted that the reforms undertaken in the member states show that "there is a broad consensus on the guidelines set out in Essen", but that "a global employment systems approach as recommended by the White Paper and by the European Council cannot always be discerned in the midst of all these reforms".

In an attempt to give a new thrust to Community employment policy, the President of the Commission, Mr Santer, brought forward this year the idea of "A Confidence Pact" (Commission of the European Communities 1996). The intention was not to launch new ideas but to secure collective action involving all relevant parties - Community institutions, national, regional and local authorities, and the social partners. An effort was made to define the responsibilities of, and the commitments required from, each of these actors for a co-ordinated strategy. In that way the Pact sought to incite the various actors to capitalise on the potential synergies offered by European integration. It placed particular emphasis on proceeding rapidly with the large scale investments in Trans-European Networks (TENs) in transport, energy and communications. It called on the Florence European Council to "launch a vast mobilisation for employment on the basis of the strategy outlined in this paper".

The communiqué following the Florence meeting on 21-22 June 1996, states that "the European Council considers that the level of unemployment must remain the top priority for the Union and its Member States". Notwithstanding these high-sounding words, however, there is nothing concrete in the communiqué to suggest the launching of "a vast mobilisation for employment". Specifically on the TENs investment, the Council merely took note of the Santer proposals, stating that it "will consider these proposals, in conformity with the imperatives of budgetary rigour and in accordance with the relevant procedures."

Implications for Ireland

Further reduction in unemployment in Ireland requires sustained strong growth in employment. Convergence towards European levels of income per capita requires continued high growth in productivity. Both objectives can be achieved simultaneously only through strong growth in output. Obviously, the latter would be easier to achieve if the European economy were buoyant.

Although economic growth in the European Union is likely to pick up in the second half of this year, the average growth of GDP in the EU in 1996 is likely to be no more than about 1½ per cent. The outlook for 1997 is somewhat brighter, but GDP growth is unlikely to be more than 2½ per cent. Consolidation is the watchword in fiscal policy in preparation for EMU, with expenditure cuts favoured over tax increases as the means of achieving the EMU borrowing criterion. The only chance of a boost to demand lies in the hope that successful fiscal consolidation would have favourable effects on confidence and long term interest rates. It is not at all clear how successfully this fiscal consolidation will proceed, given the widespread resistance to expenditure cuts evident in France, Germany and some other EU countries. Moreover, it is also unclear whether and how soon the impact of even a successful fiscal tightening on confidence and interest rates would outweigh the direct effects on aggregate demand. In this situation, the EU is left to put its faith in supply side measures (and particularly structural reform of the labour market) as the chief means of reducing unemployment - even though such measures can be expected at best to work only slowly for an area as large as the EU at a time when its own demand, and that of its major world partners, is not expanding rapidly.

Consequently, if Ireland is to continue to grow rapidly in the years ahead, it will have to do so in the face of moderate growth in the EU, and indeed in the rest of the OECD. By virtue of its strong competitive position and small scale, Ireland has accomplished this feat in recent years. The June 1996 issue of the ESRI *Quarterly Economic Commentary* predicts that Ireland can sustain a growth rate of 5 per cent per annum for the rest of this decade provided "a disciplined approach to economic management continues to be applied by both government and social partners". The next round of pay negotiations and the next Budget will be critical tests of resolve in that regard. In regard to pay, it should be stated that the Delors pay guidelines of keeping average real wage increases one percentage point below the growth rate of productivity would be too lax in Irish circumstances for the following reason. Given the likelihood that productivity (even measured with GNP rather than GDP) will continue to grow much faster here, that guideline would be compatible with a substantially faster growth of real wage rates in Ireland than in Europe. The resulting impact on employment overall would be unfavourable because the pace of productivity growth in Ireland is dominated by new or recently-established multinational enterprises with levels and growth rates of productivity so high that the indigenous employment-intensive firms, which account for the bulk of total employment, could not hope to match them. For this reason, as well as the greater scale of the employment challenge facing Ireland, a more restrictive pay target would be needed here.

Of course if we could sustain the average growth performance of the past three years (nearly 7 per cent per annum growth of GNP, divided almost equally between employment growth and productivity growth), then it would be possible to adhere to a more restrictive guideline than that of Delors while still facilitating a modest increase in real wages. Combined with restraint and increased effectiveness in public expenditure, there would be scope for income tax cuts to further boost take-home pay. Furthermore, in such a situation the ratio of employment to population would continue its recent upward trend, further accelerating the convergence in Irish income per capita to EU levels.

I am not predicting that this optimistic scenario will actually be realised. I am all too conscious that one of our persistent failings in the past has been to claim success too soon, and to grasp at the fruits of growth before we have earned them. But what I do want to highlight is that if we can now overcome this failing and sustain a disciplined approach, there is an historic opportunity to substantially alleviate the situation of the unemployed in the next five years at a relatively low level of sacrifice on the part of the employed.

In seeking to maintain its relative competitiveness, Ireland would also be unwise to ignore the increasing emphasis in Europe generally on greater flexibility in the labour market. Indeed, the willingness evident in recent years in the exposed sectors of the Irish economy and in a number of commercial state enterprises to negotiate major changes in work practices and manning levels without full compensation in pay levels has been an important factor in our performance. The chief remaining area for concern relates to the unrealistic expectations and outmoded concepts that still seem to prevail among workers in sheltered occupations and professions, including the public service. As the June 1996 *Quarterly Economic Commentary* put it:

> These concepts include the primacy of equity considerations over feasibility, a commitment to unchanging relativities between grades and between occupations, the assumption that any changes in work practices or working conditions should be fully compensated in pay rates, and the presumption that job security can be taken for granted.

Without a change in these concepts and expectations in the sheltered sector, it will be difficult to effect the tax reductions that help to sweeten the pill of adaptation for workers in the exposed sectors.

I do not wish to say that economic growth alone, if sustained long enough, will bring a complete solution to all our unemployment problems. Indeed, some hold the view that economic growth will continue to by-pass the long term unemployed, the early school leavers and other deprived groups. I would not fully share this pessimistic view. It seems to me that with so much surplus labour, employers will understandably hire first those whom they consider best qualified. If, however, in conditions of buoyant demand for labour, widespread labour shortages were to develop, then I believe that very soon some of those now branded as "unemployable" would begin to be regarded as "trainable".

Nevertheless, one must recognise that the growth of unemployment has left Ireland, and many other European countries, with a huge residue of long term unemployed, who will not be brought back into employment without special measures. Moreover, the training and motivation of the long term unemployed and early school leavers is an important way in which one can lay a basis for sustaining economic growth. A recent paper (Nickell and Bell, 1996) draws on a number of studies to argue cogently that Germany's greater success than most other countries, in coping with the decline in demand for unskilled workers, has been due to the strong emphasis in its schooling system on the bottom half of the ability range, allied to its comprehensive system of vocational training. The challenge for Ireland in this regard is to channel the necessary resources and develop the instruments to address this problem without prejudicing competitiveness in the rest of the economy. This issue, however, is a topic for another paper.

References

Commission of the European Communities (1993), *Growth, Competitiveness, Employment: The Challenge and Ways Forward into the 21st Century - White Paper.*, Office of Official Publications of the European Communities, Luxembourg.

Commission of the European Communities (1995), *The European Employment Strategy: Recent Progress and Prospects for the Future,* (Com (95) 465 final, 11.10.1995), Brussels.

Commission of the European Communities (1996), *Action for Employment in Europe: A Confidence Pact* (CSE (96)1 final, 5.6.1996), Brussels.

Nickell, S. and Bell, B. (1996), "Changes in the Distribution of Wages and Unemployment in OECD Countries " *American Economic Review,* Vol. 86 No. 2, pp. 302-308.

Copyright © 1996 by Irish Banking Review. Reprinted with permission.

8 Does the exchange rate regime affect the unemployment rate?

Ella Kavanagh

Introduction

This chapter examines the implications of the exchange rate regime for unemployment. This issue is receiving attention in Europe at present because for some countries, meeting the Maastricht Criteria for entry into a Economic and Monetary Union (EMU) in 1999 is having serious implications for their current levels of unemployment. There is also concern about the consequences of EMU for future unemployment in Europe. Although Irish government policy is that we will be among the member states eligible to participate in EMU from the outset in 1999, there is a continuing debate on the likely implications that EMU will have for Irish unemployment, particularly if the UK does not join. In this chapter, we will address this issue by reviewing the theoretical literature on the impact of different exchange rate regimes on unemployment. Although many of the comments are general, our focus is primarily on small countries and in particular, Ireland. This review will enable us to identify the economic channels and structural variables that are important in understanding the impact that the exchange rate regime has on unemployment. Finally we will provide empirical evidence for Ireland, using two macroeconometric models, HERMES-IRELAND and MULTIMOD (a world model), on how its membership in different exchange rate regimes can mediate the impact of external and domestic shocks on output and unemployment.

Theoretical literature

In this section, two strands of the literature on exchange rate regimes and unemployment are explored. The first is the "Optimum Currency Area" literature which focuses on the characteristics that a country must possess in order that the adoption of a common currency does not reduce welfare in the face of asymmetric shocks. Hence, the focus is on the impact that membership of a monetary union has for unemployment. In the light of this literature, we will review Ireland's suitability for membership of EMU. A different approach to answering the question is to focus on a particular analytical model to provide insights into how the exchange rate regime affects the unemployment rate. Using this model, we identify: the role of different disturbances (real and nominal); the channels of transmission through which the exchange rate regime has real effects; and the structural variables that are important in determining the size and the duration of the effect of disturbances on unemployment.

Optimum Currency Area literature

The optimum currency area literature[1] identifies characteristics that a country must possess in order that the loss of the monetary policy instrument does not reduce welfare when a country experiences individual country shocks. Three criteria are identified: (i) a high degree of labour and capital mobility (Mundell, 1961); (ii) a high degree of openness (Mc Kinnon, 1963) and; (iii) a diversified production base (Kenen, 1969). What this literature suggests for the macroeconomic performance of countries within a monetary union is that if countries are subject to asymmetric disturbances and if wages and prices are sticky, then unemployment will rise in those countries experiencing the shock unless there is sufficient labour mobility. It has been suggested by Bertola (1988) that fixing the exchange rate will in fact reduce labour mobility. Fixed exchange rates will result in higher income variability (due to the absence of the monetary instrument) and this reduces workers' willingness to move. This has been criticised by Branson (1988) who argues that stability of the exchange rate makes fiscal policy more effective, which will make it even easier to stabilise income and therefore increase factor mobility. In the context of the future EMU and the potential constraints on fiscal policy, Bertola's argument is more valid. Therefore, less labour mobility will result in higher unemployment if shocks are asymmetric across countries in EMU. Whether asymmetric shocks will be a feature of EMU depends on the degree to which the economic structure of potential members of EMU differs.

According to the indicators used to assess whether EU members form an optimum currency area, Ireland does not fare particularly well. In terms of similarity of trade structure and the degree of intra-industry trade, Gros (1996) ranks Ireland 10th and 11th respectively out of a total of 14 countries in the EU. This suggests that Ireland may be more susceptible to asymmetric shocks within a EMU. However these figures apply to today which raises the question whether the economic structure in Ireland will change over time and become more like mainland Europe. The very high growth rates experienced in Ireland also makes Irish real GDP and industrial growth relatively uncorrelated with other EU countries (Gros, 1996). According to Alesina and Grilli (1992), this should increase the costs to Ireland of membership of EMU. In fact, they identify Ireland as one of the countries that has most to lose from membership of EMU.[2] In contrast, due to the very high degree of trade with EU members, Ireland stands to benefit greatly from EMU particularly if the UK joins (Gros, 1996).

The significant question, in the light of EMU, is to what degree the structure of European economies will change, in other words will asymmetric shocks become more symmetric? At present views are mixed. On the one hand, trade between the industrial European nations is to a large degree intra-industry trade which means that most demand shocks will affect these countries in a similar way. The completion of the single market will continue this trend. Hence, shocks will tend to be more symmetric (De Grauwe, 1994). On the other hand, trade integration may lead to greater regional concentration of industrial activities in order for firms to benefit from economies of scale which may result in shocks having increasingly asymmetric effects. Similarly, a common monetary policy across the Union may have asymmetric effects if financial structures differ across countries. At present, there are differences in the transmission mechanism of monetary policy across EU members arising from different financing patterns of industry and households. This is discussed further below. This may lead to differences in business cycles across members of EMU. However Gros (1996) argues that financial structures are bound to converge under the impact of internal market legislation on corporate governance, accounting and disclosure rules etc. The common experience of price stability will also have an impact. For Ireland, a similar argument has been put forward by Honohan and Conroy (1994a).

A three country model

In this section, to investigate the effect that the exchange rate regime has on employment in a small open economy like Ireland, we will use a three country macroeconomic model from the international macroeconomics literature, consisting of two large countries and one small country (Marston, 1984; Argy et al, 1989; Laufer and Sundararajan, 1994). The reason for this is that Ireland is effectively linked to the UK and mainland Europe on the trade side, the UK on the labour market side and mainland Europe through the exchange rate regime. Using a three country model also allows us to investigate a much larger number of possible exchange rate regimes for the small country e.g. a composite peg arrangement, a single currency peg, a monetary union.[3] The model that we outline below by Argy et al (1989) is representative of these three country models. The individual country specifications in the model are relatively simple (see Argy (1994) for extensions) which enables us to focus on the primary linkages, both financial and real, between countries.

The three country model of Argy et al (1989) contains three markets, goods, labour and money and three different countries, one small and two large of equal size. For simplicity of exposition, we will refer to the small country as Ireland and the two large countries as the UK and Germany respectively. Ireland is assumed to trade with the UK and with Germany. The demand for Irish goods in Germany and the UK depends on income in both of these countries and the price of Irish goods in DM and sterling relative to the price of German and UK goods. The demand for domestic goods in Ireland depends again on relative prices but also on domestic income and the nominal interest rate. Hence, expectations are ignored. As Ireland is small the demand for German goods depends only on UK and German income, German prices relative to UK prices (denominated in DM) and German interest rates. The same applies to the UK.

Employment is determined in the labour market. Workers are employed up to the point at which their marginal productivity is equal to the real product wage (the nominal wage relative to the price that employers obtain for their product). Workers are concerned with their real consumption wage which is the amount of goods, domestic and foreign, that they can buy with their nominal wage. In Argy et al (1989), wages and prices are initially held constant. Because of this, an increase in the demand for domestic goods will, over the short run, cause employment to rise. However over the long run, nominal wages adjust fully to the change in consumer prices because of full indexation. For Ireland, the consumer price index combines Irish, UK and German prices. Ireland is considered large enough to determine its own price despite being a small country. In contrast, for the UK and Germany, the consumer price index consists only of UK and German prices.

Domestic nominal interest rates are determined in the money market, by the demand for money relative to the supply of money. Under the assumption of totally fixed exchange rates, the money supply is determined endogenously by the demand for money and exogenously (i.e. it is a policy variable) under the flexible exchange rate regime. Under a composite peg regime where the Central Bank targets a weighted average of the Irish pound/pound sterling exchange rate and the Irish pound/DM exchange rate, the value of the currency basket in Irish pounds is pegged via appropriate intervention operations. Financial assets are assumed to be perfect substitutes across countries (i.e. no risk premium) and capital is assumed to be perfectly mobile. The uncovered interest parity condition and the triangular currency arbitrage condition hold.

Unemployment in these type of models can only emerge if there are disturbances. The impact of a domestic disturbance on employment over the short run depends on the nature of the disturbance and the exchange rate regime. A domestic monetary disturbance (e.g. an increase in the money supply) has no effect on employment over the short run under fixed exchange rates. In contrast when it is a real disturbance (e.g. an increase in the relative demand for goods or a fiscal expansion), employment will rise under a fixed exchange rate regime. When the small country adopts a floating exchange rate regime, a monetary expansion, by reducing interest rates and depreciating the exchange rate, will increase employment. In contrast for a real disturbance, employment will remain constant or increase. An expansionary fiscal policy will, by increasing interest rates, appreciate the domestic currency and crowd out the domestic fiscal expansion. The extent of the crowding-out depends on the size of the appreciation which in turn depends on whether expectations are included into the model. These are excluded in our framework here. Note that the composite peg regime is irrelevant for a domestic disturbance in the small country.

Analysing foreign disturbances is complex under a three country model as we need to firstly examine how foreign disturbances affect the two large countries and then how they affect the small country. As noted earlier, the three countries are linked together through trade and through the financial markets. Consequently, the factors that are important in determining the choice of exchange rate regime for the small country are: (i) the division of trade between the two large countries; (ii) the nature and origin of the external disturbance and; (iii) the exchange rate regime that the large countries adopt. The impact of external disturbances on employment will be explored in more detail in our simulation results below.

This model explains how, over the short run, employment can vary relative to its full employment or natural rate. But how quickly will disturbances affect employment? What will be the size of the impact? How long will the effect of the disturbance last? The above model suggests some directions towards discovering answers to these questions. It identifies the importance of structural features of the country in determining the magnitude and the length of impact of the disturbance. These structural features include the trade pattern of the small country, the responsiveness of import and export demand to changes in the real exchange rate, the responsiveness of consumption and investment to changes in the interest rate, and the speed of wage and price adjustment. It identifies a series of channels through which the exchange rate regime can mediate the impact of a disturbance on output and employment performance. These channels are the interest rate channel and the exchange rate channel. It also highlights the importance of the origin, the nature and the degree of correlation between different kinds of disturbances for the employment effect of different exchange rate regimes.

One issue that is not addressed in this model is the impact of interest rate volatility and exchange rate volatility on output. In terms of the actual degree of volatility implied by different exchange rate regimes, the model suggests that interest rate volatility depends on the variance of the disturbances and the exchange rate regime. For example, it suggests that interest rate volatility is higher under floating exchange rates and that it depends on the reserve country(ies) under fixed exchange rates. The underlying assumption in this model is that fixing the exchange rate has credibility and is viewed as permanent. Therefore, the difficulties of maintaining the exchange rate peg which introduces additional volatility into the interest rate is ignored in the model.

The above types of models focus on how interest rates and exchange rates change relative to the equilibrium level. In the long run, exchange rates revert back to their purchasing power parity level and interest rates to their pre-disturbance level. But the model does not provide us with insights into the actual level of interest rates under different regimes. With perfect capital mobility, real interest rates should equate across countries over the long term, with the exchange rate regime affecting the speed at which real interest rates adjust.[4] Consequently, nominal interest rates will differ across exchange rate regimes due to differences in expected inflation. Empirical evidence suggests that countries which are inflation averse (independent Central Bank, anti-inflation attitude) generally have low inflation, strong currencies and low interest rates. This type of reasoning has been applied to the design of the new European Central Bank.[5]

For a small country with perfectly mobile capital and a unilateral peg, the level of interest rates is determined by the monetary policy of the reserve country. Under a composite peg regime, the domestic interest rate will be a weighted average of interest rates in the reserve countries. The choice of reserve country is very important for the small country. However this assumes that the exchange rate peg is totally credible. History suggests that "fixed" exchange rate regimes do not last forever. Therefore, there is generally an in-built devaluation risk - the "peso" effect - which adds a further premium to interest rates (Honohan, 1993). This has been a feature of the interest rates of member countries in the ERM. Interest rates in a small country may also be affected by a specific three country problem whereby the exchange rate is pegged to one country but trade is primarily conducted with the other. This has added an additional risk premium to Irish interest rates which is associated with changes in the sterling/Irish pound exchange rate (Honohan and Conroy, 1994b; Walsh, 1993).

For example, every ten pence fall in the value of sterling against the DM has tended to be associated with a 2.5 to 3.0 percentage point increase in short term interest rates. The principle advantage identified by the Baker et al (1996) of Ireland's membership of EMU is that it will remove the option of devaluation which should mean that these risk premiums on Irish interest rates will be removed.

Channels of transmission

In the previous section, we identified the following channels - interest rate channel and the exchange rate channel - through which the exchange rate regime can affect real variables in the economy such as output and employment. In this section, we wish to explore how responsive are the variables that ultimately affect employment to changes in these channels. This is of particular concern for a small country when deciding whether or not to peg its exchange rate as monetary policy for the small country is determined, not by its own domestic conditions, but by those in the reserve country(ies). This was one of the reasons for the "Currency Crisis" in Ireland in 1992/3. It is also important in the event of a EMU, where policies instigated at a European level may in fact have asymmetric effects on the members of the Union. In this section, we will also examine nominal wage adjustment given its importance in determining how long disturbances will affect employment. The final part briefly comments on whether there is a relationship between long term (equilibrium) unemployment and the exchange rate regime.

Interest rate

The transmission mechanism identified in our model is from 'an interest rate', determined in the money market, to (the demand for) investment and consumption and in turn employment. This abstracts from a number of features of the monetary transmission mechanism. Central Banks gear their policy instruments towards influencing quite closely short term interest rates (Borio and Fritz, 1995). These policy controlled rates in turn determine interest rates charged by banks and lending institutions. Consequently, an important issue in the monetary transmission mechanism is how fast (speed) and by how much (size) interest rates as charged by banks or lending institutions respond to policy controlled interest rates. The second feature of the monetary transmission mechanism is how the economy responds to changes in interest rates. This raises the issue of the maturity breakdown of debt contracts and, complementary to it, the degree of adjustability of interest rates on debt contracts. On *a priori* grounds, one would expect that, the larger the share of variable rate financing, the stronger will be the cash flow and income effects associated with monetary changes i.e. the income effect will be strong. Also the impact should be much faster, which tends to accelerate the impact of monetary policy (Borio, 1995). In Ireland, long term fixed interest rate borrowing is comparatively rare for all but the largest of companies - and the State Sector - and therefore fluctuations in short term interest rates have tended to be passed onto the smaller corporate and household borrowers (Honohan, 1993).

Interest rates affect consumption through their impact on the cost of borrowing and their effect on wealth. In relation to investment, a decline in the interest rate, by reducing the costs of capital, produces a temporary boom in investment as the industry moves to a high capital stock (Romer, 1996). The size of the stock of public debt has implications also for the impact of interest rates on the economy. If the government sets a target for the debt to GDP ratio, then higher interest repayments will induce an increase in the tax rate and/or a reduction in government expenditure.

Exchange rate

To examine the implications of changes in the exchange rate regime on employment, we will assess its effects (size and speed) on exports and imports. In this section, we will refer in our examples to the sterling/Irish pound exchange rate for ease of exposition.

The effect of a sterling depreciation on Irish exports and goods produced for the domestic market, will depend on the proportion of Irish goods in competition with UK goods either on the domestic, UK or third country markets. The way in which the exchange rate affects exports differs according to the currency in which contracts are set. For example, Irish exports could be contracted either in Irish pounds or in sterling. In the former case, a sterling depreciation will increase the price of Irish goods in the UK and reduce demand, the amount depending on the elasticity of demand for those goods in the UK. In the latter case, because the sterling price is unchanged, profits will be reduced (unless a forward hedge has been used) which may alter the exporters' willingness to supply. Whether companies have control over prices or not is also relevant. Small countries which are price takers take the world price and provide all they want at this price. Hence, the producer in deciding whether to produce, compares price (in domestic currency terms) relative to cost. In all these cases, revenue is affected. But the depreciation of sterling may also reduce costs, the size of which will depend on the proportion of costs made up by imports from the UK.

Expectations of the exchange rate play a central role in affecting business decisions and in determining the impact of the exchange rate change on output and employment. If the exchange rate change is viewed as temporary, then the impact on output and employment should be minor. In contrast if it is expected to persist, the negative effects of a sterling depreciation on output and employment will be much larger, the size of the effect depending on whether markets can be diversified, supply sources changed and/or wages renegotiated. The speed at which changes in the real exchange rate affect exports and imports is difficult to determine. A number of factors can be identified: the length of contracts (staggering of contracts may introduce a staggered adjustment, as the new circumstances will only be applied to new contracts); the use of hedging instruments and forward contracts which eliminates short term economic exposure; and the speed at which exchange rate changes are passed through into imported raw material prices and wages are adjusted.

Not only are business people affected by their expectations of exchange rates but also by the degree of uncertainty that they attach to exchange rate movements. Yet, empirical studies have failed to uncover statistical evidence that exchange rate variability has had much of a depressing effect on international trade volumes (Isard, 1995). Investment is affected by exchange rate uncertainty. Uncertainty about future exchange rates gives firms an incentive to postpone any investment (or disinvestment) in export (or import substitution) capacity that would be difficult to reverse. The reason is that if the investment is made immediately, a firm runs the risk of incurring long term cost if the home currency appreciates. On the other hand, by delaying investment, although the firm can risk sacrificing profits over the short run if the home currency depreciates, it can still choose to invest later (Isard, 1995).

Wages

In the theoretical model, the speed and the size of nominal wage adjustment are identified as the factors responsible for determining how long disturbances will affect employment. If wage contracts are partially or fully indexed, then the effects of disturbances are reduced. But if contracts are set at intervals, then disturbances may have prolonged effects as the economy is out of equilibrium for longer. Flood and Marion (1982) suggest that the optimal degree of wage indexation is itself dependent on the exchange rate regime e.g. they discover that full indexation is always optimal for the fixed exchange rate regime whereas partial indexation is generally optimal for flexible exchange rate regimes. The endogenity of the wage behaviour to the exchange rate regime can also be illustrated by empirical examples. Eichengreen notes that Italy succeeded in abolishing its wage indexation scheme (the *scala mobile*) in anticipation of European Monetary Unification (Isard, 1995). Similarly the lengthening of the wage agreement in Ireland in the late 1980s (in the renewed centralised wage agreements) may have reflected an improvement in the government's anti-inflation reputation brought about by its stronger commitment to the DM peg (Fleming, 1993).

It has also been suggested that wage adjustment in response to shocks will be much quicker in a monetary union. Horn and Persson (1988) suggest that EMU, by increasing policymakers commitment to price stability, might enhance wage flexibility (Bayoumi and Eichengreen, 1993). It has also been argued by the European Commission that implicit and/or explicit constraints on governments in a EMU will encourage workers in depressed areas in the union to modify their wage demands. One could suggest an alternative view based on the Irish case. An interesting feature of the Irish labour market is the strong linkages that exist between Irish and UK wages (Curtis and Fitzgerald, 1994). The reasons identified are: the degree of migration between the two economies; the knowledge in Ireland of UK wages which gives rise to similar demands domestically even if the bulk of the population is prohibited from moving and; the traditional close ties between the trade union movement in Ireland and Britain. One would expect that the Single Market will continue to lead to greater labour market integration.[6] At the same time, EMU will introduce greater transparency and greater conformity across countries in terms of expectations of inflation. Both of these factors may have implications for the rate at which wages adjust to domestic conditions. For example, if wages are set at a European level this could affect the speed and the degree of wage adjustment that does take place, particularly in a small country in response to disturbances.

The above suggests that the exchange rate regime has implications for wage adjustment. Causality may also run in the opposite way. Flexible exchange rates are viewed as necessary if there is little flexibility in wage and price markets. On the other hand, fixed exchange rate regimes require wage and price flexibility in response to the absence of nominal exchange rate adjustment.

Long term unemployment

There are a number of factors that affect the natural rate of unemployment (or the equilibrium rate). Regarding the determinants of equilibrium unemployment, most labour market models agree that all factors which induce wage pressure on the part of workers (e.g. union's strength, real wage aspirations, unemployment benefits etc.) and price pressures on the part of firms (e.g. desired profit margins etc.) adversely affect the level of equilibrium employment (Vinals and Jimeno, 1996). Consequently, it is generally accepted that real side variables that affect equilibrium unemployment are unrelated to the exchange rate regime. Therefore in order for the exchange rate regime to have implications for unemployment over the long term, we must appeal to hysteresis effects. Hysteresis means that long run equilibrium unemployment depends on the path followed by actual unemployment. Two sources of hysteresis are usually mentioned in the literature: insider's power in wage determination; and lower search intensity from and skill depletion in the long term unemployed. An additional factor, connected with the exchange rate, is the asymmetry of entry and exit of exporting firms. With completely symmetric entry and exit, the number of firms that close in response to a reduction in competitiveness will be equal to the number of firms that open again after a sustained period of time at the original level of competitiveness. In reality, this is not the case. Instead, only some exporters will re-enter, leaving the economy with a lower number of exporters in total (Baker et al, 1996). Hence, the minimum sustainable rate of unemployment will increase. Both flexible exchange rate regimes and pegged regimes (single peg or composite) where a country trades with two or more countries, will be affected by this phenomenon.

Empirical evidence

After highlighting some of the theoretical issues through which membership of the exchange rate regime can affect employment, we will now proceed to compare, using empirical models of Ireland and the World, the effect on Irish output and Irish unemployment of disturbances under different exchange rate regimes. Two disturbances are analysed, an unanticipated expansion in German government expenditure and an unanticipated expansion in Irish government expenditure. To examine the impact of an external shock on Ireland, we firstly identify the impact of this event on Germany and the UK using the macroeconometric model, MULTIMOD.[7] Secondly, UK and German macroeconomic performance variables generated by this model are inserted into the ESRI's Irish macroeconometric model, HERMES-IRELAND. As Ireland is small, there is no feedback from Ireland to Germany and the UK. Similarly, a domestic demand shock in Ireland will have no impact on the two larger countries and therefore HERMES-IRELAND alone can be used.

This section is constructed as follows. First, we identify the key features of the Irish model, HERMES-IRELAND. Second, we explain the modifications that were introduced into the model in order to be able to explore alternative exchange rate regimes. The following section shows how the exchange rate regime modifies the impact of the expansion in German government expenditure on Irish output and unemployment. The final section does the same for an expansion in Irish government expenditure.

HERMES-Ireland

Our discussion of the HERMES-IRELAND[8] model emphasises the linkages and channels of transmission between Ireland and the Rest of the World. In Ireland, the manufacturing sector consists of the high technology, traditional, and food processing sectors. The high technology sector is largely foreign owned, almost 100 per cent export orientated, very capital and R&D intensive, and has a high propensity to repatriate profits. The decision by multinational companies whether to locate in Ireland or indeed how much to produce from their Irish plants will depend on their expectations of "world" demand and Ireland's relative competitiveness. The traditional manufacturing sector is mainly domestically owned and tends to be more labour intensive than the other manufacturing sectors. Although less export orientated than the high technology sector, it still trades over 50 per cent of output, primarily to the UK and Germany. Again Ireland's competitiveness (relative unit labour costs) affects production in this sector. The food processing sector differs from the other sectors because of its unique dependence on the agricultural sector for its inputs and because it falls under the EC Common Agricultural Programme, CAP (Bradley and Fitzgerald, 1991). As the UK is the major export market, production here is affected by Ireland's competitiveness relative to the UK. As one would expect for a small country, domestic producers are assumed to have no market power on world markets. They behave as price takers. Prices in the manufacturing division are therefore determined externally (exogenous) and do not respond to changes in Irish cost conditions. In the non-traded sector, prices are determined by a mark up on input costs. Overall, the consumer price is a weighted average of non-energy import prices and prices in the different production sectors.

A devaluation of the Irish pound affects output and exports by increasing the profitability of Irish industrial production through lower relative unit costs. A temporary devaluation has a small effect on output. The Irish pound/DM exchange rate is important for the traditional and high technology sectors, while the Irish pound/Sterling exchange rate is important for the food processing sectors. A devaluation of the Irish pound also reduces imports by improving competitiveness and increasing domestic production relative to gross final demand.

Changes in interest rates affect housing, building and manufacturing investment. Changes in interest rates influence spending and production by altering: (i) interest repayments on the national debt; (ii) the competitiveness of the industrial sector in the long run; and (iii) investment in housing. As consumers are assumed to be liquidity constrained, consumption is determined by current disposable income excluding any wealth effects. Consequently, changes in wealth due to a change in holdings of net external financial assets (due to changes in the current account of the balance of payments) are not included in HERMES-IRELAND. Employment is a by-product of the supply of output and is therefore determined by the factors outlined above, relative factor costs, domestic and foreign demand and competitiveness. The openness and size of the Irish labour market is explicitly taken into account by the inclusion of migration in the determination of labour supply. The net outwards migration rate is determined by the unemployment rate in Ireland relative to the UK (Honohan, 1992). [9] As wages are determined by the demand and supply of labour,[10] the factors that are important in determining Irish wages are: world output; Irish prices net of income tax; the exchange rate (sterling/Irish pound exchange rate); UK wages; and UK prices net of income tax. An appreciation of the sterling/Irish pound exchange rate increases the demand for Irish labour relative to UK labour, which puts upward pressure on Irish wages. It is also assumed that wage rates take some time to adjust and an error correction process is included to account for this.

Modifications to HERMES-Ireland

Adjustments were made to the monetary and fiscal sectors of the model in order to examine the impact of unanticipated demand side shocks on Irish economic performance under different exchange rate regimes. Other than these changes, it was assumed that the economy would function very much the same as in the current model.

In the current version of HERMES-IRELAND, the monetary sector is modelled under the assumption that the exchange rate is given and that Ireland is small relative to other countries. Therefore, it could be used to examine different fixed exchange rate arrangements but was inappropriate to examine a floating exchange rate regime. Under a floating exchange rate regime, interest rates are determined in the domestic money market. Therefore the model was modified to include specifications for the demand and supply of real money balances. The supply of the (nominal) monetary base is exogenous and the short term nominal interest rate is used as an instrument to target this level of the nominal monetary base.[11]

For each of the fixed exchange rate regimes, domestic interest rates are assumed to be exogenous. Irish interest rates are equal to German (UK) interest rates under a DM (sterling) peg. Under the Composite Pegging arrangement, an equal weighting of 0.5 is given to the UK and Germany.[12] For the flexible exchange rate regime, an equation specifying the determination of the Irish pound exchange rate had to be introduced. In MULTIMOD, the uncovered interest parity condition is used to determine the exchange rate. This condition implies that, given interest rates (domestic and foreign) and expectations of the exchange rate (expectations are formed rationally), the exchange rate is determined. On average, in each year, there are zero excess returns.

Because of the size of HERMES-IRELAND, it proved difficult to introduce directly, rational expectations into the model. Instead, a path for the exchange rate is specified and the initial exchange rate change is chosen by iteration to ensure that over the sample period, excess returns are zero. It was hypothesised that the path for the exchange rate would involve an initial appreciation (depreciation) and a gradual (i.e. linear) depreciation (appreciation) of the exchange rate to reach its baseline value over the simulation period. Consequently, there may be excess returns in any one year but over the simulation period, cumulative excess returns should approach zero.[13] In this sense, the solution for the entire simulation period corresponds to a rational expectations solution.[14] It takes fifteen years for these excess returns to be eliminated.

For each of the fixed exchange rate arrangements, the Irish pound is pegged to the respective currency e.g. under the sterling (DM) peg, the Irish pound is pegged totally to sterling (DM). Under the assumption that triangular currency arbitrage holds and given the sterling, DM and dollar exchange rates taken from MULTIMOD, the Irish pound exchange rate relative to the other currencies can be determined. Under the composite pegging arrangement, the Irish pound is pegged to a weighted basket of sterling and the DM with an equal weight given to each.

The principle adjustment made to the government sector is the inclusion of a rule to ensure that government borrowing is contained to follow a non-explosive path. Thus, if the change in the exchequer borrowing requirement (as a ratio of GNP) exceeds its target change, then the income tax rate will rise in the current period. It is assumed in the simulations that the incidence of tax falls on workers. Both the foreign rate of interest and the exchange rate are important determinants of foreign interest repayments. If the Irish pound devalues, *ceteris paribus*, then the stock of Irish foreign debt denominated in Irish pounds will increase and this, together with the foreign interest rate, will increase interest repayments (in Irish pounds) on the foreign component of the National Debt. Because about two thirds of government borrowing is undertaken at fixed interest rates and at maturities of over one year, a change in interest rates will take time to affect actual interest rates (Baker et al, 1996). This will increase government current expenditure which, if not matched by tax receipts, will enlarge the exchequer borrowing requirement. As we noted above, this may lead to further increases in Irish income tax rates. As the largest proportion of foreign debt is denominated in DM, in our simulations the interest payable on the foreign debt is the German rate of interest. The exchange rate used to convert the foreign debt into domestic currency terms is a weighted average of sterling (2.1 per cent), dollar (14.9 per cent), DM (75 per cent), and yen (8 per cent) Irish pound exchange rates. The weights are given in parentheses.

An expansion in German government expenditure

MULTIMOD is used to discover the effect of a permanent increase in government spending of 5 per cent of GDP in Germany on macroeconomic performance in Germany and the UK under the assumption that the exchange rate floats between the two countries.[15] The starting date of our simulations is 1990.

An expansion in German government expenditure increases interest rates in Germany due to the expansion in absorption. Interest rates reach their peak in 1993 at 1.5 percentage points above the baseline. As a result, the DM appreciates. German GDP expands very significantly over the short term (almost 3 per cent higher than the baseline). However, after 1994, German GDP declines relative to the baseline. Three crowding out mechanisms can be identified: (i) the desire to target a particular value of the monetary base results in higher German real interest rates which crowd out consumption and investment spending; (ii) higher government spending requires higher taxes in order to maintain the debt/GDP ratio at a sustainable level. This reduces disposable income and, in turn, consumption and; (iii) the appreciation of the DM reduces demand for German exports. Over the longer term, the slow down in the rise of absorption reduces German interest rates so that by 2005, interest rates are 0.7 percentage points above the baseline due to higher expected inflation. This in turn, reduces the appreciation of the DM relative to the baseline. The flexible exchange rate regime insulates UK interest rates from the disturbance in Germany. The combination of the expansion in German demand and the depreciation of sterling increases economic activity and employment. UK prices increase slightly due to the depreciation of sterling and the expansion in GDP. This generates the expectation that a tighter monetary policy will be followed in the future which reduces inflation expectations and wages marginally.

Abstracting from the exchange rate regime, an expansion in German demand has negative effects on Irish output (GNP) after 1 year (see Figure 8.1). Three channels can be identified: (i) higher German interest rates increase interest repayments on the foreign component of the National Debt which reduces GNP relative to GDP; (ii) high interest repayments necessitate an increase in income tax rates to keep the Irish exchequer borrowing requirement within target which reduces disposable income and consumption; and (iii) German GDP expands for three years only and the expansion in UK GDP is relatively small. Over the period 1990-1995, pegging to the DM has the worst effect on output in the economy (although note that there is a small expansion in the first year). Despite the reduction in wages and in input prices which reduces domestic costs, the appreciation of the Irish pound relative to sterling and the dollar, combined with higher interest rates (imported from Germany), reduces competitiveness in both the traditional and high technology sectors. The contractionary effect on the economy is reinforced by the increase in Irish interest rates and the reduction in disposable income which reduces building activity and output in the services sector. GNP in 1995 is 2.5 percentage points below the baseline.

Figure 8.1
Irish real GNP:
German government expenditure - increase of 5% of GDP

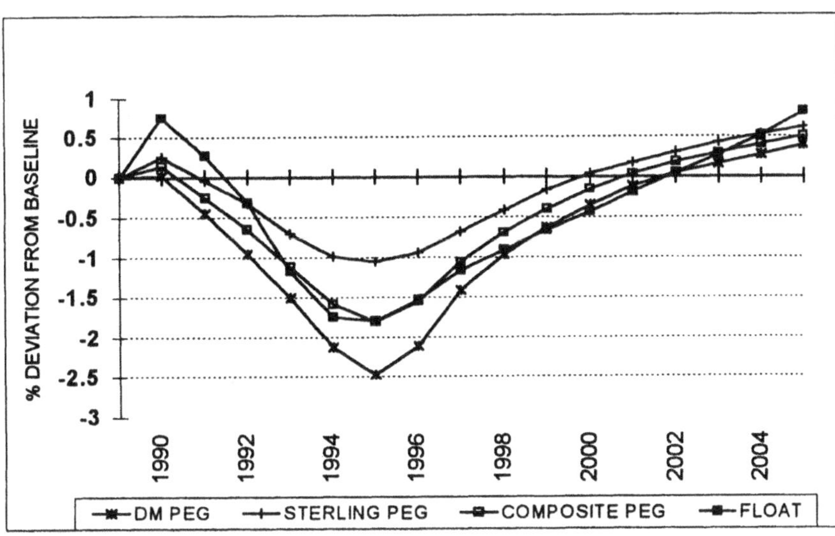

Under the floating regime, the Irish economy grows in 1990 and 1992. In response to the expansion in German government expenditure, German interest rates rise relative to Irish interest rates causing the Irish pound to depreciate relative to the DM.[16] It is hypothesised that the path followed by the exchange rate is an initial large depreciation followed by a constant appreciation until the baseline value is reached. Therefore under the floating regime, the Irish pound depreciates relative to the DM, sterling and the dollar. This sharp depreciation of the Irish pound outweighs the increase in wages and input costs thus improving output performance in the high technology and traditional sectors. Although output growth continues to be positive in the traditional sector, it declines in the high technology sector as competitiveness disimproves after 1994. Output in the manufacturing sector in general declines after 1994. In the services and building sectors, production expands initially but, after 1994, the reduction in disposable income and the increase in interest rates reduce output.

Pegging to sterling causes the smallest deviation of real GNP from the baseline. In comparison to the floating regime, the economy experiences growth in 1990 only but, over the medium term, output in the traditional sector and the high technology sector is higher. The reason for this is that the reduction in competitiveness is less under this regime (the Irish pound depreciates relative to the DM only). Interest rates rise by only 0.1 percentage points when the Irish pound is pegged to sterling. This, combined with the increase in disposable income to 1994, increases building activity and output in the services sector. Interestingly, Irish GDP increases from 1990-1995. Real GNP falls due to the large profit outflows and the interest repayments on the national debt. As we would expect, by targeting a composite currency, output performance lies midway between the DM and sterling pegs.

By 1995, the downturn in economic activity is reversed under all the exchange rate regimes. The primary reason is that profit repatriations to multinationals and the foreign interest repayments on the national debt decline which reduces the fall in GNP relative to its baseline value. The decline in wages (after 1995, Irish wages fall in line with the lower UK wages) and input prices improve cost competitiveness and the fall in taxes reduces the fall in disposable income. The decline in domestic production is reduced relative to the baseline. By the year 2001, Irish GNP rises relative to the baseline under all regimes.[17] Pegging to sterling insulates Irish GNP the most from the external shock whereas pegging to the DM has the greatest negative effect on Irish GNP.

One can see that there is a close correspondence between unemployment and output performance by comparing Figures. 8.1 and 8.2. Under the floating regime, as we would expect, the unemployment rate falls over the period 1990-1993 due to the increase in employment in the industrial sector. In contrast, pegging to the DM worsens the unemployment rate and, by 1994, it is almost 1 percentage point higher than the baseline. Over the medium term, 1993-1997, the decline in output reduces the demand for labour under the DM, composite and floating exchange rate regimes. After 1997, the unemployment rate falls under all exchange rate regimes as the rise in industrial employment outweighs the continued fall in service employment relative to the baseline.[18]

To conclude, an external shock has implications for short to medium run unemployment. Over the long term, although the ranking is sustained, the impact of the exchange rate regime reduces in importance. As before, the sterling exchange rate peg ensures the least deviation of output and unemployment from the baseline value. The floating regime does not insulate the Irish economy from the German shock.

Figure 8.2
Irish unemployment rate:
German expenditure - increase of 5% of GDP

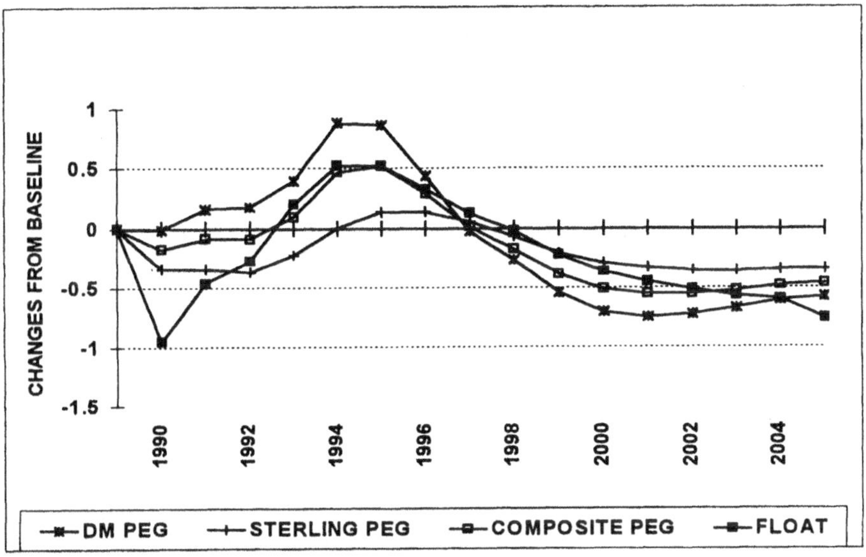

An expansion in domestic government expenditure

In this scenario, Irish government expenditure is increased by 5 per cent of GDP. Earlier we noted that economic performance in response to a domestic demand shock was found to be independent of the exchange rate peg. Consequently, two exchange rate regimes only are contrasted: floating and a DM peg.

The impact of a fiscal expansion on Irish output is almost identical under both exchange rate regimes (see Figure 8.3). Over the medium term GNP rises by up to 6 per cent relative to the baseline and by the year 2005, is almost 3 per cent above the baseline. Under the floating regime, the Irish pound appreciates. An expansion in Irish government expenditure, without an exchange rate change, will increase absorption and the demand for money which will, in turn, push up Irish interest rates relative to those abroad. Holders of Irish bonds will make excess returns relative to holders of foreign bonds. The Irish pound must appreciate for two reasons to remove these excess returns: (i) to reduce domestic demand, prices, the demand for money and in turn Irish interest rates; and (ii) to generate the expectation that the Irish pound will depreciate in the future. In 1990, the Irish pound appreciates by 12 per cent against all currencies.

Figure 8.3
Irish real GNP:
Irish government expenditure - increase of 5% of GDP

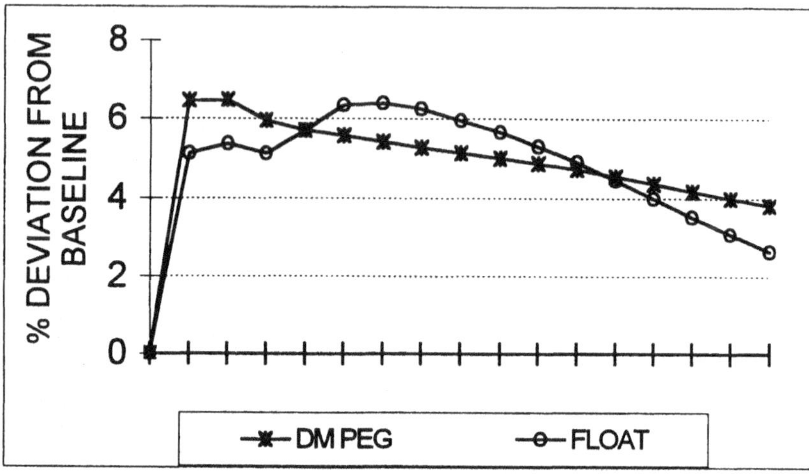

The appreciation of the Irish pound reduces the competitiveness of goods from the traditional and high technology sectors. Industrial output falls relative to the baseline as does building activity (interest rates increase post 1992). But this is totally outweighed by the expansion in value added in the government sector (public administration and defence). The rise in GDP expands in every year until 2001 but from Figure. 8.3, the rise in GNP begins to fall after 1995. This can be explained by two phenomena. Firstly, although profit repatriations from multinationals fall especially in the years 1990-1994, over time the size of the decline diminishes. Secondly, to finance the increase in government expenditure, foreign currency borrowing increases. The large appreciation of the Irish pound relative to the DM initially reduces the value of the stock of foreign debt and foreign interest repayments but after 1995, interest repayments on the foreign component of the debt increases relative to the baseline. Both of these factors reduce the expansion in GNP after 1995. Additionally, income taxes are increased to maintain the target Exchequer Borrowing Requirement throughout the period. Therefore the expansion in disposable income diminishes over time. This factor combined with the rise in domestic wages, explains the lower rise in output relative to the baseline at the end of the period.[19]

Under the DM peg, the Irish pound is unchanged against sterling and the dollar and interest rates are unchanged, as they are determined in Germany. Output rises a little in the industrial sector. It declines in the high technology sector but expands in the traditional sector due to the expansion in domestic demand. As before, the growth originates with the expansion in employment in the public administration sector and defence. The demand for services also rises. Under floating rates, there are three crowding out mechanisms: (i) appreciation of the exchange rate; (ii) high interest rates and; (iii) high taxes. Under the DM peg, the latter only crowds out public sector expenditure. In conclusion, although overall output performance is similar across the two exchange rate regimes, the exchange rate regime does matter in that different channels and sectors are affected.

As one would expect, Irish unemployment falls significantly over the medium term (up to 6 percentage points lower than the baseline – see Figure 8.4). However, by the end of the simulation period, it is almost 2 percentage points higher than the baseline under the floating regime and less than 0.9 percentage points higher under the DM peg.

Figure 8.4
Irish unemployment rate:
Irish government expenditure - increase of 5% of GDP

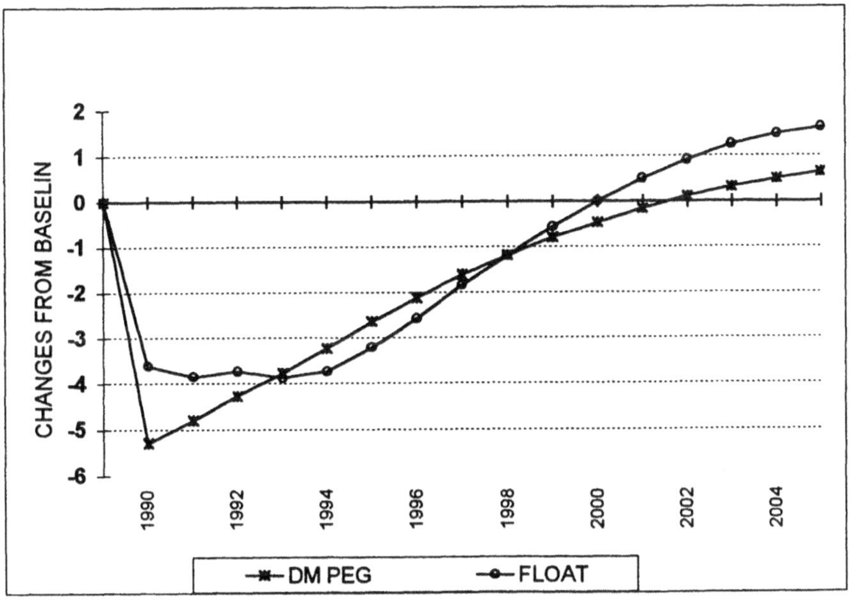

Under the DM peg, employment rises in the industrial sector due to the increase in employment in traditional and building sectors. Both of these respond to increases in domestic demand. This initial increase in industrial employment is outweighed by the larger expansion in services and in particular public sector employment. The increase in employment in both of these sectors falls over the years resulting in a smaller increase in employment by the end of the simulation period. Despite the almost constant total employment increase over the entire period, the unemployment rate rises due to the expansion in the Irish labour force. Under the floating regime, employment in the services sector and in the public sector is as above. In contrast to the DM peg, employment in the industrial sector in all years declines relative to the baseline. This arises due to the combination of an appreciating exchange rate and later the rise in nominal wages. Employment in building also falls.

Overall, the unemployment rate rises towards the end of the period due to the rise in the labour force relative to the rise in total employment. The impact of the expansion in government expenditure has different effects on sectoral employment under the two exchange rate regimes.

Conclusion

In this chapter, we investigated how the exchange rate regime can affect unemployment. We initially reviewed the theoretical literature on "Optimum Currency Areas" highlighting why Ireland is not considered to be part of a core European optimum currency area. Our examination of a three country analytical model (where two countries are large and one is small) identified the key channels through which the exchange rate regime affects the unemployment rate, the importance of the type of disturbance (whether nominal and real) and the role of structural variables in determining the size and the duration of the impact. We then examined empirically, using two macroeconometric models, the impact of unanticipated external and internal demand disturbances on unemployment and output performance in a small country - Ireland. The structure of the Irish economy plays a significant role in modifying the impact of disturbances on Irish macroeconomic performance. Key structural features include: the high level of openness; the role of the traded sector as the principle instigator of growth; the division of the manufacturing sector between the high technology and traditional sectors; the importance of the multinational sector in the determination of output and income outflows; the very large National Debt and; the linkage between the Irish and UK labour markets.

References

Alesina A. and Grilli, V. (1992), "The European Central Bank : Reshaping Monetary Politics in Europe", in Canzoneri M., Grilli V. and Masson, M.R. (eds.), *Establishing a Central Bank: Issues in Europe and Lessons from the US*, Cambridge University Press: Cambridge.

Argy V., McKibbin W. and Sielgloff, E. (1989), "Exchange Rate Regimes for a Small Economy in a Multi-Country World", *Princeton Studies in International Finance*. No. 67. Department of Economics, Princeton, NJ.

Argy V. and De Grauwe, P. (1990), *Choosing an Exchange Rate Regime, The Challenge for Smaller Industrial Countries.* International Monetary Fund: Washington.

Argy V. (1990), "Choice of Exchange Rate Regimes for a Smaller Economy: A Survey of Some Key Issues, in Argy V. and De Grauwe, P. (eds.) *Choosing and Exchange Rate Regime, The Challenge for Smaller Industrial Countries* International Monetary Fund: Washington.

Argy V. (1994), *International Macroeconomics,* Routledge: London.

Baker T. (1993), "Manufacturing Output and Employment by Market Area", *Economic and Social Research Institute Quarterly Economic Commentary,* Spring, pp. 32-56.

Baker T., Fitzgerald J. and Honohan, P. (1996), *On the Implications for Ireland of EMU*, Policy Research Series, Paper No. 28, ESRI: Dublin.

Bayoumi T. and Eichengreen, B. (1993), "Shocking Aspects of European Monetary Integration", in Torres F. and Giavazzi, F. (eds.) *Adjustment and Growth in the European Monetary Union,* Cambridge University Press: Cambridge.

Bertola G. (1989), "Factor Flexibility, Uncertainty and Exchange Rate Regimes", in De Cecco M. and Giovannini, A. (eds.) *A European Central Bank? Perspectives on Monetary Unification after ten years of the EMS* , Cambridge University Press: Cambridge.

Borio C. (1995), "The Structure of Credit to the Non-Government Sector and the Transmission Mechanism of Monetary Policy: A Cross-Country Comparison", Working Paper No. 24, BIS.

Borio C. and Fritz, W. (1995), "The Response of Short-term Bank Lending Rates to Policy Rates: A Cross Country Perspective", Working Paper No. 27, BIS.

Bradley J., Fitzgerald J., Hurley D., O'Sullivan L. and Storey, A. (1989), *Hermes-Ireland. A Model of the Irish Economy: Structure and Performance*, ESRI: Dublin.

Bradley J. and Fitzgerald, J. (1991), "The ESRI Medium Term Economic Model", *ESRI Medium Term Review 1991-1996* June, ESRI: Dublin.

Bradley J., Fitzgerald J. and Kearney, I. (1993), "Modelling Supply in an Open Economy Using a Restricted Cost Function", *Economic Modelling* , Vol. 10, No. 1, pp. 11-21.

Branson W. (1989), "Discussion", in De Cecco M. and Giovannini, A. (eds.) *A European Central Bank? Perspectives on Monetary Unification after ten years of the EMS* , Cambridge University Press: Cambridge.

Calmfors L. and Driffil, J. (1988), "Bargaining Structure, Corporatism and Macroeconomic Performance", *Economic Policy* , Vo. 67, No. 3, pp. 14-61.

Cantillon S., Curtis J. and Fitzgerald, J. (1994), *Medium Term Review 1994-2000,* ESRI: Dublin.

Currie D. (1992), "Hard-ERM, Hard ECU and the European Monetary Union", in Canzoneri M., Grilli V. and Masson, P.R. (eds.), *Establishing a Central Bank Issues in Europe and Lessons from the US* , Cambridge University Press: Cambridge.

Curtis J. and Fitzgerald, J. (1994), "Convergence in an Open Labour Market", Working Paper No. 45, ESRI: Dublin.

Danthine J.P. and Hunt, J. (1994), "Wage Bargaining Structure, Employment and Economic Integration, *Economic Journal*, Vol. 104 , No. 424, pp. 528-541.

De Grauwe P. (1994), *The Economics of Monetary Integration*, Oxford University Press: Oxford.

Fleming E. (1993), *Is there an EMS Effect in the Irish Labour Market?* M.A. Dissertation, University College, Cork.

Flood R and Marion,N. (1982), "The Transmission of Disturbances Under Alternative Exchange Rate Regimes with Optimal Indexing", *Quarterly Journal of Economics*, Vol. 97, pp. 43-66.

Gros D. (1996), *Towards Economic and Monetary Union: Problems and Prospects.* Paper No. 65, CEPS: Brussels.

Honohan P. (1992), "The Link Between Irish and UK Unemployment", *ESRI Quarterly Economic Commentary*, Spring, pp. 33-45.

Honohan P. (1993), *An Examination of Irish Currency Policy,* Policy Research Series, Paper No. 18, ESRI: Dublin.

Honohan P. and Conroy, C. (1994a), *Irish Interest Rate Fluctuations in the European Monetary System*, General Research Series, Paper No. 165, ESRI Banking Research Centre: Dublin.

Honohan P. and Conroy, C. (1994b), "Sterling Movements and the Irish Pound Interest Rates", *The Economic and Social Review*, Vol. 25, No. 3, pp. 201-220.

Horn H. and Persson, T. (1988), "Exchange Rate Policy, Wage Formation and Credibility", *European Economic Review*, Vol. 32, pp. 1621-1636.

Hughes Hallett A.J. and Vines, M. (1993), "On The Possible Costs of European Monetary Union", *Manchester School*, Vol. 61, pp. 35-64.

Kenen P. (1969), "The Theory of Optimum Currency Areas: An Eclectic View", in Swoboda A. (ed), *Monetary Problems of the International Economy*, University of Chicago Press: Chicago.

Isard P. (1995), *Exchange Rate Economics*, Cambridge University Press: Cambridge.

Laufer N.K. and Sundararajan, S. (1994), "The International Transmission of Economic Shocks in a Three-Country World Under Mixed Exchange Rates", *Journal of International Money and Finance*, Vol. 13, pp. 429-466.

Marston R.C. (1984), "Exchange Rate Unions as an Alternative to Flexible Rates: The Effects of Real and Monetary Disturbances", in Bilson J.F. and Marston, R.C. (eds.) *Exchange Rate Theory and Practice*, University of Chicago Press: Chicago.

Masson P., Symansky S. and Meredith, G. (1990), "Multimod Mark II. A Revised and Extended Model", Occasional Paper No. 71, International Monetary Fund: Washington.

McKinnon R.I. (1963), "Communications. Optimum Currency Areas", *American Economic Review*, Vol. 53, pp. 716-725.

Mundell R.A. (1961), "A Theory of Optimum Currency Areas", *American Economic Review*, Vol. 51, pp. 657-664.

Neary P. and Thom, R. (1996), "Punts, Pounds and Euros: In Search of an Optimum Currency Area", Working Paper No. 96/24, Centre for Economic Research, University College, Dublin.

Romer D. (1996), *Advanced Macroeconomics*, McGraw Hill: New York.

Tavlas G. (1993), The "New" Theory of Optimum Currency Areas, *The World Economy*, Vol. 16, pp. 663-85.

Throop A. (1994), "International Financial Market Integration and Linkages of International Interest Rates", *Federal Reserve Bank of San Francisco Economic Review*, Vol. 3, pp. 3-18.

Vinals J. and Jimeno, J. (1996), "European Unemployment and EMU", in Frieden J., Gros D. and Jones, E. (eds.), *Towards Economic and Monetary Union: Problems and Prospects*, Oxford University Press: Oxford.

Walsh B. (1993), "Credibility, Interest Rates and the ERM: The Irish Experience 1986-92", Working Paper No. 93/1, Centre for Economic Research, University College, Dublin.

Notes

1 For an exposition of some of the newer aspects of the "Optimum Currency Area" literature, see Isard (1995) and Tavlas (1993).

2 According to data by Neary and Thom (1996), a grouping consisting of France, Germany and some of its 'satellite' economies appear to be the most suitable candidates for closer monetary integration. Unambiguously, Ireland is not a member of this core.

3 An additional feature of these models is that they enable us to examine how the exchange rate regime between the two large countries affects the performance of the small country. We will not be exploring this issue in this chapter. The reader is referred to Chapter 5 of the ESRI study on the "Implications for Ireland of EMU" (Baker et al, 1996).

4 The speed of adjustment should be higher under floating exchange rates than under fixed exchange rates (Throop, 1994).

5 There is some debate in the literature whether a EMU will result in price stability. De Grauwe (1994) points out that even if the future European Central Bank has the same preferences with regard to inflation and unemployment as a low inflation country like Germany, inflation will be higher under EMU due to a higher average unemployment in the union. Currie (1992) argues that "progress towards EMU may move us towards low inflation or it may not" and depends crucially on the inflation reputation of the new Central Bank.

6 Danthine and Hunt (1994) in an extension of the Calmfors and Driffil model (1988) argue that greater economic integration, by stimulating competition, increases the trade-off between wages and unemployment i.e. the price of a given increase in wages is much higher in terms of lost markets and unemployment. The implication of this is that greater economic integration should lead to greater wage adjustment.

7 For a full description of the model, the reader is referred to "MULTIMOD MARK II: A Revised and Extended Model" by Masson, Symansky and Meredith (1990).

8 Although a description of HERMES-IRELAND was compiled in 1989 in "HERMES-IRELAND, A Model of the Irish Economy: Structure and Performance" (Bradley et al, 1989), the model has been extended considerably since then (Bradley et al, 1989; Bradley and Fitzgerald, 1991; Curtis and Fitzgerald, 1994). The reader is referred to these for a fuller description of the model.

9 The specification of the migration equation is such that when there is zero out-migration, Irish unemployment is 4 percentage points higher than in the UK (Honohan, 1992). The authors, Bradley and Fitzgerald feel that the long run migration relationship is adequately captured in the model but the timing of the short run responses may not be handled adequately by this approach.

10 The wage specification is explained and estimated in "Convergence in an Open Labour Market" (Curtis and Fitzgerald, 1994).

11 The Monetary Target Rule is taken directly from MULTIMOD.

12 Honohan (1993) suggests that a 50 per cent weight should be given to sterling, 30 per cent to the DM and 20 per cent to the dollar in a currency basket. Baker (1993) finds that, excluding both the domestic and non-UK and EC markets, the proportion of manufacturing output exported is equally divided between the UK and "Other EC".

13 The first observation is excluded in the calculation of cumulative excess returns because the shock is assumed to be unanticipated and the initial change in the exchange rate is also assumed to be unanticipated.

14 One would expect that Irish interest rates would have to exceed those abroad especially under a floating exchange rate arrangement, given interest rates and exchange rate expectations, due to the small size of Irish financial markets. International investors may perceive a higher risk attached to holding Irish securities or they may find it more difficult to acquire information about the Irish market or they may incur higher transaction costs in dealing in Irish securities (Honohan and Conroy, 1994a). The thinness of the Irish market (with its implication that by liquidating one's holdings one could drive the market against one) may also imply a premium on Irish interest rates (Honohan and Conroy, 1994a). This factor, although not added in explicitly in our simulations, may explain the length of time it takes for excess returns to be eliminated.

15 As we are concerned with the channels of transmission between Ireland and Germany and the UK, the size of the shock is necessary in order to obtain a recognisable impact on Irish macroeconomic performance. The shock that we have imposed on Germany is larger than the effect of German Reunification. Although such large shocks may distort the workings of the model, we feel that our results illustrate likely behaviour.

16 The model was initially run without changing the exchange rate. Irish interest rates declined due to the fall in Irish prices and the resultant fall in the demand for money. Therefore, this necessitated a substantial decline in the Irish pound exchange rate in order to (i) generate an expectation of the

domestic currency appreciating and (ii) increase prices, the demand for money and, in turn the rate of interest.

17 Under the DM and composite peg regimes, GDP never exceeds the baseline. GDP rises relative to the baseline under the sterling peg post-1999 and under the floating regime post-2004.

18 Under the floating regime and sterling peg, employment in the services sector declines until the year 2003. Under the DM and composite pegs, employment in the services sector declines throughout the simulation period.

19 We assumed that wages do not rise in line with higher taxes. If this effect was included, we would obtain a smaller expansionary and probably more likely a contractionary effect on Irish output over time as competitiveness is reduced.

9 Comment

Terrence McDonough

Introduction

Most considerations of Irish unemployment have approached the problem from the supply side. They have explicitly or implicitly understood the sources and solutions to unemployment to be found in the nature of the unemployed themselves. Several explanations of Irish unemployment have been offered within this framework. [1] One of the most common is a mismatch between the changing needs of the economy and the skills of the unemployed. This factor is emphasised in the innovative analysis of entry and exit into long term unemployment by Strobl and Walsh (Chapter 6 in this volume). A concern for improvements in education and training also underlies the observation of Barry and Hannan (Chapter 5) that hysteresis in unemployment can cross the generational divide. Other studies have examined the motivation of the unemployed, seeing them as systematically discouraged from seeking work by the Irish tax structure or the social welfare system. From this perspective, an essential element of the fight against unemployment is the reform of the social welfare system and the reduction of the tax burden, especially on the low paid. Even wide ranging analyses of the need for increasing competitiveness have tended to boil down to increased training, increased incentives, and wage restraint. (See Kennedy's summary of the Essen European Council plans for implementing the Delors White Paper in Chapter 7 of this volume).

Studies which have examined the demand side of the labour market have often assumed problems to be temporary or short term in nature. Unemployment arises due to external or internal shocks to a normal situation which would otherwise have been characterised by full employment. Increasing the speed of adjustment of the economy to such shocks should then improve Irish unemployment. Ella Kavanagh's paper (Chapter 8) is a sophisticated contribution to this literature.

Each of the policy prescriptions described above would probably have some positive impact on the rate of unemployment. I wish to argue, however, that none addresses the fundamental reasons why unemployment is likely to be a continuing and significant problem in the Irish economy. Further, none reflects the aggressive approach to policy and openness to new initiatives which will be necessary to face up to this problem.

The structural roots of Irish unemployment

There are three fundamental sources of the Irish unemployment problem, each of them rooted in the deep structure of the current economy. The first is the failure of the monetarist dream of transcending the business cycle, the reasons for which are to be found in the basic dynamics of the capitalist economy itself. The second is the passing of the postwar Golden Age of international capitalist expansion. The third is in the historic end of the opportunity for balanced growth.

In his presentation during the morning session of the conference, Joe Lee referred to shooting the unemployed as a solution to the problem of unemployment. One of the interesting things about this story is that shooting the unemployed as a solution, is perfectly consistent with the standard neoclassical analysis of the problem. In this view, rigidities in the labour market have held the wage above the market clearing level, creating a surplus supply of labour. In the demand and supply framework, shooting the unemployed would shift the labour supply curve back, clearing the labour market at the existing wage.

The hidden assumption in this story is that the labour market should exhibit the same behaviour as any other commodity market. This ignores the fact that what is being traded in the labour market is not beans or cricket bats but the human capacity to work. This capacity is embodied in human beings, with all the needs, aspirations and complexity which this implies. The neoclassical story says that when the supply of labour equals the demand for labour, wages should settle at an equilibrium rate. But this is no more than an assumption and is not backed by the historical evidence. On the contrary, workers bargaining power is substantially increased under conditions of full employment when the lines outside of personnel offices have disappeared and workers leaving positions can easily find work at comparable wages and conditions. As a result of this increased bargaining power at full employment, wages tend to rise, and rise faster than increases in productivity. These wage increases necessarily eat into profitability. Falling profits lead to falling investment. Falling investment leads to falling demand and the reemergence of unemployment. At positive levels of unemployment, the bargaining power of labour is weakened and wages stabilise or fall. Profits recover and the business cycle turns up again. The economy potentially grows until destabilised again by the approach of full employment. This cyclical movement is reinforced by similar dynamics around other cost factors, including the cost of raw materials and the cost of capital. It is further strengthened by the procyclical behaviour of inflation and by the development of financial fragility in periods of expansion.[2] In this scenario, shooting the unemployed merely hastens the economy along one phase of the cycle and further ammunition would be needed when unemployment re-emerges.[3]

This potential for the dynamic cycling of unemployment has been obscured by a monetarist slight of hand. Placing inflation at the forefront of policy concerns, monetarists, and with them most modern economists, have defined the non accelerating inflation rate of unemployment (the NAIRU) as the level of full employment. Since inflation can be set off by the cost push of rising wages and better working conditions, full employment has effectively been defined as a positive level of unemployment high enough to discourage demands for increased wages and improved conditions. A significant portion of unemployment has thus been eliminated simply by redefining it as full employment.

In effect when profits fall too low, business threatens to withdraw employment from the economy. This amounts to a strike by capital. Any policy proposal which deals with unemployment must recognise this threat of capital strike and the consequent continual recurrence of the short run business cycle.

In addition to the short run business cycle, capitalist economies are subject to longer run dynamics. Investment on a large scale cannot take place in the absence of secure long run profit expectations. Any long run expectations are, however, necessarily problematic. This is due to class conflict over distribution and working conditions and to the destabilising effects of competition between capitals. For this reason, long run growth demands a set of stable institutions which can moderate conflict and competition and steer these factors into non-destructive channels (see Kotz et al., 1994).

Such a set of stable institutions emerged in the period after World War II. These institutions prominently included an international order organised economically and militarily by the dominant position of the United States. Also included was a system of stable and long term collective bargaining between strong unions and basic industry. This bargaining system guaranteed a large section of labour a secure job and an income which rose in line with both prices and, crucially, productivity. The state took responsibility for guaranteeing the health of the economy and long term growth through Keynesian techniques of demand management. This institutional framework of accumulation worked so well that some economic analysts of this period have begun to refer to it as the "Golden Age" of postwar capitalism (see especially Marglin and Shor, 1990).

By the mid-1970s, the Golden Age had come to an end. The rise of the European and Japanese economies had eroded US international dominance. This loss was manifested in the end of the Bretton Woods monetary system. The Third World had entered a period of revolution and increased independence, illustrated most dramatically by the US defeat in Vietnam and the two successive oil crises. Faced with secularly rising real wages and inadequate productivity growth, business counterattacked with what United Auto Workers president, Douglas Frasier labeled "a one sided class war." Aided by rising levels of unemployment and an increasingly sympathetic government, corporations drastically weakened union power and succeeded in stalling and reversing the growth in real wages.

Keynesianism had met its Waterloo in the stagflation of the 1970s and the turn to monetarism was evident in President Carter's appointment of Paul Volcker to the US Federal Reserve Board in 1978, before the elections of Reagan and Thatcher. The international capitalist economy entered a period of stagnation and crisis. Among other things, this stagnation was evidenced by rising rates of unemployment.[4]

It may be the case that we are emerging from this period of stagnation and entering a period of renewed growth. If so, this renewed growth must be based on the construction of a new institutional structure which moderates the capitalist tendencies toward instability. This new structure may be based on the emergence of a global regime of trade and the free movement of capital and the consequent increased leverage capitalism gains both on the shopfloor and in relations with the nation state. But this new regime of accumulation will not usher in a new Golden Age. The reason is quite straightforward.

The tendency of a growing capitalism to increase productivity must be balanced by either increasing standards of consumption or increasing working class leisure. Increases in the productivity of labour mean that more product can be produced with the same amount of labour. The basic Keynesian insight holds that this increased amount of product needs to find a market. The postwar Golden age included mechanisms to ensure a market for its rising productivity in its wage bargaining system and in the Keynesian state.

A Kaleckian approach, borrowing the notion of class from Marx, observes that the income generated by production is divided between capital and labour (Sawyer, 1985, pp.72-73). Thus, increasing productivity must be accompanied by an increase in the real income of either capital or labour or both. If the increase in production accrues to capital, it must be absorbed into increased capitalist consumption or invested. There is a limit on how much capitalist consumption can be further increased. On the other hand, the money can be invested in increased production. To the extent that this is pursued through labour saving means, the problem of disposing of the increased production is merely reproduced in the next production period at a higher intensity.

The necessary conclusion from these observations is that a substantial portion of the increasing production must in some way accrue to labour.[5] This can take the form of an increasing standard of living. Alternatively, the increasing productivity of labour can express itself in producing the same quantity of goods and services but accomplishing this task in a shorter period of time. Collectively then, the labouring class would experience a shorter work week or work year.

Neither of these beneficial effects of increasing productivity can be universally observed. The new world order is founded on an increase in competition between capitals and regions of the world. Both firms and governments seek to increase competitiveness through the control of labour costs (Bryan, 1995, pp.170-8). While it is hard to make generalisations for the developed world as whole, real wages in the developed world have generally been either stagnant or have lagged behind productivity growth since the mid-1970s.

The entry of women into the labour force has tended to increase or slow the decline of the work week on a household basis.[6]

The inevitable result of rising productivity, stagnant working class standards of living, and a constant or rising length of working time is unemployment. The creation of potential free time is inherent in raising the productivity of work time. In the emerging international regime, it is tending to concentrate in a few hands, those of the long term unemployed. It is ironic that the advance of the productive forces which Marx saw as narrowing the realm of necessity and increasing the realm of freedom has instead frequently resulted in social exclusion and the grinding necessity of poverty for those expelled from the labour market, while returning precious little to those remaining at work.

The resolution of this situation can only come from an increase in the standard of living of the working class or from the sharing of the available work and its consequent income. The increasing globalisation of the world economy forestalls the first solution. While it may be in the interests of the capitalist system viewed collectively to raise incomes and so increase demand in step with increases in productivity, it is in the interest of no single firm, unprotected from international competition, to accede unilaterally to increased wage demands. In the postwar era, union organisation and social democratic government in the industrialised nations were able to force on the system a steady increase in both the private and social wage. In the present era, the balance of class forces has tipped in favour of international capital. The international market and the search for "competitiveness" guarantees strong resistance to the raising of wages and social benefits. Indeed, the most that can be hoped for in the short run is to forestall a "race to the bottom" in the standards of living in the several Western economies stemming from increasing competition for international capital investment.

Since we cannot hope for a substantial increase in working class standards of consumption, this situation can be rescued through the creation of increased leisure for working people. This can only be achieved through the redistribution of the available leisure away from those who have involuntarily hoarded it, the long term unemployed. Of course, this implies sharing the available work.

The third reason why unemployment will continue to be a problem is the passing of the historic opportunity for balanced growth. It has been argued by Samir Amin (1972) that the initial growth of the metropolitan capitalist countries can be characterised as a process of auto-centric development. This contrasts with the dependent development which Amin contends describes the development of peripheral capitalist countries located primarily in the Third World. In the case of auto-centric development, the initial industrial sector generates domestic demand. This growing demand inaugurates the mass production of consumer goods. The consumer goods industries reciprocally generate demand for the capital goods sector and further consumer goods production. A virtuous circle of continued growth ensues which is not fundamentally dependent on participation in world markets. While Amin writes from a Marxist perspective, the creation of a self-sustaining cycle of growth has been the goal of much development thinking.

Import substitution regimes were meant to kick start this process through delinking local production from world competition. Conversely, export oriented strategies have attempted to create a critical mass of industrialisation through the attraction of foreign capital, bringing advanced technologies and serving an already developed overseas market.

In the post World War II period, it appeared that several late industrialising countries (the four tigers) were able to pursue successful development through a judicious and changing combination of promoting exports, foreign investment, state intervention, protection, and the favouring of local enterprise. The experience of these countries vindicates neither the strict import substitution strategy, nor can they be meaningfully characterised as instances of free market success.[7] The question which must be posed is can they provide a model for successful development in the current period. I strongly suspect this is not the case. First, the geographically restricted character of this sort of development and the differences in the strategies from one tiger to another seem to indicate that the successful strategy is idiosyncratic and specific to particular regions with particular histories. Secondly, and more consequentially, the further integration of the international marketplace may have made auto-centric development of any complexion obsolete.

This obsolescence arises from three sources. The first is that the strategy becomes harder to pursue as more countries adopt an export oriented strategy. The second is that international competition places an upper limit on wage growth. This limits the rate at which prosperity in a leading sector can be spread to other sectors through the emergence of mass consumption. Thirdly and perhaps most importantly, participation in the international economy increasingly demands the opening of domestic markets to international foreign competition. This means that much of the demand generated by employment in the export sector is in turn directed overseas. This is hardly surprising. Orthodox trade theory predicts international specialisation as a consequence of free trade.

Orthodox trade theory also assumes a complete mobility of resources, which then flow unimpeded into the sectors favoured by trade. A moment's reflection shows that the extent to which all resources can shift to the expanding export sector is strictly limited. In the past, across the board increases in prosperity have been based in the development of multiple and reinforcing centers of growth in one country's economy. In the era of globalisation, this kind of growth process is no longer possible.

The worst case scenario is that economies of scale and the forces of agglomeration (see Jacobson and Andreosso-O'Callaghan, 1996, pp.110-113) will locate all expanding arenas of production outside of the state's borders. In order to forestall this possibility, industrial planning authorities must seek to attract a critical mass of investment in one or a few branches of the global economy so as to constitute a center of growth within the country's boundaries. In choosing such an industry or industries, the authorities will be guided partially by any natural or developed advantages the state may already possess, but must also be guided by the relative desirability of attracting leading industries. Leading industries are those whose technologies and skills lay the basis for development in the future (see Gilpin, 1987, pp.97-100). American advocates of free trade are fond of saying that it matters not if a country specialises in computer chips or potato chips. Only the most stupid industrial planner would hesitate when faced with such a choice.

In this light, the Irish economy has been exceptionally successful. Ireland has succeeded in attracting a great deal of foreign investment in the advanced electronics and computer sectors. This investment may be criticised in that much of the higher level managerial and research functions are located elsewhere. Nevertheless, it is unrealistic to think that transnational corporations are going to relocate their headquarters operations to Ireland. It has been observed that foreign investment in general has not substantially increased domestic investment or developed backward or forward linkages, but it is precisely this kind of local economic integration which is increasingly obsolete in the global economy.

Ireland's recent experience as "the Celtic Tiger" only serves to highlight the problem. Ireland has experienced high rates of growth in a few sectors but has been unable to extend this development across the bulk of the economy. As a result, the unemployment rate remains high in the face of record growth.[8]

Prescriptions

The formulation of policies to deal effectively with Irish unemployment demands that the deep roots of the problem be addressed. Solutions will involve structural change, calling for audacity and courage from policy makers. We need to change the way we understand the operation and evaluate the outcomes of the labour market. Each of the structural problems outlined above will demand a further departure from current practice.

In the first section of this chapter, I argued that the business cycle is inherent in the social dynamics of the capitalist mode of production. While it is not possible in the short run to eliminate the conflicts which create instability in the economy, it is possible to mitigate them, but only if their existence is confronted directly. It is in this arena which current practice in Ireland has already laid a partial foundation.

Ireland has considerable experience with the nationwide negotiation of income distribution and social policy. These negotiations have been pursued since 1987 under the titles of the Programme for National Recovery (PNR), the Programme for Economic and Social Progress (PESP), the Programme for Competitiveness and Work (PCW) and recently, Partnership 2000. Each of these agreements has been reached through a process of three-sided bargaining between trade unions, employers' organisations, and government representatives. The objects of the negotiation have been expanded beyond wages and working conditions to taxation and government policy. In the current round, representatives of the unemployed and other marginalised groups in society have been brought into the talks.

Curiously, Irish economists have not in general noted the coincidence of the talks process with the unprecedented growth of the economy and the equally unusual fiscal health of the state. Far from endorsing this process, economists have generally been suspicious of any process which does not privilege the free negotiation of individual contracts. It is thought that any interference at the macro societal level with the decentralised market process will only tend to keep wages and unemployment higher than they otherwise would be.[9] As I argued above, this reasoning is based in an unrealistic view of the capitalist labour market, which sees this market as tending toward static equilibrium prices and quantities. Once the labour market is seen as the center of a dynamic conflict which drives the business cycle, the constructive character of national agreements in mitigating this cycle becomes clear.

Standard economic analysis seeks to eliminate conflict by reducing all economic interaction to the voluntary contractual associations of individuals. The Irish national negotiations attempt the same thing through elaborating a concept of social partnership between the contending groups. This conception is presumably motivated by the perception that 'partners' negotiating with one another may reach agreement more easily than adversaries. Aside from the doubtful truth of this general proposition, the notion of negotiations among partners obscures the extent to which these groups have conflicting as well as complementary interests.[10]

The recent inclusion of the Irish National Organization of the Unemployed in the negotiations underscores this problem. It raises the question to what extent can the unemployed be considered partners in production. The ideological concept of social partnership is inevitably destabilised in the course of the negotiations themselves and is undermined by the unavoidable politicisation of the bargaining process when it is raised to the national level. The notion of partnership forces each of the participants to paint their sectional interests as identical with those of the community as a whole. To the extent that such a strategy succeeds for one 'partner,' the other 'partners' are forced to withdraw support from the process. The process will paradoxically be more stable and reproducable if the contending parties acknowledge the conflict in their interests along with the commonalities, and pursue their respective programmes constrained by a realistic assessment of the social context and the power and influence of their opponents. In the long run, the only way to create real social partnership is to take the idea literally and to eliminate the source of the conflict by breaking down the distinction between capital and labour. The only permanent way to do this is by resting the ownership of productive facilities with the employees who work in them, not by assuming everyone is an atomised individual, or conferring on all and sundry the title of social partner.

The tendency of the current international capitalist order to produce a lower level of employment than that produced under the Golden Age regime must be addressed directly. The Irish Times columnist John Waters tells a fable of a neighbourhood with two unemployed men and a wall to be built. The first man is hired to build the wall. After working long hours, his income is taxed to provide welfare payments to the second man who remains idle. Not only has the second man been socially excluded, but the seeds of a bitter division have been sown in the community. The solution is simple. Divide the available work between the two men.

At a societal level, this can be pursued quite simply by shortening the work week. It is often forgotten that a shorter work week has been a common way of coping with increased productivity in the past. It was the primary demand of many of the great labour movements of the nineteenth and early twentieth centuries. Later in the twentieth century, it expressed itself in the demand for a family wage, freeing all but one of the family members from the labour market. Continuing productivity growth eventually places the hours of work on the social agenda again. The penalty for not taking up this question will be continued high levels of unemployment and social exclusion.[11]

Standard neoclassical production theory treats capital as a fixed input which cannot be changed in the short run. Labour, on the other hand, is regarded as a variable input which can be altered according to the level of production. From the perspective of the individual firm, this is a perfectly sensible distinction. Yet from the point of view of society (or the nation), it is the labour force which is fixed and the amount of capital which varies over time. If the capital deployed by society is insufficient to employ all the labour, the labour does not become dormant waiting to be set in motion when new tranches of capital arrive on the scene. In order to avoid the massively negative consequences of exclusion from labour, the "excess capacity" of labour must be spread over the available labour force. A decent sense of social solidarity demands no less.

How the increased cost of such a proposal is to be allocated is a proper subject for the PCW style negotiations endorsed above. Increases in productivity associated with shorter work time will obviate some of the cost. Some of the rest will probably be shared by employers and employees. A substantial portion could be subsidised by the government, however, allocating revenues saved due to reduced social welfare spending, law enforcement expenditures, improved health, etc.

Another method of sharing work is to increase the amount of public employment. Much of the service work of maintaining the social and community infrastructure cannot be provided on the private market. Some of this work is done in the public sector, but much of it is done by non-profits and voluntary organisations. The social commentator, Jeremy Rifkin, has identified this as a third sector beyond the private and public sectors, and labeled it the civil sector. The activities of the civil sector run the gamut from social services to health care, education, research, the arts, religion and public advocacy (Rifkin, 1996). A pool of labour unutilised by the private market is an invaluable resource in addressing these kinds of community needs. This is partially recognised in the various existing community work training schemes. Yet these jobs are deliberately devalued by making them temporary, part time, poorly paid, and subject to very low standards of productivity and performance. It would be important not to see such jobs as make work, but rather as a career, providing an important and necessary service to the community. This has been partially recognised in the new programme for the incoming government. In order to acquire acceptance and dignity, this work must address recognised community needs and be adequately supervised, preferably by the community involved.

A diminution of the hours of work need not be regarded as a negative outcome. Economists have long recognised that leisure time has a positive value. In fact, it has become more important in the current era because of ongoing changes in the family structure. The family is the 'site' of much of our leisure activity. A diminution in the hours of paid work frees up more time to be devoted to the maintenance and enhancement of family life. A commitment to family means little if the primary means of its survival, the investment of adult time, is withdrawn to be overwhelmingly devoted to the market economy. Shorter work hours would facilitate the performance of family responsibilities at a time when a growing percentage of mothers are also employed in paid work. The desirable social goal of increased male involvement in child rearing and household responsibilities would be greatly facilitated by a shorter and perhaps more flexible work week.

A further issue involves the ecological health of the planet. Increased production in one way or another usually involves an increased demand on planetary resources. To the extent that natural resources are absorbed into the human economy, they become unavailable to the biological systems in which human society is embedded. When deprived of sustenance, the ecosystem must eventually enter into crisis. It is only the height of wisdom to enjoy our rising productivity in the increase of the leisured enjoyment of life, rather than in increasingly redundant consumption.

The problem of uneven development of the national economy in the context of an increasingly global world forces us to recognise that even with our best efforts, not all of the labour in society will be effectively allocated. Jobs exposed to the vagaries of the international market may be especially insecure. It is thus necessary to make provision for those members of society who are for shorter or longer periods out of work. If we come to see work as solidaristicly allocated among the citizenry, the social opprobrium must be lifted from those who are out of work through no fault of their own. The best way to accomplish this is to vest a right to income in all citizens. With everyone entitled to a minimum income, the invidious distinction between the dole recipient and the ordinary citizen is at least partially lifted. The Conference of Religious of Ireland (CORI) has developed a detailed proposal laying out how such a guaranteed income might be implemented and financed (CORI, 1994).

Conclusion

I have argued that the depth of the unemployment problem in Ireland is due to long term structural factors. Because of this, marginal interventions can at best produce marginal improvements in the situation. In the absence of fundamental changes in the way we view the operation of the labour market, unemployment, social exclusion, and its attendant social evils will continue to blight the public and private life of this island. This is guaranteed by the continued salience of the business cycle, structurally higher levels of unemployment concomitant on the passing of the postwar Golden Age, and the necessarily unbalanced growth conditioned by the global economy.

Addressing these problems will involve economic and cultural change. The utopian neoclassical vision of a world of harmonious, mutually beneficial, individual contracts must be replaced by the hard headed realisation that Irish society is economically and socially divided. While some interests are shared and conducive to easy agreement, other important interests are in conflict. It is preferable to negotiate with one's friends, but more often necessary to negotiate with one's adversaries. An acknowledgement of this fact will enforce a constructive realism in the national talks process. The recognition that wage setting and the distribution of income is an inescapably political process will open many social questions up to creative and long term solutions.

The most constructive first step in the search for solutions will be the adoption of an attitude of solidarity towards the allocation of available work and its associated income and social participation. This approach must see work and social inclusion as a right rather than the privileged outcome of private negotiation. Finally, a recognition of the rising insecurity of the global market place demands that the right to income be separated from the capacity to work. This involves guaranteeing income as a right of citizenship. It does not, however, free the individual from the obligation to contribute to society. The more successful we are in creating and fairly allocating work, the less a guaranteed income will cost. An Ireland with a substantially lower unemployment rate would of necessity be a very different place than the Ireland of today. It would be a much better place for ourselves and our children.

References

Amin, S. (1972), "Accumulation and Development. A Theoretical Model," *Review of African Political Economy*, no. 1.

Bluestone, B. and Rose, S. (1997), "Overworked and Underemployed: Unraveling an Economic Enigma," *The American Prospect*, No. 31 (March-April),. pp.58-69.

Bosch, G., Dawkings, P. and Michon, F. (1994), *Times are Changing: Working Time in 14 Industrialized Countries,* ILO: Geneva.

Bowles, S. and Edwards, R. (1985), *Understanding Capitalism,* Harper and Row: New York.

Bowles, S., Gordon, D.M. and Weisskopf, T.E. (1990), *After the Wasteland,* M.E. Sharpe: Armonk, New York.

Boyer, R. (1990), *The Regulation School, A Critical Introduction*, Columbia University Press: New York.

Bryan, D. (1995), *The Chase Across the Globe: International Accumulation and the Contradictions for Nation States*, Westview: Boulder.
CORI, (1994), *Tackling Poverty, Unemployment and Exclusion: A Moment of Great Opportunity*, Conference of Religious of Ireland: Dublin.
Gilpin, R. (1987),. *The Political Economy of International Relations,*Princeton University Press: Princeton.
Gordon, D. M. (1997), *Fat and Mean: The Corporate Squeeze of Working Americans and the Myth of Managerial "Downsizing"*, The Free Press: New York.
Gray, A.W. (ed.), (1992), *Responses to Irish Unemployment*, Indecon: Dublin.
Jacobson, D. and Andreosso-O'Callaghan, B. (1996), *Industrial Economics and Organization: A European Perspective*, McGraw-Hill: London.
Keane, C.(ed.), (1993),. *The Jobs Crisis*, Mercier: Cork and Dublin.
Kotz, D.M., McDonough, T. and Reich, M. (eds.), (1994), *Social Structures of Accumulation: The Political Economy of Growth and Crisis*, Cambridge University Press: Cambridge.
Leddin, A. J. and Walsh, B.M. (1992), *The Macroeconomy of Ireland*, Gill and Macmillan: Dublin.
Marglin, S.A. and Schor, J.B. (eds.), (1990), *The Golden Age of Capitalism: Reinterpreting the Postwar Experience*, Oxford University Press: Oxford.
McCarthy, E.J. and McGaughey, W. (1989), *Nonfinancial Economics: The Case for Shorter Hours of Work*, Praeger: New York.
McGettigan, D. (1992), "The Causes of Irish Unemployment: A Review," in *Economic Perspectives for the Medium Term*, ESRI: Dublin.
O'Hagan, J.W. (ed.), (1995), *The Economy of Ireland: Policy and Performance of a Small European Country*, Gill and Macmillan: Dublin.
O'Hearn, D. (1989), "The Irish Case of Dependency: An Exception to the Exceptions?" *American Sociological Review*, Vol. 54 (August) pp.578-596.
Rifkin, J. (1996), *The End of Work: The Decline of the Global Labor Force and the Dawn of the Post-Market Era*, Tarcher/Putnam: London.
Schor, J.B. (1992), *The Overworked American:The Unexpected Decline of Leisure*, Basic Books: London.
Sawyer, M.C. (1985), *The Economics of Michal Kalecki*, Macmillan: Basingstoke.
Sherman, H.J. (1991), *The Business Cycle*, Princeton University Press: Princeton.
Studies, (1993), *Unemployment in the Republic of Ireland, Studies*, Vol. 82, No. 325, Spring.
Yates, M. (1994), *Longer Hours, Fewer Jobs: Employment and Unemployment in the United States*, Monthly Review Press: New York.

Notes

1 See Gray (1992), Studies (1993) and Keane (1993) for collections of analyses and policy proposals. The neoclassical economics literature is usefully reviewed in McGettigan (1992).

2 A concise discussion of these issues can be found in Bowles and Edwards (1985, pp.231-296). A more extended treatment can be found in Sherman (1991).

3 It is true that a kind of full employment equilibrium would eventually be reached when a sufficient number of cycles had passed and the working population was reduced to zero.

4 For a similar analysis, see Bowles et al. (1990).

5 This insight is a major concern of the French Regulation School. See Boyer (1990).

6 Bluestone and Rose (1997) provide an excellent review of these issues for the United States. For a discussion of the complicated relationship between wages and productivity growth, see Gordon (1997, pp.144-171). In those countries where work hours have declined, the performance on unemployment has generally been better. See also Bosch et al. (1994, pp. 1-45).

7 For an interesting discussion of these issues which directly addresses the recent economic history of Ireland, see O'Hearn (1989).

8 The Tiger analogy is inappropriate in two senses. The first is that the Irish growth experience is not analogous to the Asian Tiger experience in that it is not as balanced. Secondly, the image has a king of the jungle quality in which the roaring economy scatters all before it. The actual success, while real, is more modest. Perhaps the fox would provide a better image, with its middling position in the food chain and consciousness of the hounds and horses not far behind. And, of course, one wrong turn can turn today's sleek success into tomorrow's roadkill. Additionally, Ireland's success doesn't appear to have much relation to Celtic culture in the same way that the Asian tigers have called on Eastern virtues. This said, I doubt the image of the Emerald Fox will catch on.

9 See Leddin and Walsh (1992, pp.266-7). For an exception, see O'Hagan (1995, pp.252-4).

10 The promotion of the concept of partnership in this type of national negotiation has led to opposition within the left wing of labour movements. It is unclear, however, that such negotiations undermine class consciousness to any greater extent than atomised, firm by firm bargaining.

11 Expansions of this argument can be found in Schor (1992), Yates (1994), Rifkin (1996), and McCarthy and McGaughey (1989).

For Product Safety Concerns and Information please contact our EU representative GPSR@taylorandfrancis.com Taylor & Francis Verlag GmbH, Kaufingerstraße 24, 80331 München, Germany

Batch number: 10726009

Printed by Printforce, the Netherlands